Practical Compiling with Pascal-S

INTERNATIONAL COMPUTER SCIENCE SERIES

OTHER TITLES IN THE SERIES

Programming in Ada (2nd Edn) *J G P Barnes*

Software Engineering (2nd Edn) *I Sommerville*

Handbook of Algorithms and Data Structures *G H Gonnet*

UNIX for Super-Users *E Foxley*

Introduction to Expert Systems *P Jackson*

Modula-2: Discipline & Design *A H J Sale*

The UNIX System V Environment *S R Bourne*

PROLOG *F Giannesini, H Kanoui, R Pasero and M van Caneghem*

Programming Language Translation: A Practical Approach *P D Terry*

Data Abstraction in Programming Languages *J M Bishop*

System Simulation: Programming Styles and Languages *W Kreutzer*

The Craft of Software Engineering *A Macro and J Buxton*

UNIX System Programming *K F Haviland and B Salama*

PROLOG Programming for Artificial Intelligence *I Bratko*

An Introduction to Programming with Modula-2 *P D Terry*

Cost Estimation for Software Development *B Londeix*

Parallel Programming *R H Perrott*

The Specification of Computer Programs *W M Turski and T S E Maibaum*

Text Processing and Typesetting with UNIX *D W Barron and M J Rees*

Software Development with Ada *I Sommerville and R Morrison*

Logic Programming and Knowledge Engineering *T Amble*

Performance Measurement of Computer Systems *P McKerrow*

Syntax Analysis and Software Tools *K J Gough*

Conccurrent Programming *N Gehani and A D McGettrick* (Eds)

Practical Compiling with Pascal-S

Michael Rees
University of Tasmania

Dave Robson
University of Durham

ADDISON-WESLEY
PUBLISHING
COMPANY

Wokingham, England · Reading, Massachusetts · Menlo Park, California
New York · Don Mills, Ontario · Amsterdam · Bonn · Sydney
Singapore · Tokyo · Madrid · Bogota · Santiago · San Juan

To Margot, Kathleen and Jason (MJR)

To Maggie, Glen and Jenna (DJR)

Cover graphic courtesy of Dicomed (UK) Ltd.
Typeset by Michael Rees with the UNIX troff utility and output via the Transcript package on a LaserWriter Plus kindly loaned by the Department of Information Science, University of Tasmania.
Printed and bound in Great Britain by Mackays of Chatham Ltd, Kent.

First printed 1988.

British Library Cataloguing in Publication Data

Rees, Michael
Practical compiling with Pascal-S. —
(International computer science series).
1. PASCAL.S (Computer program language)
I. Title II. Robson, Dave III. Series
005.4'53 QA76.73.P2/

ISBN 0–201–18487–7

Library of Congress Cataloging in Publication Data

Rees, Mike. 1946–
Practical compiling with Pascal-S / Michael Rees, Dave Robson.
p. cm. — (International computer science series)
Bibliography: p.
Includes index.
ISBN 0–201–18487–7 (pbk.)
1. Pascal-S (Computer program language) 2. Compiling (Electronic computers) I. Robson, Dave. 1951– . II. Title. III. Series.
QA76.73.P2155R44 1988
005.4'53—dc19 87–33348
CIP

Preface

Programming language translation was once thought to be the province of experienced language designers and systems programmers alone. However, translation techniques are now finding a home in a host of new applications. As software packages on microcomputers become increasingly powerful and the use of general-purpose products widens, applications programmers need to perform translation tasks on the end-user command languages that drive these products. Such a language is becoming known as a fourth generation language or 4GL.

Another area where programming style languages are being employed is the interface to sophisticated communication and printing devices. Document description languages are a case in point, and the PostScript language from Adobe Systems Incorporated is a good example of this. Here, document information is transmitted as a 'program' which is interpreted at the destination to produce the document image prior to printing.

This book attempts to address the needs of both traditional programming language translation and the more modern needs of 4GL and other language interpretation. It does this by adopting a subset of the Pascal programming language as a detailed case study. The reader is assumed to have programming experience, but is given an introduction to the concepts of programming language translation from scratch. A very practical approach is adopted so that readers can discover the level of complexity in terms of the code which makes up the whole translator. Some examples of alternative approaches are given where these exist, particularly where automatic tools are available to assist the programmer.

The expected readership therefore comprises students in tertiary level courses that introduce programming language translation, and programmers whose application requires translation and interpretation techniques. It is hoped that the Pascal code presented in the text can be used with little change in production programs as well as student programming exercises.

The first two chapters of the book introduce general concepts of language translation, the way languages are designed, and indicate how Pascal-S relates to the full Pascal language.

In the next seven chapters, 3 through 9, the phases of compilation are presented. The reader is led through the parts of the Pascal-S compiler source text which relate to each phase. Lexical scanning, syntax and semantic analysis, and intermediate code generation are covered. Aspects of the virtual machine architecture assumed by the code interpreter are described. This machine model is sufficiently general to suit a wide variety of interpretation requirements.

Chapter 10 gives two detailed examples of how the Pascal-S language may be extended. This gives the reader an insight into the range of changes necessary to the compiler when the language design is changed. The authors have found that these changes form excellent practical exercises for students. Rather than start from scratch on a complete compiler, which is rarely achievable in a single undergraduate course, these exercises allow students to work with a realistic translation system. It encourages skills of reading and understanding a substantial program, carefully designing changes, and giving thought to sensible testing of the end product.

The ideas in the text have been used in introductory compiler courses in four universities in England, Australia and Canada. Ideas from the students involved have resulted in several improvements in the text. Furthermore, the source text for Pascal-S has been ported to several different computer systems and well tested classroom conditions. In their respective institutions, the authors have encouraged their students to employ available tools for source code control, automatic generation of lexical scanner and syntax analysers, recompilation control and test suites. By this method the concepts of software engineering are also emphasized.

A complete source listing of the Pascal-S compiler is presented in Appendix B. This compiler is based directly on Nicklaus Wirth's Pascal-S system (N Wirth, 'Pascal-S: a subset and its implementation'. Techn. Report No. 12, Inst. für Informatik, ETH. June 1975.) The authors would like to express their thanks to Nicklaus Wirth for his kind permission to use Pascal-S in this book.

The original Pascal-S compiler has been upgraded to support more Pascal language features. A number of errors have been corrected and the operation of the interpreter changed so that it will operate on a wide range of hardware. Almost all the identifiers have been changed to make the text more readable, and a pretty printer utility has been applied for consistent layout. A considerable amount of comment text has been added to aid the reader's understanding of the program.

In addition, an index of all the identifiers used in the Pascal-S compiler is presented in Appendix C. This will substantially assist the reader in determining the exact operation of the various parts of the compiler.

Rather than rekeying the source of the Pascal-S system the complete text has been made available in machine-readable form. A 9-track magnetic tape in *tar* format can be obtained by writing to the authors for ordering details at one of the addresses given below.

Dr M J Rees
Department of Information Science
University of Tasmania
PO Box 252C Hobart
Tasmania 7001
Australia

Dr D J Robson
Department of Computer Science
University of Durham
Durham DH1 3LE
UK

(Please note that this tape is not available direct from the publisher.)

Readers may be interested to know that this book was written and typeset entirely with the aid of the AT&T UNIX operating system and associated utilities. Moreover, all creation of the text was managed and communicated over international electronic mail – the authors have not met personally since before the idea of the book was first suggested. Consequently, the authors wish to acknowledge the Universities of Southampton, Durham, Tasmania and Victoria, British Columbia, for providing network services to allow this book to be written. Our thanks also go to the network support programmers for making this possible.

Michael Rees
University of Tasmania

David Robson
University of Durham

November 1987

Contents

Preface v

Chapter 1 Introduction 1

1.1 Translation and execution concepts 2
1.2 Visual notation for translators 5
1.3 Structural overview of a compiler 7
1.4 Phase architecture 12
1.5 The compiler specification 13
1.6 Compiler construction 15
1.7 Design constraints 18

Chapter 2 Concepts of Programming Languages 22

2.1 Definitions of programming languages 22
2.2 Lexical and syntactic structure 25
2.3 Data types 26
2.4 Identifiers and names 27
2.5 Declarations 28
2.6 Data structures 29
2.7 Operators 30
2.8 Language statements 30
2.9 Program units 32
2.10 Storage management 32
2.11 The Pascal-S language 33

Chapter 3 The User Interface 35

3.1 Input/output handling 38
3.2 Source handler interface 39
3.3 Programming the source handler 42

Chapter 4 Lexical Analysis 49

4.1 Structure of the lexical analyser 49
4.2 Lexical analyser interface 50
4.3 Programming the lexical analyser 51
4.4 Automatic generation of lexical analysers 62

Chapter 5 Syntax Analysis 68

5.1 Syntax and semantics 68
5.2 Formal definition of grammar and language 68
5.3 Syntax trees 69
5.4 The Pascal-S syntax analyser 74
5.5 Syntax errors 78
5.6 Automatic generation of syntax analysers 80

Chapter 6 Semantic Analysis 90

6.1 Introduction 90
6.2 Semantic checking 90
6.3 Symbol table data structures 94
6.4 Pascal-S symbol table management 96
6.5 Entering information into the Pascal-S symbol table 99
6.6 Type checking 101
6.7 Examples 103

Chapter 7 Pascal-S Virtual Machine 108

7.1 The run-time environment 108
7.2 Stack frames 109
7.3 Variable access and the display 111
7.4 Virtual machine instructions 118

Chapter 8 Intermediate Code Generation 124

8.1 Expression evaluation 124
8.2 Code generation for basic structures 127
8.3 Procedure and function entry/exit 141
8.4 Procedure and function parameters 143
8.5 Data structures 146

Chapter 9 Pascal-S Interpreter 152

9.1 Interpretation of instructions 153
9.2 Links between the compiler and interpreter 163
9.3 Error checking 164
9.4 Post-mortem dump 165
9.5 Snapshots 167

Chapter 10 Extending the Pascal-S System 170

10.1 Enumeration types 170
10.2 Subrange types 179
10.3 Further extensions to the Pascal-S system 184
10.4 Suggested exercises and projects 185

Appendix A Pascal-S Syntax in BNF 188

Trademark notices

UNIX is a trademark of AT&T.
Transcript and PostScript are trademarks of Adobe Systems, Inc.
LaserWriter Plus is a trademark of Apple Computer Inc.
Ada is a trademark of the US Department of Defense – Ada Joint Program Office.

Addison-Wesley Publishing Company has made every attempt to supply trademark information about company names and products mentioned in this book. The trademarks listed here have been derived from a number of sources.

Chapter 1
Introduction

A programming language is a textual notation which allows a human programmer to construct **programs**, which are collections of algorithms and related data structures. Programs perform transformations on inherent or supplied input information to produce more useful data. The most common type of language used for programming today is referred to as a **high-level** or **third-generation language** (3GL).

There is not complete agreement as to exactly what constitutes the first- and second-generation language types. Machine language expressed in hexadecimal or octal form was the first programming notation available. This was easy to read by machines but very difficult for people to understand without considerable detailed knowledge and not a little patience. However, no translation was necessary as machine code can be executed directly by the machine.

Assembler languages are usually placed in the category of second-generation languages. Here, each statement corresponds to one machine code instruction. Mnemonics are used to specify the operation code and identifiers define data operands and labels.

The list of different 3GLs is very long indeed. However, only a very few are considered general enough in their application to merit popular use. A tentative 'top 10' list of languages for the mid-1980s, not necessarily in order of popularity, might be that shown in Table 1.1.

Many of the languages mentioned exist in a number of versions and continue to be developed as time goes by. It is interesting that second-generation languages are still preferred for some specialist uses, particularly where compactness of program and speed of operation are concerned.

At the time of writing the era of the fourth-generation or higher-level language (4GL) is arriving. 4GLs are very specialized indeed, and are intended to provide convenient interfaces for human users who lack in-depth computer knowledge. Many sophisticated software packages, such as databases, financial transactions and statistical analyses, include their own 4GL which is translated into lower-level operations to carry out the actions required by the user. Other 4GLs are used to specify programs in a reasonably narrow application area, such as report generation from a database. Here the 4GL text is translated into a suitable 3GL program to be treated in the normal way.

Table 1.1 Popular programming languages.

COBOL
FORTRAN
Pascal
PL/I
C
BASIC
Ada
LISP
Prolog
Modula 2

By hiding the level of detail required in 3GL programming, 4GLs aim to provide abstract facilities of direct relevance to the user with a resulting increase in ease of use. As 4GLs become more sophisticated they inevitably require the basic algorithmic features of sequence, repetition and selection. The end-user must therefore acquire a modicum of programming expertise to use 4GLs successfully.

It is just such a problem which the fifth generation of machines and languages is intended to overcome. Here, the aim is to allow the user to converse with the machine in near-natural language which is converted into a logical query. By applying an inbuilt set of logical rules a response to the user's query is generated. Noting which rules were used and the order in which they were applied can also disclose the mechanism by which the information was obtained. In effect, the machine is made to act in a human-like fashion. 5GLs are only in the development phase at present, but if the Japanese efforts in this area are successful, their realization is but a few years distant.

The techniques discussed in this book relate to the traditional treatment of 3GLs and in particular the block-structured language Pascal. However, the textual form of 4GLs is typically a good deal less complicated and the discussion will undoubtedly apply to this area as well. The same will not be true for 5GLs since the computer hardware is likely to have a very different architecture to existing machines. Hence the approach for building software will also differ.

1.1 Translation and execution concepts

To discuss the translation of programming languages a basic terminology is needed. The concept of a **translator** is fundamental. A translator is a program which accepts as input a program written in one programming language, the **source** language, and outputs the same program expressed in another language, the **object** or **target** language. If the source language is a high-level language, such as Pascal, Ada, etc., and the object language is a low-level language, such as assembly language or machine code, then the translator is called a **compiler**. (Similarly, an **assembler** translates assembly language into machine code.)

To execute a program written in source language two distinct steps are needed. These are:

(a) compile source text into object language;

(b) load and execute the object language.

Step (a), compilation, need only be performed once and subsequent executions simply employ step (b). Any changes to the source program, of course, require a further compilation. It should be noted that step (a) is rarely a single process. More realistically the object language output of the compiler is an **object module**. It needs to be **linked** with other, previously compiled, object modules such as standard functions and input/output procedures to form a single executable program. A **linker** program performs this latter process, which is usually triggered automatically at the end of the compilation step.

There is an alternative to steps (a) and (b). An **interpreter** performs a similar function to a compiler, by providing a mechanism for executing a program written in a high-level language. The interpreter program reads each source language statement, analyses it and then proceeds to carry out the operations expressed within it. This is thus a **one-step** process which appears to present a much more convenient interface to the user. The price paid for pure interpretation, however, is high compared with the two-step compilation procedure. Some of the disadvantages are:

(a) No permanent record is kept of the analysis of each statement. Where a statement is executed many times, as would occur in a repetition statement, the analysis is also repeated. This considerably slows down the overall execution rate of the source program, so that interpretation can only be considered where high execution speed is not necessary.

(b) Some of the main memory resource must be permanently assigned to the interpreter program while the user's program is being executed. This effectively reduces the amount of memory available for the data structures of the user's program.

(c) If copies of the program are to be executed on other machines, then the interpreter program must also be present. The end-users may have to purchase a copy of the interpreter before the application program can be executed.

A hybrid approach is the **translator-interpreter**. This considerably alleviates the high execution overhead and the memory size reduction of the interpreter. As before, the input is a program written in source language.

The output is an object program in a carefully selected intermediate language, which corresponds to the machine code of an idealized machine. This intermediate code is interpreted to 'execute' the user's program as the second step. Being a very simple linear list of low-level instructions the intermediate code interpreter program can be made small in size and fast in execution. Indeed, so simple is the code that it is straightforward to design a hardware processor chip to execute the code directly at typical machine code instruction speeds. This completely eliminates the problem of interpretation speed loss.

Probably the best example of the intermediate code approach is the P-code system from Softech Systems Corp. A number of translators for different languages such as Pascal, FORTRAN and BASIC all generate P-code, which is executed by a single interpreter. The translator programs themselves are also written in P-code. Notice that to transfer this software to a different hardware architecture only the P-code interpreter needs to be rewritten. A very high degree of portability is obtained at a relatively low cost in interpretation overhead.

Translation and interpretation are similar. In both methods instructions in source language are ultimately carried out by executing *equivalent* sequences of instructions in machine code. Rather than distinguishing between translators and interpreters, it is convenient to imagine the existence of a hypothetical computer or **virtual machine**. The 'machine language' of the virtual machine is an appropriate intermediate code.

As Tanenbaum (Tanenbaum, 1984) points out, it is much easier to translate one language or code into another if the target language is similar to the source. By using **multiple levels** of translation, each step from one level to the next can be made simpler and more reliable. This is illustrated in Table 1.2.

In effect, a virtual machine defines a language and vice versa. Given appropriate technology, each machine could be constructed in **hardware**. In practice, multiple interpreters and translators are written. Note that each level is a complete and independent entity, so the levels can be constructed in a modular and structured fashion.

An example of modern computer hardware built to this model is shown in Table 1.3. At each level, the technique used to support the virtual machine at the next lower level is indicated.

Hardware machines can now provide more than one microprogram, and hence more than one virtual machine, at level 1. Usually each microprogram is designed to support particular higher-level languages or specific applications. An example is the ICL Perq workstation with separate virtual machines for Pascal, C and graphics.

As the levels are ascended the choice of virtual machines usually grows. Thus each computer system can provide a (small) selection of operating systems, maybe each with a choice of assemblers. Above this, each operating system supports a wide selection of high-level languages. The even higher-level virtual machines, oriented directly to specific application areas, that are

Table 1.2 Virtual machine levels.

Level	*Virtual machine*	*Programs*
n	Virtual machine M_n, with machine language L_n	Programs in L_n are either interpreted by M_{n-1}, or translated into L_{n-1}.
2	Virtual machine M_2, with machine language L_2	Programs in L_2 are either interpreted by M_1, or translated into L_1.
1	Actual machine M_1, with machine language L_1	Programs in L_1 are executed directly by the hardware.

provided by the 4GLs have already been described.

As hardware and software technologies advance the number of levels of virtual machine can be expected to increase. The higher levels will tend towards a natural language interface while the lowest hardware levels will use customized VLSI chips with very specific capabilities.

1.2 Visual notation for translators

The variety of hybrid translators which use one or more levels of intermediate object code is such that simple textual descriptions are inadequate. Bratman (Bratman, 1961) proposed a visual notation using **T-Diagrams** which gives a clear picture of the translation process. Earley and Sturgis (Earley and Sturgis, 1970) further refined this T-diagram notation.

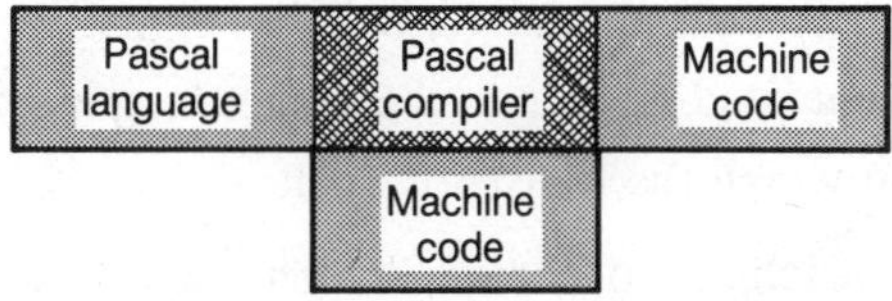

Figure 1.1 A compiler object.

Table 1.3 Virtual machine model of a computer system.

Level	*Language*
6	**Fourth generation language** ↓ Translation or interpretation (software package) ↓
5	**Problem-oriented language (3GL)** ↓ Translation (compiler) ↓
4	**Assembly language** ↓ Translation (assembler) ↓
3	**Operating system machine** ↓ Partial interpretation (system calls) ↓
2	**Conventional machine** ↓ Interpretation (micro instructions) ↓
1	**Microprogram** ↓ Hardware interpretation ↓
0	**Digital logic**

The notation gets its name from the T-shaped diagram which forms the central component. The three arms of the T describe the important attributes of any translator, namely:

(a) the language accepted as input, the source language;

(b) the language generated as output, the object language;

(c) the language in which the translator itself is written.

A true compiler in machine code form which translates a source language, say Pascal, into machine code object language would be represented as shown in Figure 1.1.

To be useful, a compiler must run on a machine able to execute the machine code of the compiler. Such a machine is represented in Figure 1.2.

Figure 1.2 A machine.

Figure 1.3 shows a source program written in Pascal.

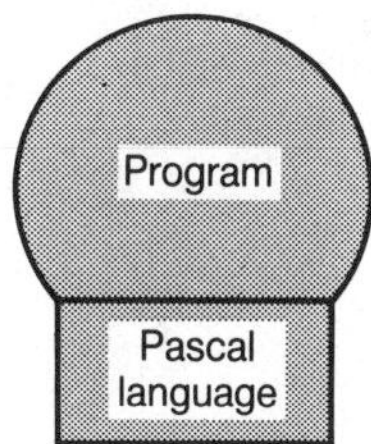

Figure 1.3 A program written in Pascal.

With this notation that encompasses machines, compilers and source programs, a two-stage compile and run would look like Figure 1.4.

A further shape is needed to describe an interpreter. A BASIC language interpreter, for example, is a very common program found on personal computers and is represented as shown in Figure 1.5.

The notation is now sufficient to describe the Pascal-S system which is the detailed case study employed throughout this book. Pascal-S can be represented as shown in Figure 1.6. A single diagram is used to indicate that the Pascal-S translator and intermediate interpreter are coresident – part of the same machine code program. Indeed, the intermediate code itself is also held in memory for the interpretation phase.

1.3 Structural overview of a compiler

Compilers were thought to be extremely difficult to write. The first compiler, for FORTRAN (1956), took 18 person-years to implement. Techniques for compiler development have improved greatly since that time, so that students can produce a compiler for a simple language in an undergraduate Computer Science compiler course.

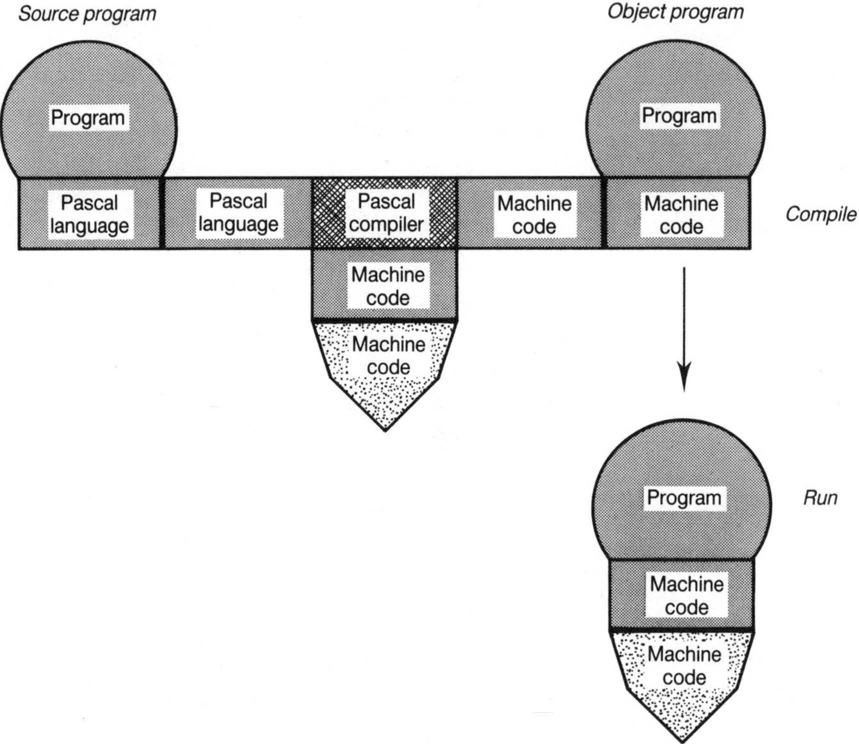

Figure 1.4 Compilation and execution.

The operation of a compiler is too complex to be regarded as a single step. It is customary to partition the compilation process into a series of **phases**. Each phase is a logically cohesive operation, that

(a) takes in one representation of the source program, and

(b) produces another representation of the program as output.

Figure 1.5 A BASIC interpreter.

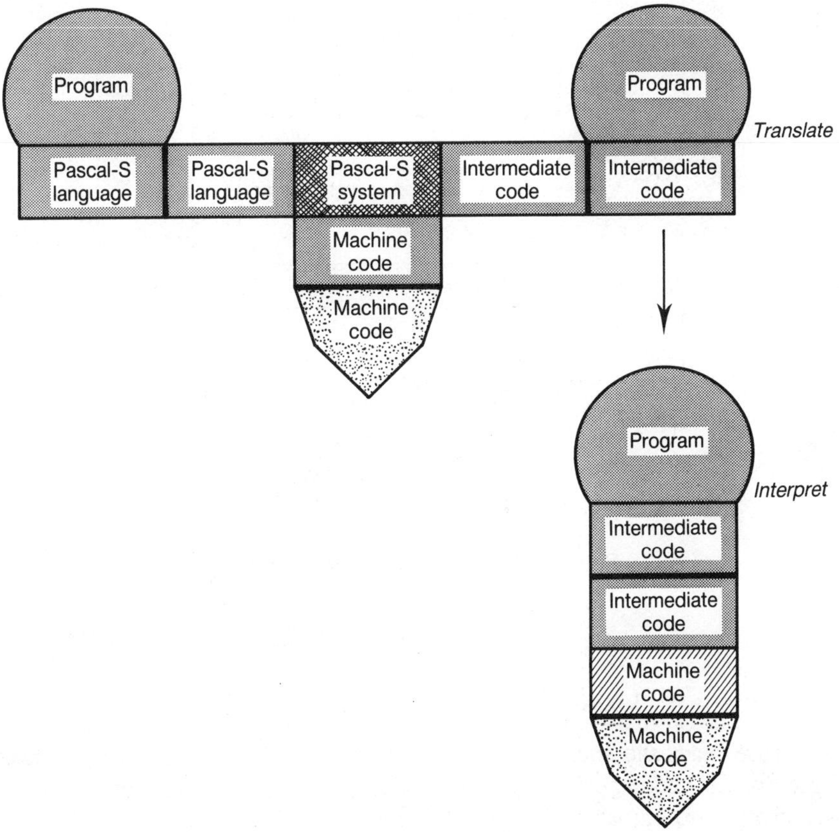

Figure 1.6 Pascal-S.

Figure 1.7 shows the basic structure for the operation of a compiler, modified from a previous design (Aho and Ullman, 1977).

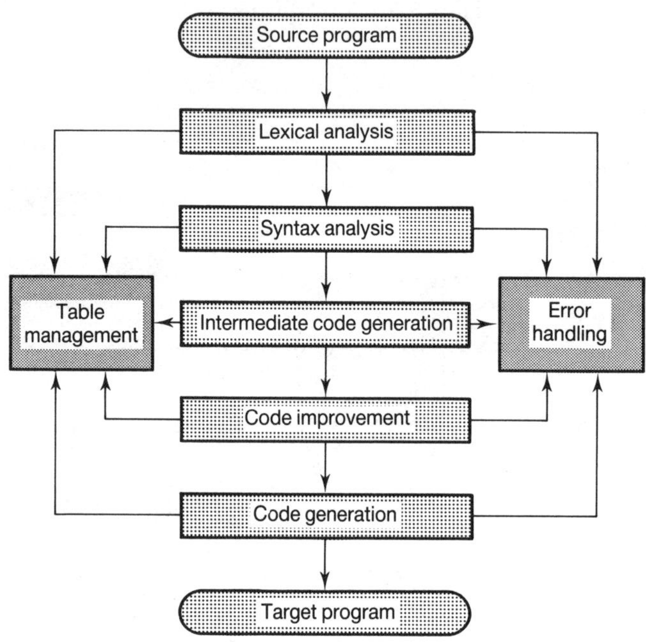

Figure 1.7 The structure of a compiler.

1.3.1 Phase 1 – lexical analysis or scanner

This phase reads the source text prepared by the user and separates characters of the source language into groups that logically belong together. The character groups are known as **tokens**. Examples of tokens are:

- keywords
- identifiers
- operators
- punctuation such as parentheses

The scanner passes on a linear stream of tokens to the next phase.

1.3.2 Phase 2 – syntax analysis or parser

The tokens from phase 1 are grouped into **syntactic structures** using the rules of syntax for the source language being translated. The whole program or module is often built as a large **syntax tree**, which is made available to the next phase. Any contraventions of the syntax rules are noted in this phase and the programmer informed via suitable **error messages**. Either interleaved with syntactic checks or implemented as a second subphase comes a series of **semantic checks** where the *meanings* of the syntactic structures are validated.

1.3.3 Phase 3 – intermediate code generator

From the syntax tree, the intermediate code generator produces a stream of simple, canonical **instructions**. These instructions usually assume some suitably simple virtual machine. An example is the stack machine, with a single hardware stack and one-address instructions. A primary design goal of this virtual machine is that it should be able to map easily onto a wide range of actual hardware.

Note that up to and including this phase, the translation is **independent** of the actual hardware machine on which the object language program will eventually execute. These first three phases are often referred to as the **front end** of a compiler.

1.3.4 Phase 4 – code improvement

This is an optional phase designed to improve the intermediate code. Improvements include savings in instruction volume and increases in execution speed. It is imperative, of course, that any changes to the intermediate code should leave the logic of the original source program unchanged. Another term for this phase is **code optimization**. It is not possible, however, to adequately define what the optimum or 'best' code version of a program should be. On the other hand, improvements to the code size or speed of execution can be accurately measured.

1.3.5 Phase 5 – code generation

The final phase produces the target code for the real or virtual machine. It is at this point that the fine details of the machine architecture are considered and utilized. Allocating memory and registers for data manipulation, selecting instructions and generating system calls to the next level of virtual machine (the operating system) are the main tasks.

Producing efficient machine code is still an extremely difficult part of compiler design and considerable research is still proceeding in this area.

1.3.6 Service routines

Two other components appear on the diagram which are not compilation phases. **Table management** or **bookkeeping** comprises a set of procedures to manipulate the **symbol table** where details of all programmer-defined and built-in symbols used within the program are kept. These procedures are called by all phases of the compiler which use the various components of the symbol table for interphase communication purposes. Bookkeeping procedures keep track of the symbolic names used by the program together with attribute information.

The **error handler** is also a set of global procedures and is invoked when flaws in the source program are detected in the various phases. The user must be informed with diagnostic messages, and special information must be passed to later phases to allow error recovery. As far as possible, *all errors* in the source program should be reported.

1.4 Phase architecture

The compiler designer has a choice of how to organize the phases of a compiler. Conceptually, each phase transforms the source text one **program fragment** (group of lexical tokens) at a time. The way in which fragments are passed to the various phases influences the overall structure of the compiler.

If each fragment goes through all phases before compilation of the next begins, the compiler is said to be **single-pass**. The entire source program is compiled in a single scan of the source text.

Conversely, if the entire program goes through one of the phases before any of it is presented to the next, it is called a **multi-pass** compiler. Each phase scans the whole program. If there are n phases, anything from 1 to n passes are possible. A **two-pass** scheme is the most common. Lexical and syntax analysis form the first pass, with the remaining phases comprising the second pass.

The decision on how many passes to use is usually influenced by the amount of main memory available. Single-pass compilers execute quickly since all the code and data are held in main memory. However, large amounts of memory are required, particularly for large source programs. Multi-pass compilers, on the other hand, can save on main memory, since the second pass can overlay the first. However, intermediate files must be used to hold the intermediate code or parse tree. This slows the operation of a two-pass compiler considerably.

1.5 The compiler specification

Welsh and McKeag (Welsh and McKeag, 1980) provide a succinct specification for a compiler. The source language version of a program is created by the programmer with the aid of a text editor of some kind. A compiler inputs this program in source language, and can produce two forms of output:

(a) the input program in object language format;

(b) a listing of the source program.

1.5.1 The input

It seems at first sight that the input is perfectly defined – the syntax definition of the source language determines exactly the set of programs the compiler may accept. This is fairly straightforward. Rohl (Rohl, 1975) puts it more succinctly: 'Any fool can write a compiler for correct source programs.'

However, a practical compiler is expected to diagnose faults in *incorrect* programs. Thus *all* possible input streams must be accepted, a considerable task.

Nevertheless, the source language definition remains the central component of the compiler's specification. The syntax definition of most programming languages can be achieved with a standard notation:- Backus-Naur Form, BNF. Apart from the syntax definition of the source language, the compiler must take into account the **semantics** of each statement of a particular source program. This is because the **form** of the program may be correct but the **meaning**, in terms of which operations may validly be performed on specific data values, may not. Formal definition of the semantics given to programs, and the semantic restraints which the language rules impose, is more difficult to specify, with no universally accepted method available.

The BNF definition of the source language greatly assists the compiler writer in determining the structure of the compiler. The semantic definitions come into the reckoning during semantic analysis and code generation.

1.5.2 The output

Two forms of output are produced:

(a) program listing;

(b) object program.

Remembering that the compiler will deal with more incorrect programs than correct ones, the qualities of the program listing and the error messages it contains may be as important as those of the object code.

The *program listing* supports two main functions:

(a) a confirmation, and permanent visual record, of the source program compiled;

(b) an indication of all the errors detected by the compiler.

No general agreement exists on the principles governing listing format and layout. This sadly neglected exercise in human-machine engineering deserves more emphasis.

The programmer expects the compiler

(a) to enforce every language rule;

(b) to find *all* violations of the language rules in a single compilation run;

(c) to generate no spurious or misleading error reports due to preceding errors.

Achieving (b) and (c) implies the compiler must resume compilation immediately on detecting each error. This is clearly impossible in some situations. However, the need for error recovery is a dominant influence on compiler design.

At run-time, when the *object program* is finally executed, there is a further possibility of malfunction due to such circumstances as arithmetic errors and memory bounds violations. These difficulties obviously constrain the design of the object program.

The target code output by the compiler is expressed in a precisely defined language, either a machine code or an intermediate language. The exact mapping from source to target code is left to the compiler writer. In choosing a suitable mapping, several attributes of the object program are taken into account:

(a) compactness or memory economy;

(b) speed of execution;

(c) security against run-time errors;

(d) run-time diagnostics.

A number of these attributes, particularly (a) and (b), and (b) and (c), are mutually conflicting, and cannot all be realized in a single object program. Some compromise is achieved according to particular priorities specified by the programmer at compilation time. (Not all compilers offer the programmer an opportunity to influence the characteristics of the generated code in this manner.)

The remaining chapters of this book take up the points raised in this section and present techniques and examples for implementing a practical compiler.

1.6 Compiler construction

With the plethora of programming languages and the wide range of computer hardware the number of different compilers that are required is very large indeed. It is hardly surprising, therefore, that over the decades many software tools have emerged for easing the compiler production process. One of the earliest tools was the **compiler-compiler** (Brooker and Morris, 1967) which inputs a textual description of the syntax of a language and outputs the skeleton code for a compiler for that language. Further information had to be provided in the form of **action routines** to be called to generate code for each syntactic construct as it was recognized. This tool therefore allows parts of a compiler to be generated automatically to address the first two phases of compilation. Lexical scanner and syntax analyser generators, as they are more properly called, are very commonly used to construct new translators of many kinds. Popular examples of such tools are *lex* (Lesk, 1975) and *yacc* (Johnson, 1975) found on the UNIX system. The widespread use of such tools can be judged from *yacc* which stands for 'yet another compiler-compiler'. Both *yacc* and *lex* generate code in C, a suitable compiler-writing language. It is hardly surprising, therefore, to find that most UNIX compilers and translators are written in C.

Another popular compiler implementation language is Pascal. This precludes the use of the *yacc* and *lex* tools. To rectify this loss, a team from the University of New South Wales have implemented equivalent tools in Pascal. The lexical analyser generator is called *aardvark* (White, 1981) and the syntax analyser generator *llama* (Dunn and Murphy, 1976). Using these tools to generate part of a Pascal translator written in Pascal is discussed in later chapters.

The trend for more recently designed 3GLs is to write the compiler in the language itself, i.e. **self-compiling compilers** (Cornelius *et al.*, 1984). Of course, for a new language no previous compiler exists. A **bootstrap** process is required to reach a self-compiling compiler using a translator for another language. Transferring existing compilers to a new computer architecture leads to similar problems, which also require a bootstrapping process.

As an example, consider the bootstrapping process to implement the first Pascal compiler (Wirth, 1971) on the CDC6000 machine at the Zurich Institute of Technology (Lecarme and Peyrolle-Thomas, 1978). The first step involved writing a compiler in the full Pascal language for a restricted Pascal subset comprising about 60% of the complete language. This restricted Pascal, P60% say, was designed to be sufficient to implement the full language compiler. Figure 1.8 shows the first object. With no compiler for any version of Pascal available, this source program was hand-translated, with all the associated scope for error, into Scallop – a medium-level systems language for which a compiler did exist. The hand-translation was converted into a P60% compiler by the Scallop compiler as shown in Figure 1.9. The resultant large, untested program was only to be used once to generate a compiler

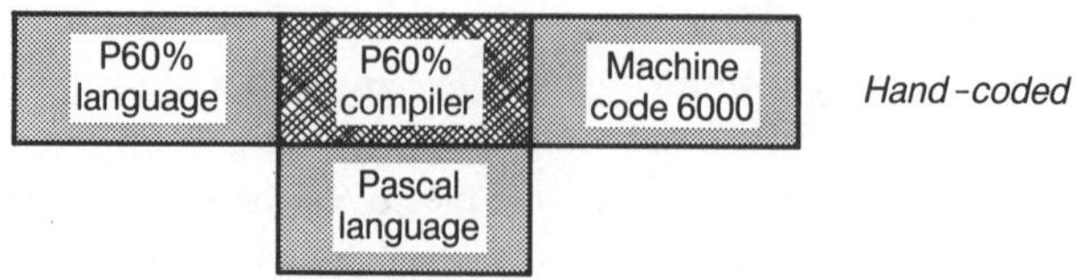

Figure 1.8 P60% compiler written in full Pascal.

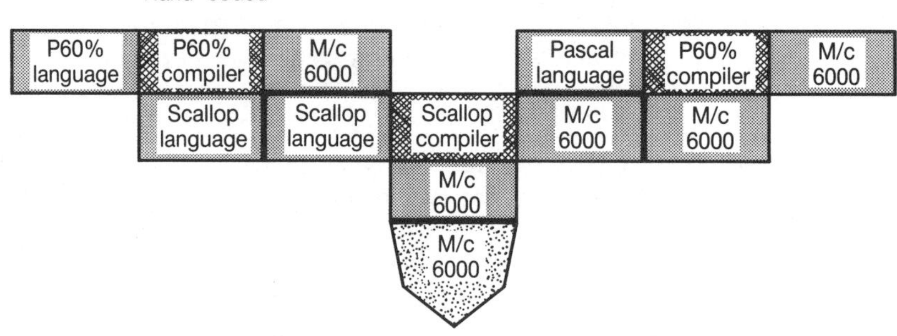

Figure 1.9 P60% compiler translated from Scallop.

for the full Pascal language written by hand in P60% – see execution 1 in Figure 1.10. As a final step, a compiler for full Pascal is written in Pascal and this first self-compiling compiler is generated by execution 2 in the same figure. For validation purposes, it is wise to perform execution 3. This should result in the same machine code for the full language compiler as that produced by execution 2. Because this process is laborious – four hand-coded compilers are produced – it is called a **full bootstrap.**

When bootstrapping a compiler from machine A to machine B, with a different architecture, a similar mechanism is used, but it is usually referred to as a **half-bootstrap**. The first step is to change the source of the compiler for machine A to generate code for machine B. What results is a compiler for machine B which executes on machine A. Such a program is known as a **cross-compiler**. Sometimes the process stops at this point because the hardware configuration of the target machine B may be insufficient to ever run a compiler itself. Examples of this abound in embedded systems applications such as domestic electrical appliances, small microcomputers and microprocessor controllers. A good many of the programs for execution on the Apple Macintosh were originally written in Pascal and compiled on the larger Apple Lisa machine.

More usually, though, the source of the cross-compiler for machine B is compiled by itself on machine A and transferred to machine B. As above,

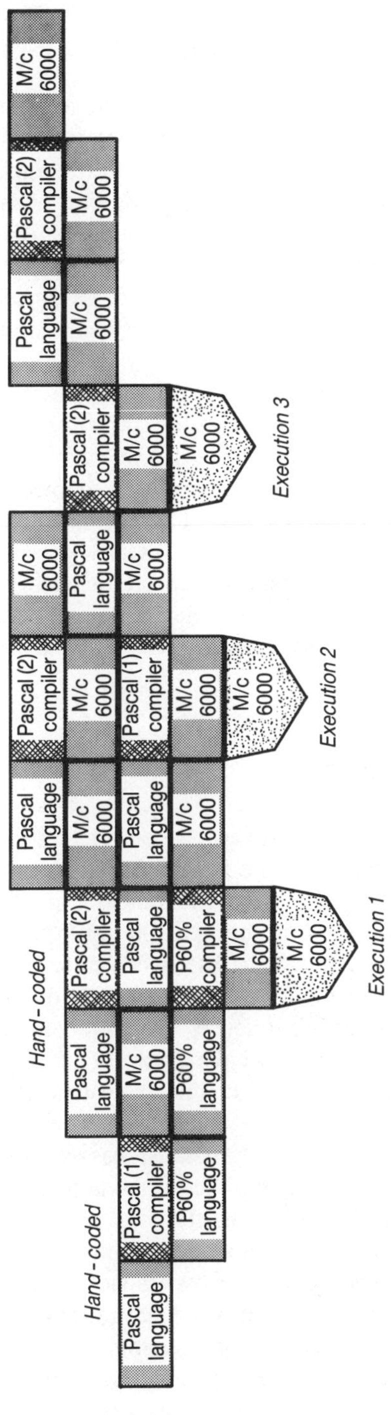

Figure 1.10 A full Pascal compiler produced with the P60% compiler.

the B compiler should be recompiled on machine B to validate the code. From this point compilations can proceed on machine B alone. This is indicated in Figure 1.11.

The microprocessor revolution resulted in a large number of new architectures requiring the bootstrapping of a great many compilers. In turn this led to the introduction of a new tool, the **portable compiler**. This simply capitalizes on the fact that all but the code generation phases, the **back-end**, of a compiler can be made machine-independent. The **front-end** can therefore be left unchanged during a bootstrap. By adopting a translator-interpreter approach, even the generation of the intermediate code can be made machine-independent. Only the interpreter itself remains dependent on the actual machine architecture.

Bootstrapping to a new machine now involves the relatively simple process of hand-coding a new interpreter for the intermediate code. The machine-independent front-end, itself expressed in intermediate code, can then be transferred across unchanged and interpreted immediately on the new machine. All programs available on the old machine then become instantly available, too. Such an approach has been used with great success by the UCSD Pascal (Bowles, 1977) system where all the compilers, utilities and most of the operating system itself are expressed in P-code. To implement the UCSD Pascal system on a new machine only the P-code interpreter needs to be rewritten.

1.7 Design constraints

As with any substantial piece of software, a compiler is subject to a number of design constraints in order to ensure it performs the task specified for it in a way acceptable to the end-user. This is definitely true of a compiler which easily takes on the status of a god in terms of the faith vested in it, by novice users in particular. They are taught to use a compiler to judge the correctness, syntactically at least, of their own programs. It does not take much to imagine the complete loss of confidence in the compilation process that occurs when the compiler is found to have errors of its own. Beginning programmers tend to lack any trust in the computer system as a whole from that point onwards.

The first design constraint therefore must be *reliability*. Guaranteeing compiler reliability starts by applying the usual approach of simple, well-structured program design. This involves the logical separation of operations and the use of well-understood techniques for their realization. Modular development and modular testing are the two most important implementation techniques. Such methods are becoming better understood and can be garnered from reputable texts on software engineering.

Fortunately, the compiler writers of today have three decades of previous development to fall back upon. The logical separation of function within

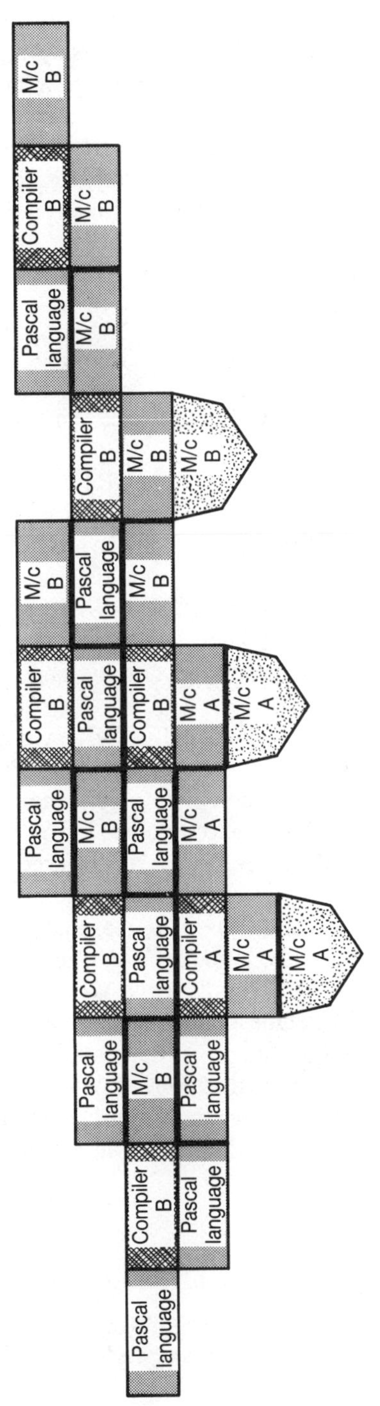

Figure 1.11 Transporting and checking a cross-compiler.

a compiler is well-known and has already been outlined in section 1.2.

Compilers, of course, are very basic tools. They are a necessary prerequisite for the generation of all other applications programs, including other compilers. The applications programs, in their turn, carry out the information processing requirements of users on which the performance of the computer systems as a whole are judged. *Efficiency* is therefore another very important design constraint for a production compiler. Such a compiler needs to address the efficiency constraints of:

(a) compilation speed;
(b) memory requirements;
(c) backing store utilization.

The choice between single-pass and multi-pass operation plays a very significant role here.

As can be seen from languages such as FORTRAN and COBOL which have appeared in many different versions over the decades, compilers need to be *flexible*. Not only does the language change over time, but the working environment is also subject to considerable modification. Operating systems evolve, too, and the compiler is expected to utilize new system facilities as they arise. Last, but probably most important of all, are the changes to the computer hardware itself as new processor designs and addressing schemes emerge.

For the compiler, machine and operating system dependency come to the fore during code optimization and generation. A fully flexible compiler will ensure that all earlier phases are completely machine-independent.

A detailed description of a true compiler for a particular operating system/hardware combination would require a much larger book than this. It would also lack generalization as far as the code generation aspects are concerned. Instead this book concentrates on a reasonably general translator-interpreter for a major subset of the popular language Pascal. The resulting discussion covers techniques which should have wide applicability for other languages. By presenting full details of the virtual machine assumed by the interpreter the reader should be able to extrapolate into the real world of machine language and system call generation without difficulty. It is hoped that the scale of effort required to construct a useful compiler will be conveyed accurately so as to show the reader the scale of problem involved with writing translators.

References

Aho, A V and Ullman, J D, *Principles of Compiler Design*, Addison-Wesley, 1977.

Bowles, K L, *Problem Solving Using Pascal*, Springer-Verlag, 1977.

Bratman, H, 'An alternative form of the UNCOL diagram', *Comm. ACM*, vol. 4, p. 142, 1961.

Brooker, R A, Morris, D, and Rohl, J S, 'Experience with the compiler-compiler', *Computer Journal*, vol. 9, pp. 345–349, 1967.

Cornelius, B J, Lowman, I R, and Robson, D J, 'Steady-state compilers', *Software: Practice and Experience*, vol. 14, pp. 705–709, 1984.

Dunn, B J and Murphy, T J, 'Llama: A compiler generator', (Honours Thesis), University of New South Wales, 1976.

Earley, J and Sturgis, H, 'A formalism for translator interactions', *Comm. ACM*, vol. 13, no. 10, pp. 607–617, 1970.

Johnson, S C, 'Yacc—yet another compiler-compiler', Computer Science Technical Report No. 32, Bell Laboratories, 1975.

Lecarme, O and Peyrolle-Thomas, M-C, 'Self-compiling compilers: an appraisal of their implementation and portability', *Software: Practice and Experience*, vol. 8, pp. 149–170, 1978.

Lesk, M E, 'Lex—a lexical analyzer generator', Computer Science Technical Report No. 39, Bell Laboratories, 1975.

Rohl, J S, *An Introduction to Compiler Writing*, MacDonald Elsevier, 1975.

Tanenbaum, A S, *Structured Computer Organisation* (Second Edition), Prentice-Hall, 1984.

Welsh, J and McKeag, M, *Structured System Programming*, Prentice-Hall, 1980.

White, B, 'Aardvark: a lexical analyser generator', (Honours Thesis), University of New South Wales, 1981.

Wirth, N, 'The design of a pascal compiler', *Software: Practice and Experience*, vol. 1, pp. 309–333, 1971.

Chapter 2
Concepts of Programming Languages

Mention has already been made in chapter 1 of the vast diversity of problem-oriented programming languages. These 3GLs vary from the free-format, block-structured languages such as Algol, Pascal and Ada to the line-at-a-time, linear-structured languages such as FORTRAN, COBOL and BASIC. The 3GL spectrum also spans the range from the more common statement-based languages to those which use a completely functional notation such as LISP and APL. Despite the diversity, techniques exist to define programming languages with sufficient clarity to allow compilers to be constructed. This chapter discusses those concepts of programming languages which have an effect on compiler design and introduces the Pascal-S language used throughout the remainder of the book.

2.1 Definitions of programming languages

Before compiler design can begin, a complete definition of the programming language to be supported must be created. An unambiguous language definition notation is required. To cater for all the categories of people involved with a particular programming language, the perfect notation would allow:

- a **language designer** to simply and clearly express what programs are valid and what these programs mean;
- a **programmer** to determine what programs could be written and exactly what data manipulation each program performs;
- a **compiler writer** to determine what source programs a compiler should accept, and what object code the compiler should produce for them.

No widely accepted notation of this nature exists to support all of these tasks. All is not lost, however, as notations do exist to describe some parts of the definition process which can be applied in a general way.

Syntax definition is one such area. A **program** is defined as a string of characters chosen from an **alphabet** of allowable characters. The **syntax** of the language consists of a set of rules expressed in a suitable notation. Examples of such notations are **context-free grammars** expressed in BNF and **regular expressions** which employ their own, simple notation. A visual notation which utilizes graphics is the **syntax diagram.** The structure of the syntax definition expressed in such a notation has a direct influence on the structure of the compiler itself. Notations for syntax definition are thus essential for compiler design.

Given a syntactically correct program, it is essential to determine the meaning of the program in order to generate the correct object code. Rules that give meaning to a program are known as the **semantics** of the programming language. No completely satisfactory means of specifying semantics exists which helps directly in defining the structure of a compiler.

To demonstrate the problem of defining semantics, consider the possible meanings of the repetition statement given in (Aho and Ullman, 1977)

for *i* := 1 **step** 10–*j* **until** 10**j* **do** *j* := *j* + 1;

Meaning 1: Evaluate the upper bound and the increment of the repetition once, before start of loop. If *j* has the value 5 at loop start, then the loop becomes equivalent to

for *i* := 1 **step** 5 **until** 50 **do** *j* := *j* + 1;

Thus a 10-fold loop results with the loop index *i* taking the values 1, 6, 11, 16, 21, 26, 31, 36, 41 and 46.

Meaning 2: Evaluate the upper bound and increment on each repetition. If *j* is again 5 at the start of the repetition, then an infinite loop results. This is because the upper bound increases without limit while the increment eventually becomes negative when *j* reaches the value 11.

Meaning 3: Change the repetition termination criterion to the loop variable being strictly less than the upper bound for negative increment values. Now the repetition terminates when *j* reaches 11 having executed the loop six times.

It is interesting to note that loop constructs adopted by the various programming languages tend to have widely different semantics, seemingly at the whim of the language designer. This leads to considerable programmer confusion when switching between languages. It was specifically to avoid such problems that the fixed repetition construct in Pascal, for example, was made extremely simple. Many other examples of widely differing semantics for the same language fragment could be given, particularly in the areas of expression evaluation and parameter passing. The need for a properly defined semantics for the language being compiled should now be obvious.

Many attempts have been made to introduce a formal notation for semantic definition. All have some merit but have tended to be too language-specific or expensive in terms of the human effort needed to define a realistic 3GL. Some approaches to semantic definition as listed in (Aho and Ullman, 1977) are:

Interpretive semantics	The semantics of machine language are defined by the hardware itself. By postulating an abstract or virtual machine, and rules for executing its machine code, the meanings of programs are defined. Virtual machines are characterized by a **state**, consisting of all data objects, their values, and the program counter. The rules specify state transitions for each language construct. The Vienna Definition Language (Wegner, 1972) was used principally to define the PL/I programming language, and is an example of interpretive semantics.
Translation	A set of rules is devised which associates with each valid program a sentence in a language whose semantics are well known. An example is a mathematical notation such as lambda calculus. Another is an existing machine language – the translator for this language becomes the semantic definition.
Axiomatic definition	Rules are defined that relate the data before and after execution of each program construct. The rules can be used to prove theorems about the input/output relation of a program. This approach also aids proofs of **program correctness**.
Extensible definition	Here primitive operations are defined whose semantics are well known. Each language construct is then defined in terms of these primitives. Good examples of this approach are to be found in the LISP and FORTH languages.
Denotational semantics	Mathematical objects corresponding to programs are defined, and rules given to perform the mapping from the programming language to the mathematical notation. Standard mathematical analysis techniques can then be used to verify the exact meaning of a particular programming language construct.

It is not necessary to use a single method of semantic definition. Several of the approaches described above can be combined to specify different parts of one language. Indeed, perusal of the international standards for such languages as FORTRAN, COBOL and Pascal will reveal a variety of the above techniques in use together with the specification of semantic rules in a natural language such as English.

The remaining sections of this chapter cover each of the major aspects of typical 3GLs and discuss the important questions which arise for the compiler writer. In each topic closer consideration is given to the Pascal language since the case study used in later chapters is a major subset of Pascal.

2.2 Lexical and syntactic structure

The set of symbols used in a programming language is called its **character set or alphabet**. Early languages such as FORTRAN and COBOL had small alphabets, as low as 48 in FORTRAN – 26 upper case letters, digits, the space (or blank) character and twelve other special characters. Most languages today accept the internationally defined ASCII or EBCDIC character sets, or subsets of these. Some languages in the Algol class, for example, regard some keywords such as **for** and **begin** as additional, individual characters in the alphabet.

Where a standard alphabet such as ASCII is used, the string representing the program can be partitioned into substrings called **lexical tokens**. Commonly used types of token are shown in Table 2.1.

Table 2.1 Token types.

Token Type	*Examples*
constants	1 2.3 4.56e6
identifiers	*a H2035B speed total_pay*
operator symbols	+ - ** **div**
keywords	**if begin procedure flex**
punctuation symbols	([{ , :

Tokens are combined into higher-level constructs such as expressions which are groupings of constants, identifiers and operators. In turn, expressions build into larger constructs such as statements, blocks and programs.

Layout constraints can have a big effect on lexical analysis. Languages such as FORTRAN require certain statement elements to be written in particular positions on the input line, reminiscent of the strict layout of some assembly languages.

The treatment of *blanks* is another major issue. In some languages such as Algol, blanks are simply used to aid readability for the human programmer. The compiler itself ignores blanks completely. Other languages treat blanks as token separators, so their presence or absence affects the syntactic structure. Pascal is such a language.

a **div** *b*

in Pascal is an example of the integer division operator. A blank is required after the first operand, *a*, and the keyword, **div**.

2.3 Data types

A basic building block of programming languages is the set of **data elements** to which operators can be applied. More complex **data structures** are then constructed from the basic data elements. Considerable variety exists:

- *Numerical data.* This includes integers, reals, complex and multiple precision numbers.
- *Logical data.* Most languages have a Boolean (logical) data type and possibly a bit string type. Both can be subjected to logical operations such as *and*, *or* and *not*.
- *Character data.* Character strings are complicated data structures as they may naturally vary in length during program execution. Early languages either failed to recognize the need for this data type or included very basic facilities for single characters or fixed-length strings. Pascal falls into this category. Other languages permit a range of string facilities such as character and string types, where the strings have dynamic length during execution.
- *Pointers.* These are data elements whose values allow access to other data elements. The general facility is

  p := addr(x)

  which means *p* 'points to' *x*. Writing

  *y := p^*

  means assign to *y* the data element pointed at by *p*. Pointers allow the programmer complete freedom to design novel, dynamic data structures to suit the particular application. Unfortunately, unless very carefully controlled, they also give enormous scope for misuse. Pascal has pointer types but restricts each pointer to refer to a specific data element type. Also, **pointer values** can only be created by calling a special procedure, *new*, which also controls the memory allocated to the data element pointed at. Even so Pascal is not immune to pointer problems, with scope for *dangling* pointers (to non-existent memory) and *hidden* pointers (which can no longer be accessed).

- *Labels*. Some languages permit a data type whose value is the position of a statement within the program, to allow a direct transfer of control to be specified. Pascal is not such a language but label constants are allowed. A specific label identifier, a number, can be placed before any statement. Statements of the form

  goto *label*

  allow the transfer of control to be actioned.
- *Sets*. Pascal is one of the very few languages to introduce the *set* as a data type. Sets record the presence or absence of each *member* of the set. Set members belong to a specified type which must have a (small) finite number of possible values.
- *Enumerated data*. Pascal was the first mainstream language to enable the programmer to define *enumerated* types. Each component value of the type is given a name, and an ordering within the type. The number of values in the type corresponds to the number of names defined.

2.4 Identifiers and names

Each memory cell has a **name**, which usually corresponds to a variable in a programming language. In turn, each name is denoted by an **identifier**, which is a string of characters. The same identifier may denote different names at different places in the program or at different times during program execution.

Each name possesses a **value** and **attributes**. The value may be numerical, or it could be an input-output relationship if the name is a procedure, for example. The attributes determine:

(a) the possible *values* that the name may have,

(b) the *operations* that may be applied, and

(c) the effect of those operations.

A name is represented, at the implementation level, by a portion of memory. (A name may represent different locations at different times while the program is running. For example, a recursive procedure in which an integer *FACTORIAL* is declared may have several instances of *FACTORIAL* in memory at one time. The name *FACTORIAL* refers to the location of the most recently activated instance. Conversely, the same location may have several names. When procedure *P(X)* is called by *P(A)*, the name *A* in the calling procedure may denote the same location as the name *X* of *P*. This will depend on the parameter-passing convention of the particular programming language.) This location contains a sequence of bits indicating the value, and sometimes a **data descriptor** or **dope vector**, which indicates how the bits are to be decoded. Data descriptors allow the size of the data structure to change during execution.

The attributes of a name determine its properties. The most important attribute is its **type**, which defines:

(a) the *values* the name may take,

(b) the way its value is *represented*, and

(c) the *operations* that may be performed on the name.

Other attributes of a name may determine its **scope**, i.e. where in the program its value is accessible.

Pascal is a strongly typed language. Every data element must have a built-in or programmer-defined type. Every type either has a name with an associated identifier or is defined *in situ*, when it is referred to as an anonymous type.

Another named object with which a Pascal compiler must deal is the **constant**. Constant identifiers can be used anywhere in a Pascal statement where a numerical, logical or character constant value can appear. The compiler must essentially perform a textual substitution by replacing the constant identifier by the actual value of the constant.

2.5 Declarations

Depending on the particular programming language, attributes of a name may be determined: **implicitly**, **explicitly**, or by **default**. For example, in FORTRAN, any identifier beginning with one of the letters in the range I to N inclusive is implicitly of type integer. Where partial attributes are explicitly declared, others may be assumed by default. Most modern 3GLs, with a proper emphasis on program correctness, insist on **explicit declaration**.

The act of associating attributes to a name is referred to as **binding**. Most binding is done at compile time when the compiler reads the declarations – this is **static binding**. Some languages, such as POP-2, APL and SNOBOL, allow **dynamic binding** – that is, binding at run time. In these circumstances, the value of an identifier may literally change its data type while the program is executing.

There are a number of substantial benefits to static binding despite the protests of some programmers when they are forced to explicitly declare the type of every identifier. (Languages like BASIC and FORTRAN, for example, make automatic assumptions about attributes.) Static binding allows considerable **type checking**, i.e. semantic checks that make sure no illegal mixing of types takes place in expressions. In addition, type checking allows efficient code to be generated since no checks at run time are necessary, which is the case for dynamic binding.

2.6 Data structures

A data structure is a set of primitive data elements together with a set of **structural relations** among its components. By allowing data structures to be defined in terms of other structures, including themselves, recursive data structures are possible. Examples of such structures are lists and trees. Other common structures are arrays, queues, stacks, and strings.

Every data structure requires a set of manipulation functions:

(a) **constructors** to create instances of structures;

(b) **destructors** to reclaim memory occupied by structures;

(c) **selectors** to access structures.

An *array* is a collection of elements all of the same type laid out in a multi-dimensional structure. The measure of the distance along each dimension is called the **index** or **subscript**.

The upper and lower bounds of each index may be known at compile time (a **fixed-size** array) or determined at run time (an **adjustable** array).

One of the design constraints of Pascal was that the size of every data structure should be known at compile time. Consequently, all Pascal arrays are fixed in size. (Level 1 of the ISO Pascal Standard (ISO 7185) allows a variant of this rule in the form of **conformant arrays**. Procedures and functions can be declared which take array parameters whose magnitude is not known at compilation time – a form of adjustable array.)

Logically, a *record structure* is like a tree, with the **fields** of the record being the children of the root, the **subfields** being the children of these, and so on. As with fixed-size arrays, records are implemented as a block of memory. The length and offset of each field from the start (or base) of the record are determined at compile time.

In addition to fixed-size records, Pascal allows the length of the *last* field in a record to vary according to the value set in one of the other fields. This type of record is referred to as a **variant record**.

Character strings can be treated as one-dimensional arrays whose data elements are characters. However, strings naturally vary in length and, indeed, may be completely empty. Dynamic memory allocation is required for adjustable strings, together with a data descriptor indicating the current length. Such a facility can lead to significant management overhead at run-time if memory use is to be maximized. Routines to carry out the allocation also occupy memory. It is perhaps for these reasons that Pascal allows only string constants to be declared which can be output as messages or assigned to variables whose type is a suitably dimensioned array of single characters. Programmers are forced to use fixed-size character arrays to manipulate strings and construct their own handling procedures.

2.7 Operators

It can be said that the richness of a language is determined by its operators. A number of the general-purpose 3GLs such as PL/I and Ada allow programmers to further enrich the extensive set of built-in operators by defining their own.

The commonly found types of arithmetic operator are:

(a) **binary infix**: e.g. x + y;

(b) **unary prefix**: e.g. –x;

(c) **unary postfix**: e.g. x++ (postincrement).

There are no operators of type (c) in Pascal. Operators are combined with numeric operands to form an **arithmetic expression.** When evaluated, an expression yields a single numeric value. Rules for expression construction can be stated as:

(a) A single data reference is an expression, i.e. data element name, identifier, constant or data structure selector.

(b) If • is a binary infix operator and E1 and E2 are expressions, then E1•E2 is an expression.

(c) If • is a unary prefix operator and E is an expression, then •E is an expression. Similarly for E• if • is a unary postfix operator.

(d) If E is an expression, then so is (E).

Conditional expressions evaluate to *true* or *false* and are composed of arithmetic expressions and **relational operators.** Apart from the exponentiation operator, Pascal supports the four basic arithmetic operators and a full set of relational operators. In addition, operators are provided to manipulate sets, a feature rarely found in other languages.

As well as the rules for the syntax of expressions, semantic rules are required to define the order of evaluation for expressions which contain several operators. The notion of **operator precedence** levels is used to indicate which operators are allowed to group their operands first. Different languages sadly use different precedence schemes.

2.8 Language statements

After expressions, the next largest construct in most 3GLs is the **statement. Assignment** statements are the most common statement type in programming languages. The basic structure is:

data element := *expression*

where := is the **assignment symbol.** (In a very few languages, the assignment symbol is regarded as another operator which can appear in any expression; assignment takes place as part of expression evaluation.)

The location and value represented by a name are two distinct concepts. Both are used in a single assignment statement. The value to be assigned is known as the **r-value**, whereas the location to receive the value is the **l-value**.

Some rules clarify the concept:

(a) Every name has an l-value.

(b) If *A* is an array, the l-value of *A[i]* is the location reserved for the *i*th element of the array. The r-value is the value stored there.

(c) The constant 2 has an r-value but no l-value.

(d) If *P* is a pointer, its r-value is the location to which *P* points and its l-value is the location in which the value of *P* itself is stored.

Apart from assignment, statements fall into the following types:

- **Sequence.** A compound statement which can be treated as a single unit at a higher level in the program structure. Pascal notation is:

  begin
  statement$_1$;
  statement$_2$;
  . . .
  statement$_n$
  end

- **Selection.** A decision-making statement which offers one or more alternative courses of action. There are two such statements in Pascal:

  (a) **if** . . . **then** . . . **else**
  (b) **case** . . . **of**
  . . .
  end

- **Repetition.** A looping statement which causes other statements to be repeated zero or more times. Three such statements are provided in Pascal.

  (a) **for** . . . **do** . . .
  (b) **while** . . . **do** . . .
  (c) **repeat** . . . **until** . . .

- **Control transfer.** A statement which interrupts the normal linear sequence of statement execution and directs it to resume at a specified statement. Control may or may not subsequently return to the point of interruption. Pascal provides the **goto** statement for direct transfer of control, and the *procedure call* for subroutine execution.

- **Input/output**. A statement which allows data values to be imported or exported from the program execution environment. The Pascal language does not contain such statements. Input and output are performed by procedure calls.

2.9 Program units

These form the major building blocks for programs and are the highest-level structures. They are often referred to as **subprograms**. Two types of subprograms are **procedures** and **functions**. More modern languages incorporate higher-level subprograms such as tasks, modules, packages, monitors and classes.

Splitting programs into separate units creates the problem of the **scope** of names. Common practice is to adopt static scope rules which can be checked and enforced at compile time. Pascal uses such an approach.

More esoteric languages such as SNOBOL and APL, which allow dynamic binding, are forced to adopt dynamic scoping. Here, the scope of names can vary during program execution depending on which data objects are bound to which names.

A second major problem area is **parameter passing**. Three different approaches are:

- call-by-reference;
- call-by-name;
- call-by-value.

Pascal adopts only the first and last mechanisms.

2.10 Storage management

Several techniques are available for allocating memory for data values during program execution. Where the language permits, **static storage allocation** can be used. Here the size and location of all objects are known at compile time, so fixed-size memory areas can be allocated prior to program execution. FORTRAN is an example of such a language.

Block-structured languages, of which Pascal is one, deliberately delay the allocation of memory for local variables until a particular subprogram is called. This calls for **dynamic storage allocation** and **deallocation** during program execution. Fortunately, the order of memory allocation follows the order of subprogram call and a simple stack allocation mechanism can be used. Recursive subprogram call is also supported this way.

Supporting adjustable and dynamic data structures requires the more sophisticated dynamic storage allocation of various types. The overhead in managing the data space can be high, and careful selection of efficient schemes is required. Pascal requires dynamic storage for pointer variables which must have permanently allocated memory for the data structures pointed at. A completely separate memory area, referred to as the **heap**, is needed to support this requirement.

The major topics of language specification have been briefly covered in this chapter. Techniques adopted for compiler construction are given in the remaining chapters for a substantial subset of the Pascal language called Pascal-S. In the main, specific mechanisms are shown without mentioning all the available alternatives. For these, the reader is directed to another, more detailed text such as (Aho *et al.*, 1986). The discussion will now concentrate on the particular problems of constructing a translator for Pascal-S.

2.11 The Pascal-S language

Pascal-S (Wirth, 1981) is a subset of the full Pascal language described in (Jensen and Wirth, 1975). The language features which Wirth chose for Pascal-S correspond to those which usually are taught in an introductory programming course in Pascal. Indeed, the first implementation of Pascal-S was used for this very purpose. The interpretive approach was chosen deliberately because 'it allows for a simple compiler and dense [intermediate] code'. From a student programming point of view, Pascal-S offers a short **program amendment** cycle of program edit, translate and test. For most programs written on an introductory course the speed of program execution is unimportant and interpretation is acceptable. Wirth thought it important that Pascal-S be a strict subset of Pascal so that Pascal-S programs could be compiled with a full Pascal compiler without change. These differences are summarized for reference purposes in Table 2.2.

Table 2.2 *Omissions from Pascal-S.*

Data types	enumerated, subrange and pointer
Data structures	variant **record**, **packed**, **set** and **file**
Statements	**with** and **goto**
Declarations	**label**, procedure/function parameters
Input/Output	*put* and *get*

In (Wirth, 1971) it is argued that the power of a programming language was determined by the allowed data types and associated operators. In this context, the power of Pascal-S can be judged by its inclusion of only four data types, integer, real, boolean and char. The enumerated and subrange types of Pascal are omitted. In addition, Pascal-S only supports unpacked array and non-variant record data structures. Missing are the set and file structures as well as pointer and hence all dynamic data structures.

Since the essence of well-structured programs relies on procedures and functions, Pascal-S retains all the features of Pascal except that procedure and function parameters cannot be used. To reinforce the structured program concept, the **goto** statement is omitted from Pascal-S and therefore the **label** declaration statement. One other statement not included in Pascal-S is **with**.

With the **file** data type missing, Pascal-S input/output is necessarily restricted to the standard files **input** and **output**, and with no file variables the *put* and *get* procedures are redundant.

The complete listing of the Pascal-S system is presented in (Wirth, 1981). This, Wirth says, 'proves that compiler *and* interpreter can be described in a machine-independent, well-structured form that nevertheless is effectively machine-translatable.' Another benefit of the Pascal-S listing is its brevity. For this reason and because Pascal-S is still a substantial language, the authors have adopted Pascal-S as the case study for this book.

Changes have been made to the original Pascal-S source to:

- increase the readability, with more meaningful identifier names;
- add debugging features for both programmer and compiler writer;
- improve the operation of the lexical scanner;
- make the interpreter more portable.

A complete, pretty-printed source listing and an extensive cross-reference are provided in the appendices so that the use of all identifiers in the source can be determined.

References

International Standards Organisation, 'ISO standard: specification for the computer programming language Pascal', 7185, 1983.

Aho, A V and Ullman, J D, *Principles of Compiler Design*, Addison-Wesley, 1977.

Aho, A V, Sethi, R, and Ullman, J D, *Compilers: Principles, Techniques and Tools*, Addison-Wesley, 1986.

Jensen, K and Wirth, N, *Pascal User Manual and Report*, Springer-Verlag, 1975.

Wirth, N, 'The design of a Pascal compiler', *Software: Practice and Experience*, vol. 1, pp. 309–333, 1971.

Wirth, N, 'Pascal-S: a subset and its implementation', in *Pascal - The Language and Its Implementation*, ed. D W Barron, pp. 199–260, Wiley, 1981.

Wegner, P, 'The Vienna definition language', *Computing Surveys*, vol. 4, pp. 5–63, 1972.

Chapter 3
The User Interface

The traditional interface provided by a compiler is the file containing the source text of the user's program. Using a software tool such as an editor program, the programmer builds one or more files containing the source program. At this point the compiler is called upon, and provided no errors are detected in the translation process, the end result is a file or files holding the object program, which is executed to test its validity.

If changes to the run-time behaviour of the object program are either necessary or desired, the complete edit-compile-execute cycle must be repeated. Indeed, the cycle often reduces to just edit-compile when syntax or semantic errors are detected by the compiler. This is the interface assumed by the Pascal-S compiler used as a case study throughout the remainder of this book.

The successive execution of the editor, compiler and user's program can easily become tedious if inordinate delays or long command sequences are involved. Not all operating systems environments are sympathetic to a programmer's needs in this regard. Simple facilities such as automatic program execution following successful compilation, and automatic editor activation with the screen positioned at the first error, can considerably ease programmer frustration. Of course, these facilities are very much dependent on the particular operating system being used.

A completely different approach to these problems is increasingly to be found in the provision of **syntax-directed editors** or **program synthesizers** (Lakos and McDermott, 1982). Here, the traditional screen editor is changed so that it will only accept text which forms a syntactically valid source program in a chosen language. Indeed, such software tools go much further than that. For program and statement constructs, the syntax-directed editor automatically provides the necessary keywords and other symbols which must occur for each construct. The user is left to type only the program-specific information such as identifiers, data structures and expressions. All input is checked for syntactic correctness before the program can be saved for compilation. Some sophisticated syntax-directed editors perform semantic checks as well.

To perform their task, these software tools must maintain a syntax tree of the program being edited and, if semantic checks are included, a symbol table as well. Indeed, a syntax-directed editor effectively incorporates most of the checking code of the front-end of a compiler. To maintain the visual interface on the terminal screen, the editor must retain the source text at appropriate points in the tree. Even comments, which are normally discarded during compilation, must be kept for editing purposes.

Being, in effect, a combination of editor and part-compiler, the code of a syntax-directed editor is extensive and consumes substantial amounts of processing time. Its memory requirements for data, too, are large. Bear in mind the need to store in a readily accessible form not only the source text but also the syntax tree and possibly the symbol tables as well. Despite these prodigious resource requisites there are several benefits which accrue to the programmer:

1. Syntax errors are completely eradicated from the program creation process, so saving a considerable number of traditional compilation cycles.
2. The source text is automatically displayed in structured (indented) form, since the structure is always known, so doing away with the need for pretty printers.
3. The programmer's view of the program can be contracted from the details of the source text to just the procedure structure, either globally or locally. On command, the editor can 'zoom' into the source text again at an appropriate point. The user thus gains a better impression of the overall, or macro, framework of the program. A good example of this facility is to be found in the Eliot syntax-directed editor (Jesshope *et al.*, 1985). After issuing the command to enter zoom mode the window on the text changes to provide a structural view of the program overall by procedure and function. In the case of the Pascal-S compiler source this would look something like that shown in Figure 3.1. The level of indentation indicates the degree of nested declaration. In this way, the structure of a large program can be shown in a very concise way. Facilities are provided to select one of the displayed procedures or functions and resume editing from that position.
4. The translator program needed to generate an executable object program is appreciably smaller and faster than a traditional compiler, since, at worst, only semantic checks are necessary before code generation can begin.

With memory size becoming less of a problem as semiconductor developments progress, syntax-directed editor use will spread more widely.

Program construction aids need not stop at syntax-directed editors. With the addition of code generation (and maybe extra semantic checking), the compiler can be completely incorporated into the editor. These facilities are referred to as **incremental compilation** (Atkinson *et al.*, 1981). As each textual alteration is made to the program, object code is generated (or regenerated) for all statements affected by the change. Thus the object program is built incrementally. In exchange for even more memory resource the programmer now gains the exceedingly useful ability to execute the object

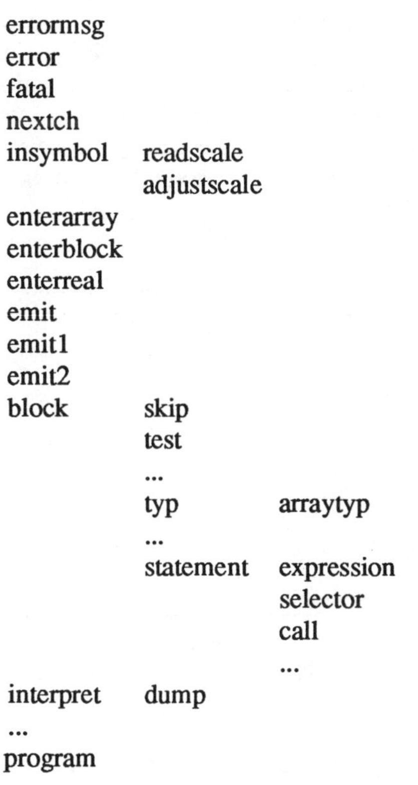

Figure 3.1 View of a large program.

program *in situ*. The compilation cycle ceases to exist. At any moment, the user may make changes to the source program and execute the equivalent object program using *one* software tool.

While straightforward in concept, incremental compilers raise difficulties of code optimization and execution efficiency of the object programs they generate. Incorporation of standard run-time library code is a problem as is the linkage to other user-written, pre-compiled routines. Problems of this kind are still being researched but the emergence of such integrated tools for production use cannot be far away.

3.1 Input/output handling

For a conventional compiler, such as Pascal-S, expecting to input a source program in text-file format, the input/output specification is given in Figure 3.2. (Note that the translator for the Pascal-S language described in this and later chapters is a translator-interpreter according to the definitions given in Chapter 1. Although strictly incorrect, the Pascal-S translator-interpreter will be referred to as the Pascal-S compiler for the sake of conciseness. More simply, where context makes it obvious, the compiler will be denoted by Pascal-S alone.)

Input

- source program

Output

- object program
- listing
- error messages

Figure 3.2 Compiler input/output specification.

All of these inputs and outputs must be represented in a suitable format on physical storage media of some kind. Their specific format is therefore dependent on physical i/o devices. Since device-independence is a compiler objective, the first refinement is to isolate the device dependencies within **interface device handlers** such as:

input handler This converts the device-dependent source program held typically in one or more text files into a device-independent form, namely a single **character stream.**

listing handler This composes a device-oriented listing format taking into account the vagaries of a line printer by collating the source program character stream with the errors detected by the compiler.

code handler This constructs a device-oriented representation of the object program in memory-image loader format from the device-independent object code emitted by the code generation routines of the compiler.

The first decomposition of the compiler into modules is shown in Figure 3.3. An interface handler is interposed between the single input and two output

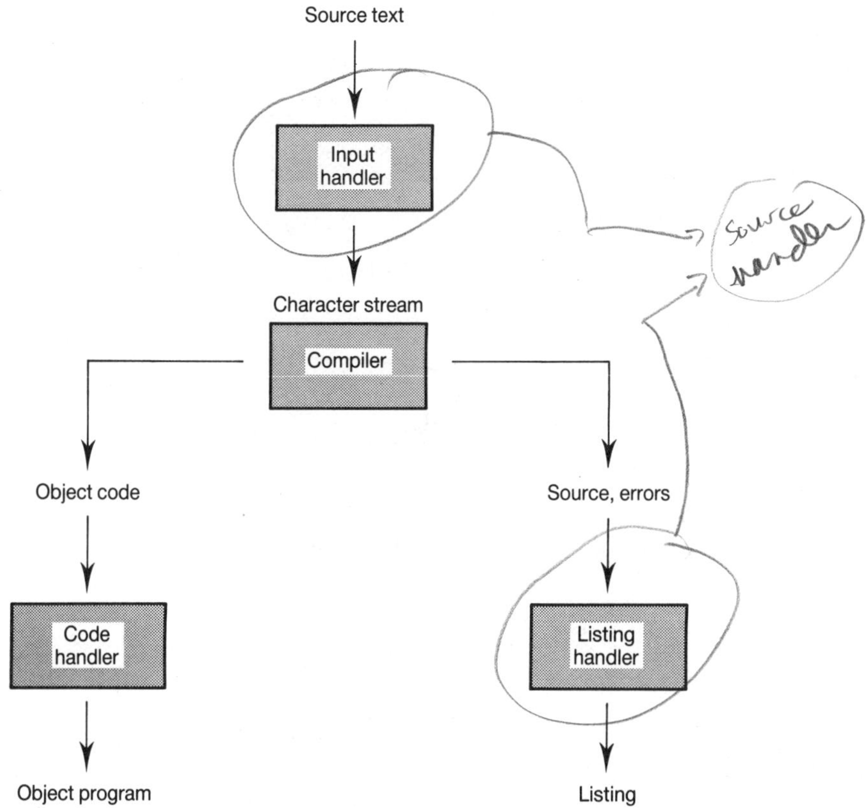

Figure 3.3 Modules of a compiler.

streams in a simple one-on-one fashion.

While such a straightforward design will work correctly, it has an inherent inefficiency. Note that the input handler and output handler each process the source program. These two scans of the source must be avoided. The two handlers must be merged into a single **source handler**. With this change the model design now becomes that of Figure 3.4. The device dependencies of the source program and listing are now contained within the single source handler module. Its interface with the compiler now becomes two-way. The source character stream is passed to the other compiler modules and error messages, if any, flow back to the source handler to be incorporated into the listing.

Any buffering schemes dictated by the operating system for text input and output are encapsulated within the source handler. The listing is a simple superset of the source program. Knowing this, the source handler can minimize the inter-buffer copying which would be required with separate input and

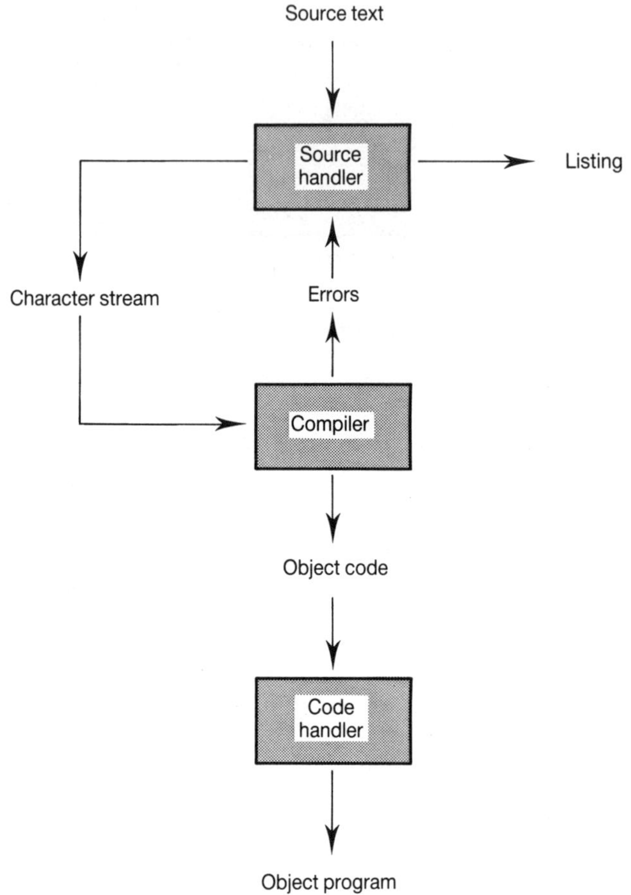

Figure 3.4 Modified compiler design.

listing handlers.

Pascal-S does not adopt the above model for handling the object code in its entirety. Being a translator-interpreter it generates the intermediate code directly into main memory. The built-in interpreter reads the code directly from there. Thus no physical output is generated for the object code. It would be a very straightforward matter to construct a code handler which takes the intermediate code and stores it in a suitable file format. Some information from the symbol table would also need to be stored in the file. A free-standing interpreter program would simply read from the file and interpret the code in association with the symbol table values.

3.2 Source handler interface

Pascal-S is itself written in Pascal. For text files, the procedures *read* and *write* are available to input and output single characters. Additional boolean functions *eoln()* and *eof()* are used to determine line breaks and end-of-file conditions.

The source handler must generate a single stream of characters from physical files which are probably record- and block-oriented. A sufficient interface is to make available the **current character** in the global variable

lastcharread : *char*;

together with the ability to determine its successor whenever it is required. This is provided by calling the procedure

procedure *nextch*;

For error reporting, each error must report to the source handler the *nature* and *position* of the error. Since the source handler must by definition be aware of the current character position, the problem reduces to reporting only the cause of the detected error. It is important to realize that the position of the error is not necessarily related to the current character position. No assumptions can be made as to how the compiler actually detects errors. The source of error may be *anywhere* in the character stream already scanned by the compiler.

At the source handler interface level, the nature of the error can be represented by a simple numeric code, giving the source handler the opportunity to map this into an explicit text message. This task is performed by the Pascal-S procedure

procedure *errormsg*;

only at the end of the complete scan of the source program. The error number alone is output at the point of the error. A brief error message is output at the end of the listing corresponding to all those error numbers detected.

A more elaborate scheme would be for the compiler to keep track of the ordinal position of each character, and express each error position in these terms. Then, the source handler could relate this information to an exact line and character position in the source program, even if this were a position well behind the current point of the scan.

3.3 Programming the source handler

Efficiency must be the keynote when programming the source handler since it directly affects the overall compiler execution speed. The procedure *nextch* which also controls the output of the source program listing will be the most frequently called procedure – once for each character in the source text.

A first model for *nextch* is given in Figure 3.5. This simply converts a sequence of text lines into a single stream of characters.

```
if previous text line exhausted then begin
  read and list next line;
  initialize character pointer;
end;
position character pointer;
update contents of lastcharread;
```

Figure 3.5 Outline design for *nextch* procedure.

Refining the first model, *nextch* expands into the code given in Figure 3.6. The character array *line* is used as a buffer to hold each line of input. Its current length is given by *currentlinelength* and the number of characters read from the buffer so far is held in the variable *charactercount*. No output buffer is required since each character read is immediately output to the listing.

As with all initial designs, considerable additional refinement is necessary to take into account further facilities and treatment of special cases. For *nextch* the list of refinements is not trivial. Additions must handle:

- *Numbering output lines.* For ease of reference and editing it is usual for a compiler to number the output lines as it generates the listing. Pascal-S performs this prior to reading the next line of source. In addition it outputs the amount of intermediate code generated up to that point in the compilation to indicate the size of object program being produced.

- *End-of-file.* For a syntactically correct program the compiler will call *nextch* until the closing '.' is found. No attempt will be made to read beyond the end of the input file.

  For source programs with syntax errors, the general case, reaching a file's end is a real possibility which must be dealt with in the code of *nextch*. The real problem is the course of action to take when this

```
procedure nextch;
begin

  if charactercount = currentlinelength then begin

    currentlinelength := 0;
    charactercount := 0;

    while not eoln(source)) do begin
      currentlinelength := currentlinelength + 1;
      read(source, lastcharread);
      write(listing, lastcharread);
      line[currentlinelength] := lastcharread
    end;

    writeln(listing);
    readln(source);

  end;

  charactercount := charactercount + 1;
  lastcharread := line[charactercount]

end; (* nextch *)
```

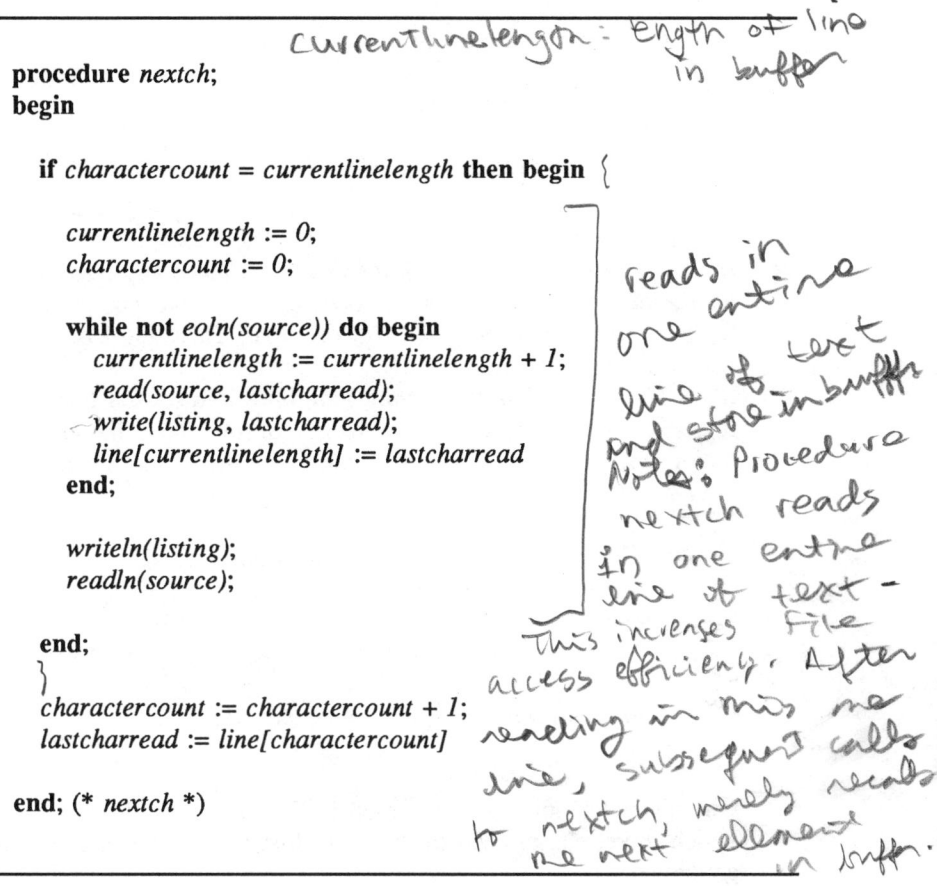

Figure 3.6 Initial code for *nextch* procedure.

erroneous situation is detected. There is no doubt it is a fatal error which must cause the compilation to halt in as graceful a way as possible. If at every call of *nextch* we had to check that end-of-file has not been reached there would be an intolerable overhead. Reluctantly, the problem must be solved with the use of a *goto* statement within *nextch* to terminate execution after suitable error messages have been output. The code segment becomes:

```
if eof(source) then begin
  writeln;
  writeln('program incomplete');
  errormsg;
  goto 99 (*terminate program*)
end;
```

- *Input buffer overflow.* It is unreasonable to place any restriction on the length of input lines when the operating environment places no such limit, as in the case of UNIX, for example. There must be provision to handle lines of any length.

  This is handled by splitting long lines into several lines in the listing, each being the maximum length of the input buffer, *line*. The major change is an additional check in the main input/output loop which now reads

```
while (currentlinelength < maxinputline - 1)
    and (not eoln(source)) do begin
  currentlinelength := currentlinelength + 1;
  read(source, lastcharread);
  write(listing, lastcharread);
  line[currentlinelength] := lastcharread
end;
```

  One character position is reserved in the buffer for the space character which represents the end of the input line in the character stream being generated.

- *End-of-line translation.* Where a sequence of text lines is being converted into a single character stream it is usual for the first character on a line to follow immediately after the last character in the preceding line. In other words the line end is ignored. However, the Pascal language treats line ends as separators so that the program fragment

```
if x > 1 then y := 0;
```

  is equivalent to

```
if x > 1 then
y := 0;
```

  Thus *nextch* must translate end-of-line into a space character. The code to achieve this is

```
if eoln(source) then begin
  readln(source);
  currentlinelength := currentlinelength + 1;
  line[currentlinelength] := ' ';
end;
```

- *Error message handling.* All error messages detected by the compiler while scanning a source line must be output before the next line is listed. Each message should include a visual indicator of the exact point of the error within the line. Pascal-S adopts this convention but simply prints the error number at the point of error. At the end of the listing the correspondence between the numbers and the messages is output. As many messages as possible are output on the same line with additional lines being used where necessary. An example of error message output is

```
b = a * a :
 ^51
   ^ 0 ^ 0
          ^ 6
```

where variable *a* is assumed to be undefined.

The procedure

```
procedure error (n : integer);
```

is called by the compiler to report all errors. The parameter indicates the error number which is output following the '^' character. Variables

```
errcount : integer;
errpos   : integer;
```

are used to keep a count of the total number of errors and the column position of the last error message output, respectively.

A further facility is to output all lines in error together with their error messages on the programmer's terminal as well as in the listing. Syntactically correct lines should not appear on the terminal, however. The variable

```
linewrittentoscreen : boolean;
```

is set to indicate when the source line must be output on the screen in the event of an error. The set variable *setofallerrors* records all the different error numbers that have occurred. This information is used by the *errormsg* procedure at the end of the listing to provide a table of error numbers and messages.

With all these considerations taken into account the source handler code expands to that shown below.

```
   procedure error (n : integer);

(* Prints error numbers under the point of detection of the error,
   both on the standard output and in the file associated with the
   'listing' file variable.
*)

   var
      i : integer;

   begin
      errcount := errcount + 1;

      if not linewrittentoscreen then begin
         write(linecounter : 4, ' ', locationcounter : 5, ' ');

         (* Write out the current source line *)
         for i := 1 to currentlinelength do
            write(line[i]);

         writeln;
         write(' ' : 9);
         write(listing, ' ' : 9);
         linewrittentoscreen := true
      end;

      if charactercount <= errpos then begin
         writeln;
         writeln(listing);
         write(' ' : 9);
         write(listing, ' ' : 9);
         errpos := 0;
      end;

      write(' ' : charactercount - errpos, '^', n : 2);
      write(listing, ' ' : charactercount - errpos, '^', n : 2);
      errpos := charactercount + 3;
      setofallerrors := setofallerrors + [n]
   end (*error*);
```

```
procedure nextch;

(* Read the next character from the source, deal with eof and ignore eoln. *)

begin

  (* First check to see whether we have processed all the characters in
     the array line.
  *)
  if charactercount = currentlinelength then begin
    (* We have processed all the characters in the array line. *)
    if eof(source) then begin
      writeln;
      writeln('program incomplete');
      errormsg;
      goto 99 (*terminate program*)
    end;

    (* Check to see if the previous line has errors. If so, terminate
       those lines both on standard output and in the file associated
       with the file variable 'listing'.
    *)
    if errpos <> 0 then begin
      writeln;
      writeln(listing);
      errpos := 0
    end;

    (* As we read the next line of input into the array line, put it
       straight out to the file associated with 'listing'.
    *)
    write(listing, linecounter : 4, ' ', locationcounter : 5, ' ');
    currentlinelength := 0;
    linecounter := linecounter + 1;
    linewrittentoscreen := false;
    charactercount := 0;

    while (currentlinelength < maxinputline - 1)
        and (not eoln(source)) do begin
      currentlinelength := currentlinelength + 1;
      read(source, lastcharread);
      write(listing, lastcharread);
      line[currentlinelength] := lastcharread
    end;
```

```
      writeln(listing);

      if eoln(source) then begin
        readln(source);
        (* Replace end-of-line with space *)
        currentlinelength := currentlinelength + 1;
        line[currentlinelength] := ' ';
      end;

    end;

    (* The array line contains 'unread' characters, the first of which can
       be returned to insymbol.
    *)

    charactercount := charactercount + 1;
    lastcharread := line[charactercount]
  end; (* nextch *)
```

Note that from the initial simple logical design, *nextch* has expanded ten-fold in order to cater for special cases and guarantee robustness. This is fairly typical of a good many procedures within a compiler which attempt to deal with user-supplied source text which is always liable to be in error.

References

Atkinson, L V, McGregor, J J, and North, S D, 'Context sensitive editing as an approach to incremental compilation', *Computer Journal*, vol. 24, pp. 222–229, 1981.

Jesshope, C R, Crawley, M J, and Lovegrove, G L, 'An intelligent Pascal editor for a graphical oriented workstation', *Software: Practice and Experience*, vol. 15, pp. 1103–1119, 1985.

Lakos, C A and McDermott, T S, 'Interfacing with the user of a syntax-directed editor', Technical Report R82–3, Dept of Information Science, University of Tasmania, 1982.

Chapter 4
Lexical Analysis

The source handler discussed in the previous chapter provides a single stream of characters representing the source program. It is the purpose of the lexical analyser (also known as the scanner) to group adjacent characters in the input stream into lexical **tokens** or **symbols**. Apart from character set considerations, the lexical analyser is entirely free of dependence on any particular machine hardware.

4.1 Structure of the lexical analyser

The scanner provides a very similar interface to the source handler in that a stream of tokens is passed to the remainder of the compiler. For Pascal-S this takes the form of a single procedure

procedure *insymbol*;

which updates the global variable

sy : *symbol*;

to the last lexical symbol read from the input stream. Apart from *nextch*, calls to *insymbol* are the most numerous and it is essential that the code of the scanner be reasonably efficient.

The only error detectable by the source handler is the premature encounter of the end of the source file which must lead to termination of compiler execution. In contrast, the recognition of lexical tokens depends on the syntax rules of the source language being compiled. When a composition rule for a token is breached, the scanner must report the (non-fatal) error, using the mechanism provided by the source handler, and resume the lexical analysis. Sensible error recovery in these circumstances linked to the need for fast execution is not easily achieved and can lead to somewhat unstructured algorithms as will be seen below.

Just as the source handler isolates input/output device dependencies, so the lexical analyser encapsulates character set considerations. The syntax and semantics analyses are only concerned with lexical symbols *per se*. How these symbols are actually represented in the input stream is known only to the scanner.

4.2 Lexical analyser interface

Some of the source language syntax rules relate to the definition of lexical symbols. Pascal-S provides a typical example. A simple definition of a lexical symbol expressed in BNF is shown in Figure 4.1.

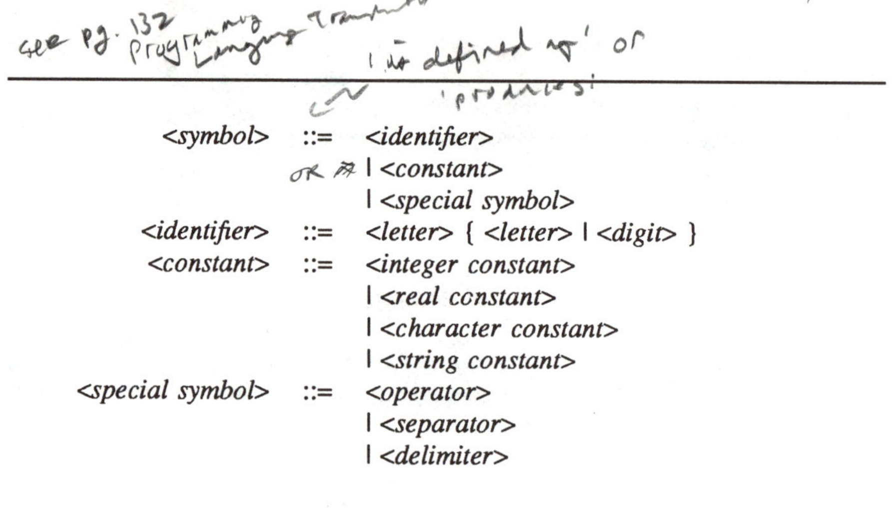

<symbol>	::=	*<identifier>*
		| *<constant>*
		| *<special symbol>*
<identifier>	::=	*<letter>* { *<letter>* | *<digit>* }
<constant>	::=	*<integer constant>*
		| *<real constant>*
		| *<character constant>*
		| *<string constant>*
<special symbol>	::=	*<operator>*
		| *<separator>*
		| *<delimiter>*

Figure 4.1 Definition of a lexical symbol.

Since a lexical symbol can be defined in the same way as the remainder of the source language one may be tempted to combine the scanner with the syntax and semantic analysis. Apart from losing the isolation of character set dependence it turns out that the syntax of lexical symbols is extremely simple. This allows a much more straightforward technique to be used for symbol scanning, warranting its separation from other parts of the compiler.

Although the syntax rules for symbols given above are adequate for recognition purposes, additional processing is required to take account of the semantics of symbols. For example, most languages, including Pascal-S, reserve certain identifiers for use as reserved words. It is the task of the scanner to determine whether an identifier is one of these keywords or not.

As well as the **type** of each symbol, the scanner must record the **value** of symbols representing constants. In addition, the **spelling** of user-defined identifiers must be retained. Another problem is the maximum spelling length for comparison purposes. The *insymbol* procedure passes back this information in a set of global variables shown in Figure 4.2. The settings of these

```
lastidentread : alfa;
lastintegerread : integer;
lastrealread : real;
ordvalofchar : integer;
lengthoflaststring : integer;
posinstringtable : integer;
```

Figure 4.2 Variables set by *insymbol*.

variables depend on whether a user-defined identifier or constant symbol was read.

identifier	The variable *lastidentread* contains the spelling of the identifier. *alfa* is a character array with an upper limit of *numofsigchars* characters. If the name of the identifier is longer than this it is truncated. At the same time, all upper case letters are converted to lower case as Pascal-S does not distinguish between cases.
integer constant	The variable *lastintegerread* holds the value of the integer constant.
real constant	The variable *lastrealread* holds the value of the real constant.
character constant	In the case of a single character constant, the variable *ordvalofchar* is set to the ordinal value (ASCII character code) of the constant.
string constant	Two variables are involved in this case. *lengthoflaststring* is set to the string length and *posinstringtable* gives the starting position of the stored string in the table *stringtable* set aside for holding all the string constants encountered in the source program.

4.3 Programming the lexical analyser

The task of the *insymbol* procedure is to encode the symbol just recognized in the variable *sy*. Pascal enumerated types are most appropriate for this task. Thus from the above syntax rules for symbols the type *symbol* can be defined as shown in Figure 4.3.

```
symbol =   (
           { identifier }
              ident,
           { constants }
              intcon, realcon, charcon, string,
           { arithmetic operators }
              plus, minus, times, idiv, rdiv, imod,
           { logical operators }
              notsy, andsy, orsy, eql, neq, gtr, geq, lss, leq,
           { separators }
              lparent, rparent, lbrack, rbrack,
              comma, semicolon, period, colon,
           { assignment }
              becomes,
           { keywords }
              constsy, typesy, varsy,
              programsy, funcsionsy, prosedurersy,
              arraysy, recordsy,
              beginsy, ifsy, casesy, repeatsy, whilesy, forsy,
              endsy, elsesy, untilsy,
              ofsy, dosy, tosy, downtosy, thensy,
           { subrange }
              deadcolonsy);
```

Figure 4.3 Type *symbol* derived from syntax rules.

For Pascal-S the syntax rules for identifiers and keywords are identical. (Nearly all programming languages employ keywords to define constructs in the language and face a problem in distinguishing them from identifiers with the same spelling.) The alternatives open to the language designer are (a) to require programmers to distinguish such symbols in some way; (b) to require no distinction other than context between these symbols and identifiers of the same spelling; (c) to require no physical distinction between these symbols but to forbid the use of identifiers of the same spelling. Pascal employs option (c). An additional syntax check is necessary whenever an identifier is encountered in order to detect keywords.

Between any two lexical symbols **layout characters** (blanks, tabs and newlines) may occur. These characters must be ignored by the scanner. Fortunately, the source handler procedure *nextch* automatically removes newline characters and replaces them with spaces. The problem for the scanner reduces to removing all blanks and tabs between symbols.

Rewriting the syntax rules for lexical symbols as given in Figure 4.4 dictates the exact structure of the code for *insymbol*.

<symbol> ::= *<letter>* { *<letter>* | *<digit>* } |
<digit><rest of numeric constant> |
′ *<character>* { *<character>* } ′ |
<= | <> | < |
>= | > |
:= | : |
.. | . |
(* | (|
<single character symbols>

Figure 4.4 Rewritten syntax rules for lexical symbols.

From this syntax it can be seen that the next character scanned indicates which lexical symbol, or small set of symbols, exists in the input stream. In essence, a single case statement is all that is required. The skeleton of *insymbol* is:

```
while lastcharread = layout character do nextch;
case lastcharread of
    'a'..'z', 'A'..'Z':        scan identifier or keyword;
    '0'..'9':                  scan numeric constant;
    '''':                      scan character or string constant;
    '<':                       scan <=, <> or <;
    '>':                       scan >= or >;
    ':':                       scan := or :;
    '.':                       scan .. or .;
    '(':                       scan comment or (;
    set of valid chars:        set symbol appropriately;
    set of invalid chars:      generate error message;
end;
```

Where a comment opening delimiter, '(*', is encountered all characters will be ignored up to and including the closing delimiter, '*)'. At this point no lexical symbol will be to hand, necessitating a repetition of the complete code for *insymbol*.

A similar remark applies to the discovery of an invalid character. After outputting a suitable error message, the body of *insymbol* must be repeated.

It is always possible for the source file to contain non-printable control characters from the ASCII set. Filter code which outputs an error message and ignores the control characters must be added.

The upgraded *insymbol* now becomes:

```
procedure insymbol;
var
  symbolfound : boolean;
begin (*insymbol*)
  repeat
    symbolfound := true;
    (* Catch control characters except tab (note ascii dependency.) *)
    while (lastcharread < ' ') and (lastcharread <> chr(ordvaloftabchar)) do
    begin
      nextch;
      error(24)
    end;
    (* Ignore spaces or tabs (note ascii dependency). *)
    while (lastcharread = ' ') or (lastcharread = chr(ordvaloftabchar)) do
      nextch;
    (* The deadcolon symbol is .. This may have been detected during
      numeric constant processing.
     *)
    if swalloweddeadcolon then begin
      swalloweddeadcolon := false;
      sy := deadcolonsy;
      nextch
    end
    else begin
      if lastcharread in ['A' .. 'Z', 'a' .. 'z'] then
        handle identifier
      else if lastcharread in ['0' .. '9'] then
        handle numeric constant
      else
        (* Deal with characters which can be simply formed into symbols. *)
        case lastcharread of
          ':' :
            begin
              nextch;
              (* Check for the assignment operator := *)
              if lastcharread = '=' then begin
                sy := becomes;
                nextch
```

```
      end
      else sy := colon
   end;
'<' :
   begin
      nextch;
      if lastcharread = '=' then begin
         sy := leq;
         nextch
      end
      else if lastcharread = '>' then begin
         sy := neq;
         nextch
      end
      else sy := lss
   end;
'>' :
   begin
      nextch;
      if lastcharread = '=' then begin
         sy := geq;
         nextch
      end
      else sy := gtr
   end;
'.' :
   begin
      nextch;
      if lastcharread = '.' then begin
         sy := deadcolonsy;
         nextch
      end
      else sy := period
   end;
'''' :
   handle character constant;
'(' :
   begin
      nextch;
      if lastcharread <> '*' then
         sy := lparent
      else begin (* Comment *)
         nextch;
         repeat
            while lastcharread <> '*' do
```

```
                    nextch;
                  nextch
                until lastcharread = ')';
                nextch;
                symbolfound := false; (* Try for another symbol *)
              end
            end;
          '+', '-', '*', '/', ')', '=', ',', '[', ']', ';' :
            begin
              sy := specialsymbol[lastcharread];
              nextch
            end;
          '$', '%', '^', '_', '?', '&', '{', '}',
          '\', '~', '`', '"', '#', '!', '|' :
            begin
              nextch;
              error(24); (* These characters not permitted*)
              symbolfound := false;
            end
        end; (*case*)
    end
  until symbolfound;
end (*insymbol*);
```

The code of *insymbol* is designed to leave the character input stream positioned at the character immediately following the last character of the current symbol. The only exception to this rule is the treatment of the '..' symbol when it follows a numeric constant, as in the declaration:

line : **array***[1..10]* **of** *char*;

The code which handles the detection of a numeric constant will happily read the first '.' in expectation of a real value. Only when the second '.' is encountered is it obvious that an integer value is intended. No mechanism to 'put a character back' in the input stream is provided, so instead a special flag variable, *swalloweddeadcolon,* is set to true. An extra section of code is inserted in the **repeat** loop of *insymbol* to check this flag and take appropriate action if it is set.

The flag variable *symbolfound* is set to true at the start of the main loop of the scanner procedure and is used to determine when to terminate the loop. The only situation where the loop will be executed more than once is when either a comment or an illegal printable character is encountered.

For those characters which can start more than one symbol, the code develops into a nested **if** statement testing for all the possibilities. Rather than needing a separate assignment statement for each character which forms a special symbol on its own, the symbol type is placed in the array

specialsymbol : **array** *[char]* **of** *symbol*;

with one entry for each such character. Determining the symbol type is as simple as

sy := *specialsymbol[lastcharread]*;

It has been assumed that the Pascal-S compiler will execute in an environment which employs the ASCII character set. This automatically introduces some dependencies into the code, and this is noted in associated comments wherever it occurs.

For conciseness, the parts of *insymbol* which handle identifiers and constants have been omitted in the above listing. These omissions are now discussed in turn. The code to handle identifiers and keywords is:

```
(* identifier or keyword. Build it up in the array lastidentread.
   Only the first 'numsigchars' are put into the array. The
   rest are ignored.
 *)
count := 0;
lastidentread := '          ';
repeat
   if count < numofsigchars then begin
      count := count + 1;
      if lastcharread in ['A' .. 'Z'] then
         lastcharread := chr(ord(lastcharread) - ord('A') + ord('a')
            );
      lastidentread[count] := lastcharread
   end;
   nextch
until not (lastcharread in ['A' .. 'Z', '0' .. '9', 'a' .. 'z']);
(* Check to see if the identifier is a keyword. *)
(* Binary search. *)
lower := 1;
upper := numofkeywords;
repeat
   middle := (lower + upper) div 2;
   if lastidentread <= keyword[middle] then upper := middle - 1;
   if lastidentread >= keyword[middle] then lower := middle + 1
until lower > upper;
if lower - 1 > upper then
   sy := keywordsy[middle]
else sy := ident
```

Pascal-S allows user-specified identifiers to be of any length but only treats the first *numofsigchars* as significant. The programmer is free to use both upper and lower case letters in identifier names but Pascal-S always converts them to lower case. As each character in a name is read it is stored in the array *lastidentread* to the maximum significant length. Additional characters in the name are discarded.

Once the spelling of the identifier has been captured it must be checked against the keyword list. The list consists of two arrays

```
keyword : array [1..numofkeywords] of alfa;
keywordsy : array [1..numofkeywords] of symbol;
```

keyword holds the spellings of the keywords in alphabetical order, and *keywordsy* holds the corresponding symbol value. A simple binary search algorithm is implemented for searching the keyword list. *sy* is set to the appropriate value from *keywordsy* if a keyword is found, otherwise it is set to *ident*. The code to handle numeric constants is:

```
(* Number. *)
numofintegerdigits := 0;
lastintegerread := 0;
sy := intcon;
(* Build up the integer character by character. *)
repeat
  lastintegerread := lastintegerread * 10 + ord(lastcharread) – ord
    ('0');
  numofintegerdigits := numofintegerdigits + 1;
  nextch
until not (lastcharread in ['0' .. '9']);
if (numofintegerdigits > maxnumofsigdigits) or (lastintegerread >
integermax) then begin
  error(21); (* Too big *)
  lastintegerread := 0;
  numofintegerdigits := 0
end;
(* Check to see if real number or a dead colon (..). *)
if lastcharread = '.' then begin
  nextch;
  if lastcharread = '.' then
    swalloweddeadcolon := true
  else begin
    (* Have a real number of the form 3.3 or 3.3e–2. *)
    sy := realcon;
    lastrealread := lastintegerread;
    exponent := 0;
```

```
        (*Build up part following decimal point, but before
          the exponent.
        *)
        while lastcharread in ['0' .. '9'] do begin
          exponent := exponent - 1;
          lastrealread := 10.0 * lastrealread + (ord(lastcharread) -
            ord('0'));
          nextch
        end;
        if (lastcharread = 'E') or (lastcharread = 'e') then
          readscale;
        if exponent <> 0 then
          adjustscale
      end
    end
    else if (lastcharread = 'e') or (lastcharread = 'E') then begin
      (* Have a real number of the form 3e3 *)
      sy := realcon;
      lastrealread := lastintegerread;
      exponent := 0;
      readscale;
      if exponent <> 0 then
        adjustscale
    end;
  end
```

The code for handling numeric constants is typically the most error-prone component of the lexical analyser. This is because great care must be taken when building the actual value of the constant to ensure that arithmetic overflow does not occur or, if it does, the condition is noted. A programmer can easily enter valid numeric values which lie outside the representational capability of the machine on which the compiler runs.

In the above code the maximum integer value is held in the constant *integermax* and constants which exceed *maxnumofsigdigits* in length are checked. However, the checks come *after* the statements which accumulate the numeric value, such as:

```
lastintegerread := lastintegerread * 10 +
        ord(lastcharread) - ord('0');
```

It is assumed that overflow may occur, the program will continue to run, and that an erroneous value will result. Eventually checks like:

```
if (numofintegerdigits > maxnumofsigdigits)
   or (lastintegerread > integermax) then ...
```

will reject the value as being too large. On machines where arithmetic overflow causes fatal program termination a different algorithm will be needed.

The code has to take into account the following types of numeric constant in Pascal-S:

```
123
123.456
123.456e7
123e7
```

An initial assumption is made to expect an integer constant and begin the conversion character by character. Suitable nested *if* statements cater for the other eventualities. Where fractional parts and exponents are involved the two procedures *readscale* and *adjustscale*, which are declared locally within *insymbol*, perform the necessary scaling. Their contents can be consulted in the full compiler listing given in Appendix B.

A problem faced by the numeric constant handler was mentioned above, namely the occurrence of a '..' symbol following an integer constant. It is not until the second '.' is read that the subrange symbol is detected. At this point an integer constant is returned and the *swalloweddeadcolon* flag set to true.

The code to handle string constants is:

```
  function endofstring : boolean;
(* Check for single quote to end string.
  Allow adjacent single quotes through.
*)
  begin
    nextch;
    if lastcharread = '''' then begin
      nextch;
      endofstring := lastcharread <> '''';
    end
    else endofstring := false;
  end (*endofstring*);
begin
  (* Start of string or character constant. All strings
    are stored contiguously in stringtable, with their
    starting position and length passed back to insymbol's
    caller.
  *)
  stringlength := 0;
  while not endofstring do begin
    if lastcharinstringtable + stringlength = stringtablemax
```

```
        then
          fatal(7);
        stringtable[lastcharinstringtable + stringlength] :=
          lastcharread;
        stringlength := stringlength + 1;
        if charactercount = currentlinelength then
          (*end of line*)
          stringlength := stringlength - 1;
      end; (* while *)
      (* Have now put all characters of string into stringtable.
        Check to see if only character constant.
      *)
      if stringlength = 1 then begin
        sy := charcon;
        ordvalofchar := ord(stringtable[lastcharinstringtable])
      end
      else if stringlength = 0 then begin
        error(38); (* Null string not permitted *)
        sy := charcon;
        posinstringtable := 0
      end
      else begin
        sy := string;
        posinstringtable := lastcharinstringtable;
        lengthoflaststring := stringlength;
        lastcharinstringtable := lastcharinstringtable +
          stringlength
      end
    end;
```

To cater for the variable number and length of string constants, a separate table

stringtable : **packed array** *[1..stringtablemax]* **of** *char*;

is set aside for their storage. Each string constant is represented by its length, in *lengthoflaststring*, and the starting position *posinstringtable* in the string table where its characters are stored. As the string is scanned it is placed in the next available position in the string table indicated by *lastcharinstringtable*, which is another global variable. Before each character is stored a check is made to prevent the string table overflowing, in which case a fatal error results.

If the length of the string is exactly one character then a character constant is returned with its ordinal value in *ordvalofchar*. An error is flagged if a null string of length zero is encountered.

One special case which breaks the rule that a newline terminates the symbol is the string constant, which can span several lines. The whole point of detaching the source handler as a separate procedure is to isolate input device characteristics such as line ends. However, in converting a newline into a space the source handler would introduce an extra character for each newline included in a string constant.

Although breaking the rules for structured programming as mentioned earlier in this chapter, *insymbol* must be given access to end-of-line information. Because the source handler design uses global variables for efficiency, it turns out to be very easy.

if *charactercount* = *currentlinelength* **then**

will perform the necessary check.

As can be seen, the code for the lexical analyser occupies about 350 lines of Pascal – about 10 per cent of the total compiler code.

4.4 Automatic generation of lexical analyser

As was pointed out earlier in the text, the structure and content of the scanner procedure is almost wholly dictated by the syntax rules for lexical symbols. It is therefore very straightforward to generate lexical analysers for new languages. Indeed, software tools which read in the syntax of the lexical symbols can automatically generate scanner code. A good example of such a tool is the *lex* utility (Lesk, 1975) available as part of the UNIX system. Given the syntax of the lexical tokens in a suitable variant of BNF this utility outputs a suitable scanner in the C language.

A software tool equivalent to *lex* is *aardvark* (White, 1981) which operates in the same fashion but generates a lexical analyser in the Pascal language. To demonstrate the ease with which a scanner can be produced by *aardvark* we consider a simple program used to typeset the Pascal source code in this book. As can be seen from the many code fragments, most of the Pascal text is set in italics with keywords emboldened and most punctuation is set in a Roman (upright) font. What was required was a program to input plain Pascal source and output it again incorporating additional escape sequences so that the typesetting utility would perform the necessary font changes.

The program, referred to as *embold*, was produced in a little under two hours' work using *aardvark* and its sister tool *llama*, which generates a syntax analyser and is described in more detail in the next chapter. *embold* must input a character stream, split it into Pascal tokens, recognize keywords and punctuation, and output the character stream interspersed with appropriate font change escape sequences. Obviously, *embold* must be aware of the syntax of comments and strings so that they may be set totally in italic font even if words corresponding to keywords appear within them.

aardvark inputs a number of text sections most of which are passed on to *llama* which is responsible for creating the final Pascal program. Essentially *aardvark* outputs, unchanged, all sections apart from '&token'. This contains the definition of the tokens to be recognized. *aardvark* replaces this section with a parameterless procedure

procedure *llexan*;

which, when called, returns the next token in the global variable

llnextsymbol : *llterminal*;

In essence, *llexan* is equivalent to the *insymbol* procedure described in section 4.1 and *llnextsymbol* is equivalent to *sy*.

The token definitions in the form 'tokenname = expression .' for *embold* are shown in Figure 4.5.

```
&token
 digit = <0-9> .
 letter = <a-zA-Z> .
 NUMBER = digit { digit } .
 IDENT = letter { letter | digit } .
 SPACE = " " .
 TAB = tab .
 ENDLINE = eoln .
 PUNCTUATION = "~ " | "!" | "#" | "$" | "%" | "%" | "^" | "&" | "*" |
               ":" | ";" | "_" | "-" | "+" | "=" | "
               "<" | ">" | "," | "." | "?" | "/" | "|" | "
               ":=" | "<>" | ".." | "<=" | ">=" .
 QUOTE = "'" .
 OPENCOMM = "(*" .
 CLOSECOMM = "*)" .
 LBRACE = "{" .
 RBRACE = "}" .
 DELIM = "[" | "]" | "(" | ")" .
```

Figure 4.5 Token definitions.

Expressions make use of explicit symbols enclosed by '"' and operators for alternation ('|'), optional ('[' and ']'), zero or more repetitions ('{' and '}') and classes ('<' and '>'). All these components within an expression are concatenated by the implicit catenation operator.

Token names to be recognized by the *llexan* procedure are specified in upper case. An example token definition is

NUMBER = digit { digit } .

which can be interpreted as 'a digit followed by zero or more digits'. 'digit' is an example of a supplementary definition

digit = <0–9> .

which is not one of the set of tokens returned by the *llexan* procedure.

When *aardvark* inputs the token definitions given in Figure 4.5 it produces the output intended as input for *llama.* Embedded in this output is the code for the *llexan* procedure, an abridged version of which is:

```
procedure llexan;
 . . .
function next(statecode : statetype; onc : aachordrange) : integer;
begin
   next := errorstate;
   case statecode of
      1 : if (onc = 9) then
               next := 391
            else if (onc = 32) then
               next := 307
               . . .
     14 : if (onc = 42) then
               next := 715;
        2, 3, 4, 5, 6, 8, 15, 16, 17, 18, 19 : (* no transition *)
   end
end (* next *);
function token(code : tokentype) : llterminal;
begin
   case code of
      1 :  token := NUMBER;
      2 :  token := IDENT;
            . . .
     12 :  token := DELIM;
     13 :  token := llEND
   end
end (* token *);
```

```
begin (* llexan *)
   . . .
   lastfinalstate := errorstate;
   while state <> errorstate do
   begin
      . . .
      state := next((state div 4) mod 20, aabuff[aacurr]);
      . . .
   end;
   . . .
   llnextsymbol := token(recognized);
   . . .
end (* llexan *);
```

aardvark adopts a state table approach to recognizing tokens. When it is executed for the token definitions already described, a summary of the number of states and associated information is output as shown in Figure 4.6.

```
 13   tokens (127 max)
  0   actions (127 max)
  2   classes used (20 max)
154   NFA states generated
 19   DFA states generated (255 max)
 10   transitions optimized by case label merge
```

Figure 4.6 Summary output by *aardvark*.

The table definition itself is encapsulated in the local function

function *next(statecode : ...) : integer*;

which defines the transition from one state to the next. Mapping from a numeric code to an enumerated type representing the set of token names is undertaken by the local function

function *token(code : tokentype) : llterminal*;

The main body of *llexan* contains the scanning control and the setting of the next token recognized in *llnextsymbol*. *llexan* occupies 140 lines of Pascal.

As well as *llexan*, a collection of constants, types, variables, functions and procedures are generated by *aardvark* for use in fine-tuning the action of the lexical scanner. These can be used for such purposes as accessing the characters making up the tokens themselves, error handling, input/output control, etc.

The main program code for *embold* is:

```
begin
  llexaninit;
  initkeywords;
  commentlevel := 0;
  instring := false;
  while llnextsymbol <> llEND do begin
  llexan;
  case llnextsymbol of
  NUMBER, DELIM : italic;
  IDENT : if comment or instring then
            italic
          else if keyword then
            embold
          else
            italic;
  OPENCOMM, LBRACE : begin
              roman;
              commentlevel := commentlevel + 1;
            end;
  CLOSECOMM, RBRACE : begin
              roman;
              commentlevel := commentlevel - 1;
            end;
  PUNCTUATION : if not comment then
                roman
              else
                italic;
  QUOTE : if not comment then begin
            backslash;
            roman;
            instring := not instring;
          end else
            italic;
  SPACE, TAB : italic;
  ENDLINE : writeln;
  llEND : ;
  end;
end;
```

The initialisation procedure *llexaninit* is also generated by *aardvark* and must be called before the first use of *llexan*. *initkeywords* sets up an array of keyword spellings to be checked by the *keyword* function to distinguish keywords from other identifiers. The procedures *roman*, *italic* and *embold* output the current token surrounded by font escape sequences. Note that for this application, tokens for space, tab and end-of-line are needed because the output layout must exactly match the input. For translation purposes, of course, these tokens would be discarded as would all comments.

aardvark generates a special *llEND* token when the end of the input is reached. The **while** statement uses this to terminate the loop.

---

procedure *initkeywords*;
procedure *roman*;
procedure *italic*;
procedure *embold*;
procedure *backslash*;
function *comment* : *boolean*;
function *keyword* : *boolean*;
main program

Figure 4.7 Hand-written procedures and functions.

In summary, *embold* was produced by providing token definitions and Pascal code for the procedures and functions listed in Figure 4.7 – about 160 lines of code out of a total of 480. In effect, *aardvark* and *llama* generated two thirds of the final program. A more realistic fraction for a full compiler would be less than half but still a large part of the overall code. This approach does demonstrate that lexical and syntax analyser generators can be used for any application employing programming language-like input. Many 4GL systems in areas like databases, electronic publishing, statistical analysis, etc. fall into this category.

References

Lesk, M E, 'Lex—a lexical analyzer generator', Computer Science Technical Report No. 39, Bell Laboratories, 1975.

White, B, 'Aardvark: a lexical analyser generator', (Honours Thesis), University of New South Wales, 1981.

Chapter 5
Syntax Analysis

5.1 Syntax and semantics

Syntax analysis is the phase in the compilation process which checks whether the arrangement of symbols in the input conforms to the rules of the language being compiled. Syntax analysis is followed by semantic analysis which is concerned with checking whether the symbols are used correctly. The interface and interaction between these two phases has to be clear in order to fully understand their relationship.

The language features of Pascal do not require that semantic analysis should necessarily follow syntax analysis – they may take place in parallel, and it would be more efficient if they did.

The semantic analysis will require some representation of the user's program which will have to be supplied by the syntax analysis phase. If semantic analysis takes place after syntax analysis is complete then this representation will involve the entire program, usually in the form of a syntax tree. If however, semantic analysis takes place in parallel with the syntax analysis, then the semantic analysis can be hung on the bones of the syntax analysis. This is the approach adopted by the Pascal-S system.

5.2 Formal definition of grammar and language

Before looking in detail at the Pascal-S system's syntax analysis phase, we shall look more generally at the process of syntax analysis. As discussed earlier, the syntactic rules are often expressed in the form of syntax diagrams or in Backus-Naur form. We shall use the Backus-Naur notation introduced earlier as a basis for more formal concepts.

A **production** or **rewriting rule** is an ordered pair (U,x), usually written

$$U ::= x$$

where U is a symbol and x is a non-empty finite string of symbols. U is the

left part, and *x* the **right part** of the production.

A **grammar**, *G[Z]*, is a finite non-empty set of rules. *Z* is a symbol which must appear as the left part of at least one rule. It is called the **distinguished** symbol. All the symbols used in left parts and right parts form the **vocabulary** *V*. As an example, suppose the grammar *G1[<number>]* is composed of the following rules

```
<number>     ::= <num>
<num>        ::= <num> <digit> | <digit>
<digit>      ::= 0 | 1 | 2 ... 8 | 9
```

then

V = {0, 1, 2, ... 8, 9, *<digit>*, *<num>*, *<number>*}

Given a grammar, *G*, those symbols appearing as a left part of a rule are called **non-terminals** or **syntactic entities.** They form the set of non-terminals *VN*. Those symbols not in *VN* are called **terminal** symbols. They form the set *VT*. Thus

V = *VN* union *VT*

Let *G* be a grammar. The string *v* directly produces the string *w*, written

$v => w$

if we can write

$v = xUy$
$w = xuy$

for some strings *x* and *y*, where *U* ::= *u* is a rule of *G*. *w* is said to be a **direct derivation** of *v*, or is **directly reduced** to *v*. We can use this notation to show that the string '34' is a legal string of the grammar *G1* above. This is done by showing that we can derive the string '34' from the distinguished symbol *<number>*. Figure 5.1 illustrates the derivation. A legal string of the language is known as a **sentence**.

5.3 Syntax trees

Syntax trees are an aid to understanding the syntax of sentences of the language. As an illustration, Figure 5.2 gives the tree for the derivation of the sentence '34' for the grammar *G1*. Starting with the distinguished symbol

v		*w*	*x*	*y*
<number>	=>	*<num>*	*empty*	*empty*
<num>	=>	*<num><digit>*	*empty*	*empty*
<num><digit>	=>	*<digit> <digit>*	*empty*	*<digit>*
<digit><digit>	=>	3 *<digit>*	*empty*	*<digit>*
3 *<digit>*	=>	34	3	*empty*

Figure 5.1 Derivation of string '34'.

<number> => *<num>* => *<num><digit>*
=> *<digit> <digit>* => 3 *<digit>* => 34

Figure 5.2 Syntax tree for the derivation of string '34'.

<number>, a branch is drawn downward to indicate a direct derivation of the next node – see Figure 5.3.

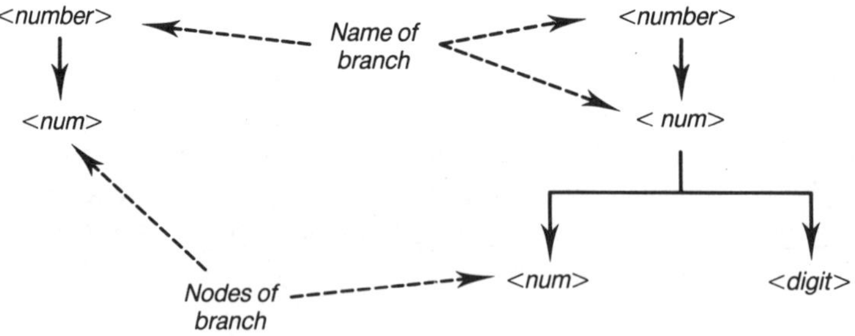

Figure 5.3 Graphical form of the syntax tree.

This process is continued in Figure 5.4 until the terminal symbols in the source are encountered. This method of proceeding from the distinguished

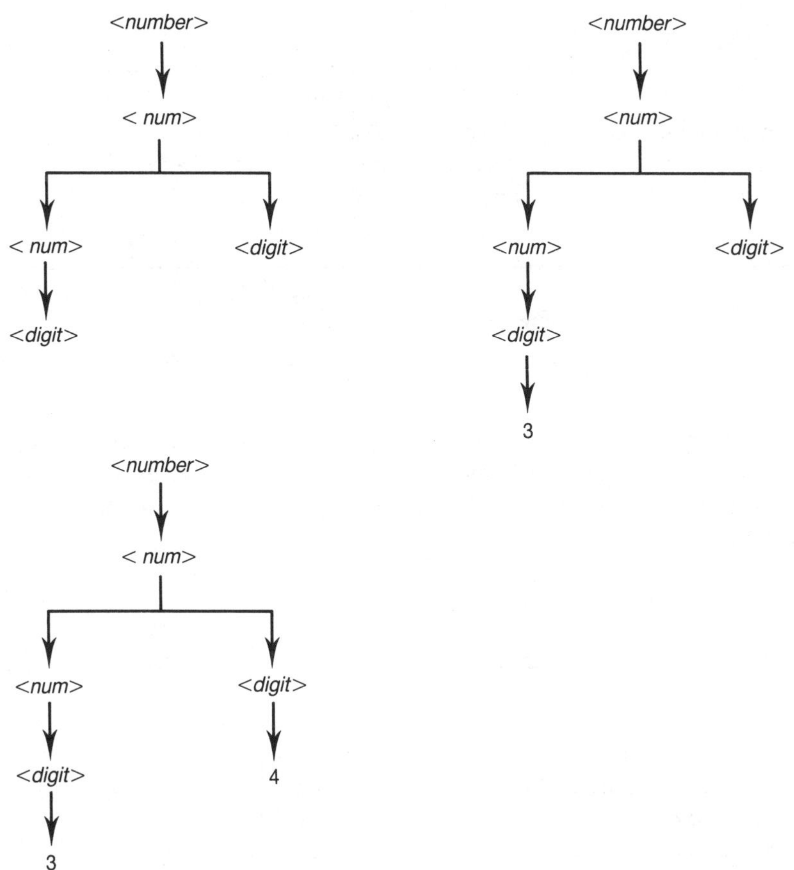

Figure 5.4 Expansion of syntax tree to terminal symbols.

symbol and applying rules of the grammar until the source symbols are matched is known as **top-down** or **descending** analysis.

An alternative approach is to consider groups of symbols in the input stream, and attempt to match them with groups in the right part of one of the rules of the grammar. If this can be done, then such groups are **reduced**, that is replaced by the symbol in the left part of the rule. Repeated application of this procedure will ultimately lead to a single symbol. This is **bottom-up** or **ascending** analysis.

As an example of bottom-up analysis, consider the simplified grammar shown in Figure 5.5. As we shall be matching the right-hand sides of the above rules against the input string we shall rewrite the rules the other way round, so that the aim is to produce the distinguished symbol *<program>*.

<program>	::= *<block>*
<block>	::= *label* : *< block>* | *<unlabelled block>* | *statement*
<unlabelled block>	::= *<block head>* ; *<block end>*
<block head>	::= *begin decln* | *<block head>* ; *decln*
<block end>	::= *<block>* ; *<block end>* | *<block>* end

Figure 5.5 Simple grammar.

The grammar becomes that shown in Figure 5.6. Note that pairs of rules 4 and 4a, 6 and 6a start with the same symbols. This is a fairly common occurrence. The problem now arises as to which reduction to apply when we have those symbols in the input string.

1.	*<block>*	=> *<program>*
2.	*label* : *<block>*	=> *<block>*
3.	*<unlabelled block>*	=> *<block>*
4.	*<block head>* ; *decln*	=> *<block head>*
4a.	*<block head>* ; *<block end>*	=> *<unlabelled block>*
5.	**begin** *decln*	=> *<block head>*
6.	*<block>* ; *<block end>*	=> *<block end>*
6a.	*<block>* **end**	=> *<block end>*
7.	*statement*	=> *<block>*

Figure 5.6 Rewritten grammar.

For example, consider the parsing of the following string:

label : **begin** *decln* ; *decln* ; *statement* **end**

The goal is to either reduce the above string to *<program>*, in which case the string is legal, or to show that no further reduction is possible, in which case the string does not conform to the rules of the grammar. Initially, the goal is to reduce the string to *<program>*. Only rule 1 produces *<program>* and so we institute as subgoal 1 the left-hand side of rule 1, namely *<block>*.

Rules 2, 3 and 7 produce *<block>*. Rule 7 clearly cannot be applied because the first symbol of the string is not *statement*. Rule 3 is not so straightforward. The left-hand side is *<unlabelled block>* and we should check that this cannot start with the symbol *label* (for this we cannot rely on the phrase *<unlabelled block>* which implies that it cannot start with the symbol *label*).

We note that *<unlabelled block>* is only produced by rule 4a, which starts with *<block head>*. In turn *<block head>* is produced by rule 4 – the first symbol is *<block head>* – or rule 5, which starts with the symbol *begin*. Thus we can conclude that rule 3 cannot start with the symbol *label* and apply rule 2. Hence we can match the first two symbols of the input string, *label* against the first two symbols of the left-hand side of rule 2.

We then need to match *<block>* against the remainder of the input string, namely:

begin *decln* ; *decln* ; *statement* **end**

We make this subgoal 2. As we have already seen, rules 2, 3 and 7 produce *<block>*, but this time we can disregard rules 2 and 7 as they do not start with the symbol **begin**. Thus subgoal 3 is the left-hand side of rule 3, namely *<unlabelled block>*. This is only produced by rule 4a, so the left-hand side of rule 4a becomes subgoal 4. This starts with *<block head>* which is produced by rules 4 and 5 and this is where our major difficulty arises.

Suppose we apply rule 5, match the symbols **begin** *decln* and so satisfy the first part of subgoal 4. We could then match the ';' in rule 4a, but the next symbol in the input string is *decln* and no rule starts with that symbol. Thus we have to undo all the actions taken since selecting rule 5 and take the other choice at that point, namely rule 4.

This is known as **backtracking** and can be very costly to implement in a syntax analyser. Continuing this example and applying rule 4, we make the left-hand side of rule 4 subgoal 5. This starts with *<block head>* which means we have a choice of rules 4 or 5 again. Selecting rule 5, we match the symbols **begin** and *decln* and then the ';' and *decln* and so satisfy subgoal 5.

Returning to subgoal 4, which is the left-hand side of rule 4a, we have now matched *<block head>* and the input string is now

; *statement* **end**

Thus we can now match the ';' symbol and then try to match the remainder against *<block end>*. This is produced by rules 6 and 6a, both of which can start with the symbol statement. Rule 6a is the correct choice, selection of rule 6 would lead to backtracking. Rule 6a starts with *<block>* and only one of the rules which produce *<block>* starts with *statement*, namely rule 7.

Thus we match *statement* and so return to rule 6a and match the symbol **end.** This satisfies subgoal 4, which in turn satisfies subgoal 3 and produces *<unlabelled block>*. This satisfies subgoal 3 (the left-hand side of rule 3), which in turn satisfies subgoal 2 (the left-hand side of rule 2). Finally, this satisfies subgoal 1 (the left-hand side of rule 1) and so we have produced the distinguished symbol *<program>* and hence the string is legal.

The implementation of a bottom-up syntax analyser usually involves a stack. The bottom-up parser has two basic operations involving the stack. Firstly input symbols are shifted onto the stack and secondly the right-hand sides of rules are matched against the symbols on the top of the stack. If a match is found, then the matched symbols are replaced on the stack by the left-hand side of the rule. These two operations have meant that bottom-up parsing is sometimes referred to as **shift-reduce** parsing.

The difficulty with bottom-up parsing is the avoidance of backtracking, caused by the selection of the incorrect reduction. The solution to this problem is outside the scope of this book and the interested reader is referred to other books (Hunter, 1985) and (Aho *et al.*, 1986) for a more detailed treatment.

5.4 The Pascal-S syntax analyser

A top-down syntax analyser for Pascal-S can be constructed directly from the syntax rules. With this method no syntax tree is actually constructed but the calling of the various analysis procedures mirrors the structure of the syntax tree.

In order to ensure strict adherence to the actual syntax, a set of conventions is followed:

(a) Each syntax rule is to be translated into a procedure with a name corresponding to the left part, and a body to perform the analysis corresponding to the right part.

(b) The analysis causes the input of the longest sequence of symbols which form a valid construct, reporting an error if no such sequence is found;

(c) Each procedure leaves *sy*, the last symbol read by the lexical analyser, updated to the first symbol not in the construct.

Thus, given the rule specified in Figure 5.7 (which is not one of the Pascal-S rules), the procedure shown in Figure 5.8 would result.

What takes place in the body of each analysis procedure depends on the structure of the rule in question. As can be seen from the above example, if a particular symbol, such as *var*, is required then it is just a matter of looking at *sy* to see if it contains that symbol. If what is required is a non-terminal construct, such as *<vardeclaration>*, then a call to the procedure analysing that construct should be made.

```
<block>          ::= [ const <constdeclaration> ]
                     [ type <typedeclaration> ]
                     [ var <vardeclaration>
                     [ procedure | function <procorfuncdec> ] <body>
```

Figure 5.7 Rule for *block*.

```
procedure block;
  begin
  if sy = constsy then
    constdeclaration;
  if sy = typesy then
    typedeclaration;
  if sy = varsy then
    variabledeclaration;
  if sy in [procsy, funcsy] then
    procorfuncdec;
  body
  end; (*block*)
```

Figure 5.8 Recognition procedure for *block*.

If repetition is involved, as in:

<case label> ::= *<constant>* { , *<constant>* }

then this can be implemented as a loop as shown in Figure 5.9, where *insymbol* is the name of the routine which forms the next symbol and assigns it to *sy*.

If a number of alternatives exist, as in the rule in Figure 5.10, then this can be implemented as a case statement, each arm of which contains a call to the appropriate analysis procedure. The case selector can be the value of *sy*

```
procedure caselabel;
  begin
  constant;
  while sy = comma do
    begin
    insymbol;
    constant
    end
  end; (*caselabel*)
```

Figure 5.9 Recognition procedure for repetition.

(we shall assume for the present that *sy* contains a value for which there is a corresponding label). Note, however, that for this to work no alternative must start with the same symbol. The alert reader will have noticed that the rule above does not satisfy this condition as *<assignment>* and *<procedure call>* both start with an identifier. The Pascal-S system gets round this difficulty by performing a semantic action, namely searching the symbol table to see if the identifier is a variable or a procedure, in order to determine which alternative to take.

```
<visible statement>  ::= <assignment> |
                         <procedure call> |
                         <compound statement> |
                         <while statement> |
                         <for statement> |
                         <repeat statement> |
                         <if statement> |
                         <case statement>
```

Figure 5.10 Rule with alternatives.

Constructs with an empty alternative can cause further difficulties. An example is given in Figure 5.11. If a symbol could be the starter of one of the alternatives and could also follow *<statement>* in the input, then the analyser does not know whether to choose the alternative in question or to select the empty alternative. Thus to avoid this problem the syntax rules must not allow a symbol to be a starting and following symbol of a construct which has an empty alternative.

<statement> ::= *<assignment>* |
<procedure call> |
<compound statement> |
<while statement> |
<for statement> |
<repeat statement> |
<if statement> |
<case statement> |
<empty>

Figure 5.11 Rule with empty alternative.

The above guidelines enable the translation of the syntax defining the language into an equivalent set of syntax procedures. To analyse a complete program, the procedure corresponding to *<program>* is called. This, in turn, calls other procedures, so producing a gradual tracing of the conceptual syntax tree of the program being analysed. The tracing is accompanied by a symbol-by-symbol acceptance of the program each time a leaf of the tree is identified.

For those constructs which are recursive in form, such as expressions and statements, the procedures automatically call themselves recursively. Because of this, and the fact that analysis proceeds from top to bottom, the analyser is referred to as a **recursive-descent analyser**.

The analyser operates in a deterministic manner, deciding on the analysis path by inspection of the current input symbol. A set of syntax rules meeting these conditions is known as an LL(1) grammar, i.e. top-down without backup, examining all symbols processed so far and one more symbol to the right (the current symbol).

5.5 Syntax errors

This section has been heavily influenced by an excellent discussion of syntax error recovery in (Welsh and McKeag, 1980).

So far, the discussion of recursive-descent syntax analysis will only be acceptable up to the detection of the first syntax error. Then the analysis is likely to get out of step, and will either

(a) loop seeking a non-existent symbol, or

(b) produce a stream of irrelevant error messages.

Synchronization between the analyser and symbol stream must be enforced over as limited a range of symbols as possible. As the syntax analyser is written in terms of procedures it is natural to try and enforce synchronization at procedure entry and exit.

To enforce synchronization at the start of the procedure *S* corresponding to the syntax rule <*S*> is fairly straightforward. The set of symbols which are legitimate starters for <*S*> is known, so a preliminary check is made, such as that given in Figure 5.12, where *skipto* is a routine which skips symbols until one is found in the set passed as a parameter. Thus if there are erroneous symbols before a starting symbol this code will work satisfactorily. However, this simple method has a fundamental flaw in that the starting symbol for <*S*> may not be present and this may cause the above code to loop.

```
if not (sy in starters) then
   begin
   error(4);
   skipto(starters)
   end;
```

Figure 5.12 Preliminary check for starter symbols.

The solution to this problem is to add the set of legal following symbols to the set of symbols being looked for by the procedure *skipto*. Thus if a legal follower is discovered then synchronization can take place by leaving the current syntax analysis procedure. As the checking for synchronization takes place in numerous places within the syntax analyser, the Pascal-S system provides the procedures *skip* and *test* as shown in Figure 5.13. These routines can be called from any of the syntax analysis routines.

```
procedure skip (fsys : symset;
                errornum : integer);
(*Report error and skip over symbols looking for any symbol
  contained in fsys (the set of legal following symbols).
*)
begin
  error(errornum);
  while not (sy in fsys) do
    insymbol;
end (*skip*);

procedure test (legalsymbols, legalfollowingsymbols : symset;
                errornum : integer);
(*Test to see if current symbol is in a set of legal symbols and
  call skip if it is not.
*)
begin
  if not (sy in legalsymbols) then
    skip(legalsymbols + legalfollowingsymbols, errornum);
end (*test*);
```

Figure 5.13 Procedures *skip* and *test*.

The set of legal following symbols will not be known by any of the syntax analysis procedures – it will depend on where a procedure was called from and what other syntax analysis procedures are awaiting completion. Thus the set of legal following symbols is passed as a parameter to each syntax analysis procedure. Each such procedure thus has its own set of following symbols and when it calls another syntax analysis procedure, it adds further following symbols to its own set and passes the new set onto the called procedure. These extra symbols are determined by the location of the call within the procedure. As an example consider the code for the repeat statement given in Figure 5.14 where the following symbols passed to *statement* are *untilsy* and *semicolon* which are both likely following symbols to *statement* in this context.

Note that *repeatstatement* itself has no parameter specifying the following symbols. This is because it is called from the procedure *statement* and its following symbols will be the same as those passed to *statement*.

```
procedure repeatstatement;
var
  untilexpitem : item;
  locofrepeat : integer;
begin
  if tracing then
    writeln('Entering repeatstatement');
  locofrepeat := locationcounter;
  insymbol;
  statement([semicolon, untilsy] + fsys);
  while sy in [semicolon] + statbegsys do begin
    if sy = semicolon then
      insymbol
    else error(14);
    statement([semicolon, untilsy] + fsys)
  end;
  :
  :
```

Figure 5.14 Procedure showing additions to following symbol set.

The set of following symbols can also be used to enforce synchronization at the exit from each syntax analysis procedure. As an example, consider the call to the *skip* procedure with the argument *fsys* in the last few lines of the procedure *constant* shown in Figure 5.15. Thus when leaving a syntax analysis procedure we are assured that *sy* contains a value that the calling procedure expects.

5.6 Automatic generation of syntax analysers

The automatic generation of syntax analysers is now a well known technique and can greatly assist with the production of a compiler. These generators take a grammar, usually in some restricted form of BNF, and produce a parser. They will also often allow the insertion of semantic actions within the grammar, so that when a particular rule has been recognized, then a certain action can take place. For instance, after recognizing the correct syntax for a declaration, the semantic action could be to insert the names found in the declaration into the symbol table. Alternatively, when a certain statement has

```
                    :
                    :
          else if sy = realcon then begin
            theconstant.typeofconstant := reals;
            theconstant.ordinalvalue := sign * lastrealread;
            insymbol
          end
          else skip(fsys, 50)
        end;
        test(fsys, [], 6)
      end
    end (*constant*);
```

Figure 5.15 Procedure fragment with check for following symbols.

been recognized, the semantic action could be the generation of code to implement that statement.

Generators exist which will produce both top-down and bottom-up recognizers. One of the first and most famous top-down generators is SID (Syntax Improving Device) developed by Foster in (Foster, 1968). The most well-known bottom-up recognizer is probably *yacc* (Johnson, 1975), which is available within the UNIX system and which produces a parser written in C. *Llama* (Dunn and Murphy, 1976) is a similar tool which produces a bottom-up parser written in Pascal, and this system will be used to illustrate some of the benefits of these generators.

As an example consider the grammar in Figure 5.16. This grammar is a simplified form of a subset of the Pascal-S grammar and the string in Figure 5.17 is a legal string of the language generated by the grammar.

Llama has a strict input format and the grammar has to be transformed according to the following rules:

(a) Every rule ends with a period.

(b) The symbol ::= is replaced by =.

(c) The angle brackets < and > are omitted.

(d) All terminal symbols have to be different from Pascal keywords and entered in a section beginning with *&term*.

(e) The rules are entered in a section beginning with *&gram*.

<statement> ::=	*<assignment statement>* |
	<compound statement> |
	<while statement> |
	<repeat statement> |
	<empty>
<assignment statement> ::=	*id* := *<expression>*
<compound statement> ::=	**begin** *<statement sequence>*
	end
<statement sequence> ::=	*<statement>* { ; *<statement>* }
<while statement> ::=	**while** *<expression>* do
	<statement>
<repeat statement> ::=	**repeat** *<statement sequence>*
	until *<expression>*
<expression> ::=	*exp*

Figure 5.16 Simple grammar example.

Applying these rules the grammar is:

```
&term
      beginsy, endsy, repeatsy, untilsy, whilesy, dosy, expsy, semicolonsy
&gram
statement =              assignmentstatement |
                         compoundstatement |
                         whilestatement |
                         repeatstatement |
                         empty.
assignmentstatement =    id becomes expression.
compoundstatement =      beginsy statementsequence
                         endsy.
statementsequence =      statement |
                         statementsequence semicolon statement.
whilestatement =         whilesy expression dosy
                         statement.
repeatstatement =        repeatsy statementsequence
                         untilsy expression.
expression =             exp.
```

```
begin
    repeat
        while exp do
            begin
            id := exp;
            id := exp
            end;
        repeat
        until exp;
    id := exp
    until exp
end
```

Figure 5.17 Legal string conforming to simple grammar.

Llama is a syntax analyser generator and does not incorporate the lexical analysis phase. A user-designed lexical analyser can be inserted into the file in a section beginning with *&proc*, or the user can use a lexical analyser generator such as *aardvark* which is described in Section 4.4. When *aardvark* and *llama* are used in conjunction, the input file would first be run through *aardvark* which would produce a lexical analyser in the appropriate section in the file. The resulting output will then be the input to *llama* which would produce a Pascal program as output. This output would have to be compiled in order to produce an executable syntax analyser.

Aardvark requires the terminal symbols to be in a section beginning with *&token* and a user-supplied error routine to deal with unexpected symbols. With these modifications the input file to *aardvark* is:

```
&token
    separator = " " | tab | eoln.
    beginsy = "begin".
    endsy   = "end".
    repeatsy = "repeat".
    untilsy = "until".
    whilesy = "while".
    id = "id".
    becomes  = ":=".
    dosy    = "do".
    exp   = "exp".
```

```
    semicolon = ";".
&gram
statement =             assignmentstatement |
                        compoundstatement |
                        whilestatement |
                        repeatstatement |
                        empty.
assignmentstatement =   id becomes expression.
compoundstatement =     beginsy statementsequence
                        endsy.
statementsequence =     statement |
                        statementsequence semicolon statement.
whilestatement =        whilesy expression dosy
                        statement.
repeatstatement =       repeatsy statementsequence
                        untilsy expression.
expression =            exp.
&proc
procedure aaerror;
    begin
    writeln('Unexpected input symbol found by lexical analyser');
    halt
    end; (*aaerror*)
```

The results of executing *aardvark* followed by *llama* on this file is a Pascal program of 796 lines, which is too large to reproduce here. *Llama* assumes the grammar is in LALR(1) form, which is a more general form than the LL(1) form discussed earlier and this will allow the syntax analyser to parse the input deterministically without backup.

As discussed earlier, a bottom-up parser operates by either shifting the current input symbol onto a stack or by taking the right-hand side of a rule from the top of the stack and replacing it by the left-hand side of the rule. With this particular grammar, *llama* produces an analyser which contains 24 different states and a record of which states have been passed through is entered on the stack with the symbols. *Llama* has a number of options and one of these allows a trace of the operations performed on an input string. Thus each shift and reduction and its effect on the stack can be observed. As an example consider the legal input:

```
begin
repeat
  id := exp
until exp
end
```

With tracing switched on, *llama* gives the output shown below (the symbols *llstart* and *llEND* are internal *llama* symbols marking the beginning and end of the input).

```
stack entries:
                 1    llstart
state: 1  symbol: beginsy  action: shift  goto: 2
stack entries:
                 1    llstart
                 2    beginsy
state: 2  symbol: repeatsy  action: shift  goto: 3
stack entries:
                 1    llstart
                 2    beginsy
                 3    repeatsy
state: 3  symbol: id  action: shift  goto: 5
stack entries:
                 1    llstart
                 2    beginsy
                 3    repeatsy
                 5    id
state: 5  symbol: becomes  action: shift  goto: 16
stack entries:
                 1    llstart
                 2    beginsy
                 3    repeatsy
                 5    id
                 16   becomes
state: 16  symbol:    exp  action: shift  goto: 14
stack entries:
                 1    llstart
                 2    beginsy
                 3    repeatsy
                 5    id
                 16   becomes
                 14   exp
state: 14  symbol:    untilsy
action: reduce "expression =exp"  goto: 21
stack entries:
                 1    llstart
                 2    beginsy
                 3    repeatsy
                 5    id
                 16   becomes
                 21   expression
```

```
state: 21  symbol:     untilsy
action: reduce "assignmentstatement = id becomes expression"  goto: 7
stack entries:
                       1    llstart
                       2    beginsy
                       3    repeatsy
                       7    assignmentstatement
state: 7  symbol: untilsy
action: reduce "statement = assignmentstatement"  goto: 11
stack entries:
                       1    llstart
                       2    beginsy
                       3    repeatsy
                       11   statement
state: 11  symbol:     untilsy
action: reduce "statementsequence = statement"  goto: 13
stack entries:
                       1    llstart
                       2    beginsy
                       3    repcatsy
                       13   statementsequence
state: 13  symbol:     untilsy  action: shift  goto: 19
stack entries:
                       1    llstart
                       2    beginsy
                       3    repeatsy
                       13   statementsequence
                       19   untilsy
state: 19  symbol:     exp  action: shift  goto: 14
stack entries:
                       1    llstart
                       2    beginsy
                       3    repeatsy
                       13   statementsequence
                       19   untilsy
                       14   exp
state: 14  symbol:     endsy
action: reduce "expression = exp"  goto: 23
stack entries:
                       1    llstart
                       2    beginsy
                       3    repeatsy
                       13   statementsequence
                       19   untilsy
                       23   expression
```

```
state: 23  symbol:     endsy
action: reduce "repeatstatement = repeatsy
statementsequence untilsy expression"  goto: 10
stack entries:
                    1    llstart
                    2    beginsy
                    10   repeatstatement
state: 10  symbol:     endsy
action: reduce "statement = repeatstatement"  goto: 11
stack entries:
                    1    llstart
                    2    beginsy
                    11   statement
state: 11  symbol:     endsy
action: reduce "statementsequence = statement"  goto: 12
stack entries:
                    1    llstart
                    2    beginsy
                    12   statementsequence
state: 12  symbol:     endsy  action: shift  goto: 17
stack entries:
                    1    llstart
                    2    beginsy
                    12   statementsequence
                    17   endsy
state: 17  symbol: llEND
action: reduce "compoundstatement = beginsy statementsequence
endsy"  goto: 8
stack entries:
                    1    llstart
                    8    compoundstatement
state: 8  symbol: llEND
action: reduce "statement = compoundstatement"  goto: 6
stack entries:
                    1    llstart
                    6    statement
state: 6  symbol: llEND  action: accept
```

Llama also allows the insertion of semantic actions. The nature of these actions is more fully discussed in the following chapters. However, to illustrate their use within *llama*, suppose that the original grammar is altered to allow different identifiers and that after recognizing an assignment statement it is required to check that the identifier on the left-hand side is declared. Suppose that this can be accomplished by calling a boolean function called *declared* which takes the name to search for as a parameter. A problem arises as to how this function is to be passed the name of the identifier that has been found in the input. *Aardvark* and *llama* solve this problem by associating attributes with symbols. Thus an identifier can have a name attribute which can be accessed in the semantic actions. Given the rule:

$x = y\ z$

then the name attribute of y and z can be accessed as *$1.name* and *$2.name* respectively. The name attribute of x can be accessed as *$$.name*. The token section of the file has to be modified so that *aardvark* will record the name in the attribute. The modified input to *aardvark* and *llama*, with the semantic actions enclosed within '&(' and ')&', is:

```
&token
        separator = " " | tab | eoln.
        beginsy = "begin".
        endsy   = "end".
        repeatsy = "repeat".
        untilsy = "until".
        whilesy = "while".
        id = "a" &( $$name := 'a' )& | "b" &( $$name := 'b' )& |
              "c" &( $$name := 'c' )& | "d" &( $$name := 'd' )&.
        becomes  = ":=".
        dosy    = "do".
        exp   = "exp".
        semicolon = ";".
&attr
        id : (name : identifier);
&gram
statement =             assignmentstatement | compoundstatement |
                        whilestatement | repeatstatement | empty.
assignmentstatement = id becomes expression
                              &( if not declared($1.name) then
                                          writeln($1.name,' not declared');
                              )&.
compoundstatement = beginsy statementsequence endsy.
statementsequence = statement |
                        statementsequence semicolon statement.
whilestatement = whilesy expression dosy statement.
repeatstatement = repeatsy statementsequence untilsy expression.
expression = exp.
&type
                        identifier = 'a'..'d';
```

```
&proc
procedure aaerror;
     begin
     writeln('Unexpected input symbol found by lexical analyser');
     halt
     end; (*aaerror*)
function declared(name : identifier) : boolean;
     begin
     declared := false;
     (* This would be replaced by code to search
       the symbol table. *)
     end; (*declared*)
```

Assuming an input of

```
begin
  a := b + c;
end
```

llama generates:

```
a not declared
b not declared
c not declared
```

This is a very small example of the use of a syntax analyser generator. No coverage has been given to the subject of error recovery within *llama* and for this and further details of the features of *llama*, the reader is referred to the tutorial by Robinson and Hayes.

References

Aho, A V, Sethi, R, and Ullman, J D, *Compilers: Principles, Techniques and Tools,* Addison-Wesley, 1986.

Dunn, B J and Murphy, T J, 'Llama: A compiler generator', (Honours Thesis), University of New South Wales, 1976.

Foster, J M, 'A syntax improving device', *Computer Journal*, vol. 11, pp. 31–34, 1968.

Hunter, R, *Compilers: Their Design and Construction Using Pascal,* Wiley, 1985.

Johnson, S C, 'Yacc—yet another compiler-compiler', Computer Science Technical Report No. 32, Bell Laboratories, 1975.

Robinson, K A and Hayes, I, 'A tutorial on Llama: a Pascal translator generator', Teaching Document, University of New South Wales, 1986.

Welsh, J and McKeag, M, *Structured System Programming,* Prentice-Hall, 1980.

Chapter 6
Semantic Analysis

6.1 Introduction

The syntax analysis phase analyses the arrangement of symbols in the input stream and checks whether the arrangement conforms to the rules of the language being compiled. The semantic analysis phase looks more closely at the symbols and carries out checks such as whether an identifier used in an expression has been declared or whether the two side of an assignment statement have compatible types. To perform this sort of analysis, the semantic analyser must build up a table of identifiers and their attributes. This table is commonly known as the **symbol table**. During the analysis of a Pascal-S program, the symbol table is built up as the declarations are analysed.

The attributes required to be stored for identifiers are:

(a) the declared class of usage of the identifier, i.e. whether it is a constant, type, variable, procedure or function. The class of usage may be represented by an enumerated type:

$$object = (konstant, atype, variable, prozedure, funktion)$$

(b) for type, constant, variable and function identifiers, the associated type itself.

The association of each identifier with its attributes must involve the maintenance of some record of the form shown in Figure 6.1. These records are held in a data structure which should allow fast access in order that searches of the symbol table can be completed efficiently.

6.2 Semantic checking

The semantic analysis of identifiers involves:

(a) creating a new identifier record as it is declared, and recording its attributes;

```
symtabletype = packed record
                   name : alfa;
                   obj  : object;
                   typ  : types;
                   ...
                   end;
```

where

types = (notyp, ints, reals, bools, chars, arrays, records)

Figure 6.1 Record of symbol attributes.

(b) locating the entry for a particular identifier on each of its subsequent occurrences, and inspecting its attributes.

For block-structured languages such as Pascal, the process is complicated by the fact that more than one entry for an identifier may exist, and the appropriate entry, as determined by the scope rules, must be selected. For example, consider the program shown in Figure 6.2.

The scope of the global real constant *i* stretches between lines 3 to 5 and 13 to 16, whereas the local variable *i* is in scope between lines 8 and 12. The symbol table must record information about both uses of the identifier *i*. If *i* is accessed within the procedure *p* the semantic analyser must access the symbol table entry of the integer variable *i*. If *i* is accessed outside *p*, then the semantic analyser must access the information corresponding to the real constant *i*.

As a procedure or function can contain several local procedures or functions, the number of accessible blocks – or levels – can go up and down several times when processing a user's program. An example is given in Table 6.1.

In order to distinguish between names with different scopes, the level at which the identifier is declared is stored as part of the identifier's entry in the symbol table. The level is passed to *block* as a parameter and at every call the level is increased by one in order to deal with the rising and falling of the number of accessible blocks.

Searching of the symbol table commences from the current block and if the required identifier is not found, the search continues at the next accessible level. Thus all the symbol table entries declared at the same level, which

```
program scope(input, output);
const
  i = 27.6;
    :
    :
procedure p(s : integer);
  var
    i : integer;
  begin
    :
    :
  end; (*p*);
begin (*main program*)
  :
  :
end.
```

Figure 6.2 Example program.

must be unique, are chained together. In order to record which blocks are currently accessible at any point, the semantic analyser also uses a stack, known as the *display* stack, which contains indexes to the identifier declared first at each block level. Thus when an identifier is discovered during the processing of a statement, the semantic analyser takes the top element of the display stack and searches that level for the identifier. The index to the top element of the display stack is given by the value of the current static block level. If no match is found, then the element one below the top of the display stack is used and this continues until either the identifier is found or the display stack is exhausted, in which case the identifier is inaccessible.

The symbol table in Pascal-S is called *symboltable*, and is arranged so that user symbols are all stored and none discarded. The array *display* is used as a stack indexed by level. Each element of *display* points to the first user symbol in *symboltable* at that level.

arraytable holds in each entry sufficient information to define a vector. Thus when an array name is stored in *symboltable*, there will be one or more corresponding entries in *arraytable*, one for each dimension.

In Pascal, each block is necessarily uniquely associated with a procedure or function. An additional table, *blocktable*, is used to hold additional information about each block. *blocktable* is also used in analysing record

Table 6.1 Example program showing lexical levels.

Level 0	→	*pre-defined identifiers*
		program *source(input, output)*;
Level 1	→	**const** ...
		type ...
		var ...
		procedure *global1(...)*;
Level 2	→	**const** ... **type** ... **var** ...
		procedure *local1(...)*;
Level 3	→	**const** ... **type** ... **var** ...
		procedure *local2(...)*;
Level 4	→	**const** ...
		begin ... **end** (**local2**);
Level 3	→	**begin** ... **end** (**local1**);
Level 2	→	**begin** ... **end** (**global1**);
Level 1	→	**function** *global2(...)* ... ;
Level 2	→	**const** ...
		begin ... **end** (**global2**);
Level 1	→	**begin** (**main**)
		...
		end.

declarations, which are treated like blocks.

Routines to achieve the management of the symbol table in the Pascal-S system are:

procedure *enter*	enter identifier into the symbol table
procedure *enterblock*	start new block
function *locinsymboltable*	locate identifier in the symbol table

The *enter* procedure checks that the identifier has not already been declared at this level and if not, it enters the identifier name into the symbol table. The *locinsymboltable* function which locates identifiers will normally return the position in the symbol table of the requested identifier, but if it is not present, it signals an error.

Note that in a true compiler all usage of the identifier entries takes place between the opening and closing of the scope in which they were declared. It is possible to reclaim the storage occupied by local identifier entries when closing the scope. In an interpreter with run-time debugging features relating back to variable names, such as the Pascal-S system, all symbol table entries are kept.

6.3 Symbol table data structures

There are various ways of constructing a symbol table. Usually the choice is between a sequential structure such as an array and some form of dynamic data structure such as a linked list or binary tree.

One solution is to use an array of records with each record containing all the attributes of a single identifier. Identifiers would be inserted in the next free entry in the array and each record would also contain a field indicating the index of the next identifier declared in the same block. (Identifiers declared in the same block would not necessarily occupy contiguous entries in the array. For example, consider two procedures *p* and *q* declared at the same level. The entries in the symbol table for the identifiers *p* and *q* would be separated by any identifiers declared in *p*.)

The array could be searched sequentially from the first entry declared at any particular level. This simple solution, which is similar to the one used by the Pascal-S system, suffers from the disadvantage that access to the identifiers declared at a particular level is relatively slow. As the list of identifiers is inserted in the table in the order in which they were discovered in the input stream, the searching process starts at the first entry and continues until the last or until the identifier is found. The Pascal-S system starts the search at the last identifier declared at that level and proceeds to the first, but the problem is the same. If the list contains *n* identifiers, the average number of comparisons required, assuming the identifier is present, is *n*/2.

An alternative approach, adopted by many compiler writers, is to use hashing. With this technique, identifiers are not inserted in the table in the order that they occur, but according to the result of applying what is known as a **hashing function** to the name of the identifier. Thus the result of the hashing function is an index into the array. Clearly the number of possible identifiers is immense and there cannot be a unique entry in the array for each identifier. Thus, there has to be a strategy for dealing with the situation when applying the hashing function to an identifier name results in an index to a non-empty entry in the array (this is known as a **collision**). There are two major strategies for solving this problem, namely **rehashing** and **chaining**.

6.3.1 Rehashing

There are several rehashing methods and the reader is referred elsewhere (Morris, 1968) for a detailed coverage of all the alternatives, but to give the flavour of the strategies in this area two major alternatives are briefly discussed:

Linear rehash This is the probably the oldest and simplest solution. When a collision occurs a fixed number is added to the result of the hashing function and the modulo *n* operation, where *n* is the size of the array, is applied to yield an entry within the bounds of the array. If this new position is also full, the operation is repeated. The problem with this strategy is that separate chains can quickly become intertwined (this is known as **clustering**) which results in a greater number of comparisons before an entry is found.

Add-the-hash rehash Here the original hash value is added and the modulo *n* operation applied. This lessens the chance of two separate chains becoming entangled.

6.3.2 Chaining

With this technique the symbol table does not contain the identifiers themselves but pointers to them. Thus when the first identifier is entered into the symbol table a pointer to the name and its attributes is entered into the appropriate entry in the symbol table. This is shown in Figure 6.3.

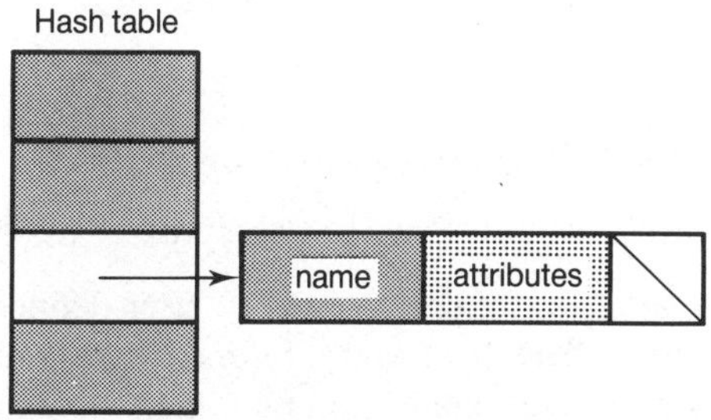

Figure 6.3 First entry in chained hash table.

If another identifier hashes to the same entry a list would be formed as indicated in Figure 6.4.

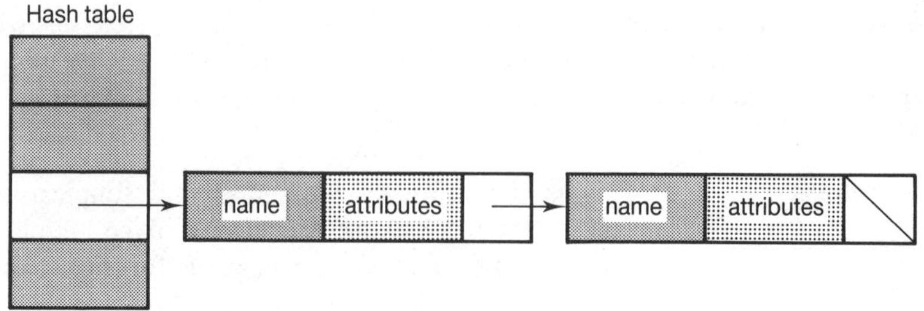

Figure 6.4 Two entries at same location in chained hash table.

Rehashing can become slow when the symbol table fills up. If the table fills up completely, extending the table can involve a complete reconstruction of the entire table. Chaining, however, will avoid these sorts of problems.

Using dynamic storage avoids the problem of the size of the symbol table entirely. The table could be held as a linked list, but this would mean that access would be slow. A better alternative would be to represent the symbol table as a binary tree, an approach adopted by the implementers of the Pascal-P system (Nori *et al.*, 1981).

6.4 Pascal-S symbol table management

The Pascal-S system does not use a dynamic data structure to represent the symbol table. This is probably due to Wirth's aim that the system could easily be translated into a language such as FORTRAN which does not possess such facilities.

6.4.1 Pascal-S symbol table data structures

A summary of the arrays used in Pascal-S to represent the symbol table is:

blocktable contains one entry for every user-defined function or procedure. The first entry refers to the imaginary block surrounding the main program, and contains standard const, type, var and procedure/function names. The second entry refers to the main program, that is the global variables. *blocktable* is also used for record declarations. Each record is regarded as a block and has an entry in *blocktable*. Each *blocktable* entry contains 4 fields:

indexsymtaboflastobj points to the most recent entry in *symboltable* of an identifier declared

	at this level. This allows all identifiers declared in the same block to be chained together.
indexsymtablastparam	points to the last parameter associated with a function or procedure. If this block is not a function or procedure, *indexsymtablastparam* points to the preceding function or procedure name.
spaceforparams	number of storage units on the stack required to hold the parameters and housekeeping information.
variablesize	number of storage units required to hold the housekeeping information plus parameters plus local variables.

display is a one-dimensional array with one entry for every block level in the main program. The maximum level to which procedures may be nested is one less than the length of *display*. Each entry in *display* points to an element in *blocktable*, being the block in scope at that level. There is a second array named *display* within the Pascal-S system. The other one is used within the interpreter and its functions are discussed in Chapter 9.

symboltable is the main symbol table array. Every identifier defined in the program is entered in *symboltable*, together with the predefined identifiers. Identifiers appear in their order of declaration. Each field of the record contains:

name	first *numofsigchars* characters of identifier name
link	pointer to the *symboltable* entry for the identifier declared immediately prior to this one at the same static level. The first entry at each level has a link of zero.
obj	the category of the identifier, that is *konstant, variable, atype, prozedure* or *funktion*.
typ	indicates the data type of the identifier, that is *notyp* (procedure), *ints, reals, bools, chars, arrays* or *records*.
ref	used for various purposes:

typ	*obj*	*ref*
arrays		points to *arraytable* entry
records		points to *blocktable* entry
	prozedure or *funktion*	points to *blocktable* entry

normal used to distinguish between variable and value parameter access in procedures and functions.

adrr has a variety of uses depending on the settings of other fields:

obj	*typ*	*adrr*
konstant	ints	actual value of constant
konstant	reals	pointer to *realconsttable*
konstant	bools	ordinal value
konstant	chars	ordinal value of char
atype	any	storage units to hold this type

field identifiers	offset from record base
procedures/functions	code start address
simple variables	stack frame offset
records/arrays	total storage units
value parameters	stack frame offset
var parameters	stack frame offset of address

lev static level number at which identifier was declared.

arraytable records information on arrays. Each entry refers to a single-dimension array – multiple-dimension arrays require several entries.

inxtyp type of the index of the array.

eltyp element type.

elref if *eltyp* is *arrays*, then this is a pointer to *arraytable* for that array.

low	value of the lower bound.
high	value of the upper bound.
elsize	number of storage units required for each element of the array.
size	the number of storage units required by the whole array.

stringtable	holds all the literal strings to which the user program refers.
realconsttable	holds all the real constants used in the user program.
code	holds all the intermediate code.

All of the tables discussed above are implemented as arrays of fixed length. It is not easy to determine the optimum size of these tables, if any such sizes exist. The maximum size of each table is currently declared as shown in Figure 6.5.

```
symboltablemax          = 200;
blocktablemax           = 30;
arraytablemax           = 40;
maxlevel                = 10; (*max size of display*)
stringtablemax          = 100;
realconstanttablemax    = 30;
maxamountofcode         = 1000;
```

Figure 6.5 Maximum table sizes.

If the tables were implemented as linked lists of pointers instead of arrays, greater flexibility would be achieved.

6.5 Entering information into the Pascal-S symbol table

Information is entered into the Pascal-S symbol table while parsing declarations. The identifier names must precede their type and this causes minor problems when inserting items into the symbol table. Consider the input:

```
var
    i, j, k, l : array [1..20] of integer;
```

The names are read first and either have to be held in a list until their type has been discovered and then entered into the symbol table or, are entered immediately after they have been read and the type information is entered later. The latter method is the one used in the Pascal-S system and since the symbol table is an array and new items are added after previous entries, it is a simple matter to record the position of *i* in the symbol table and then at a later stage alter the entries of *i*, *j*, *k*, and *l*.

The chief procedure in the parsing of declarations is *typ*, which is called whenever a type is expected, that is from *typedeclaration* and *vardeclaration*. The permitted types in Pascal-S are a subset of those in Pascal, but can still be complex. Consider Figure 6.6. *table* is an array type and each element of the array is a record. Thus the array element type involves a further type definition.

```
type
     table = array [1..10] of
                record
                name : array [1..4] of char;
                date :
                     record
                     day, year : integer;
                     month : array [1..20]
                          of char
                     end
                end;
```

Figure 6.6 Program fragment with type declarations.

This suggests that the *typ* procedure ought to be implemented in a recursive fashion in order to handle this self-embedding. This is the case and, when handling the types of array elements and the fields of records, a recursive call is made.

Standard types such as *integer* and *boolean* have already been entered into the symbol table, so they are handled in the same way as user-declared type identifiers; that is, information is extracted from their symbol table entry and returned to the caller of *typ*.

typ has a local procedure, *arraytyp*, to deal with arrays, but records are handled within the body of *typ*. In the case of arrays, information about the array is stored in *arraytable*. The information stored is the lower and upper bounds, the type of the index and elements and a reference to the elements.

If the type is a two-dimensional array, this reference will be an index into another entry in *arraytable*.

Information about records is stored in both *symboltable* and *blocktable*. The fields of the record are stored within *symboltable*, but their level is one greater than other entries at this level, such as the name of the record. This is in order that the field names can only be located in the symbol table in the situation where they are preceded by a record name of the appropriate type. An entry is made in *blocktable* so that this 'block' can be searched in this situation.

6.6 Type checking

Pascal and Pascal-S are languages which require the compiler to perform type checking at compile time. In the original description of Pascal (Jensen and Wirth, 1975) the kind of type checking required was unclear.

Consider the two types in Figure 6.7. Are these equivalent types? In other words, if there were variables of type *p* and *q*, could they be treated as having the same type? A language which treats *p* and *q* as equivalent types is said to support the **structural equivalence** of types and a number of early Pascal compilers implemented type equivalence using this approach.

```
p =  record
       i : integer;
       c : char
     end;
q =  record
       k : integer;
       l : char
     end;
```

Figure 6.7 Two type declarations.

In the standard definition of Pascal (ISO 7185) two variables are said to be of equivalent type only if they are declared with the same name or within the same anonymous type. This is known as **occurrence equivalence.** Thus in the above example, *p* and *q* are not equivalent types. Consider the example in Figure 6.8. Here *r* and *s* are of equivalent type and *t* and *u* are also equivalent types.

```
type
      names = packed array [1..10] of char;
var
      r, s : names
      t, u : record
             i : integer;
             c : char
             end;
```

Figure 6.8 Four type declarations.

Note that other languages such as Ada are even more strict and support the **name equivalence** of types, so that in the above example *t* and *u* would not be considered to be of equivalent type.

Pascal-S predates the ISO definition of Pascal, but implements the occurrence equivalence rather than the structural equivalence of types. Type checking takes place throughout the syntax analysis framework and the code required is dependent on the type found. In the case of standard types a simple comparison of the type expected and the *typ* field in the symbol table is often sufficient. However, this simplistic approach needs to be amended in certain situations. For instance, in the procedure *assignment,* the type of the right-hand side has to be checked against the type of the left-hand side. The right-hand side of the assignment is handled by the procedure *expression* and this may call some of its local procedures depending on the complexity of the expression. Thus type information has to be exchanged by procedures and this is made up of a record which is of the type:

```
item = record
       typ : types
       ref : index
       end;
```

The *ref* field in both *item* and *symboltable* is used when the *typ* field indicates a user-defined type such as an array or record has been encountered. The *ref* field in this case will be an index into *arraytable* and *blocktable* respectively and it is this index which is used to check for occurrence equivalence of types. If the types of two arrays are equivalent, then the values in the *ref* field will be equal.

6.7 Examples

The best way to fully understand the workings of the Pascal-S symbol table is to examine the contents of the compiler's tables after it has analysed some example programs. The compiler has an option to output these tables and some examples will now be discussed.

6.7.1 Example 1

This first example illustrates the contents of the tables when a constant and an array type are encountered.

```
program first(input,output);
const
  max = 27;
type
  tables = array [1..max] of integer;
var
  table : tables;
  i : integer;
begin
end.
```

Consider the output shown in Table 6.2 produced by the Pascal-S system when the debugging option is switched on.

Notes

(a) Entries in the Pascal-S tables which are of enumerated type such as *obj*, *typ* and *normal* (*nrm* in the above table) are represented in the above output by their ordinal values.

(b) There are two entries in *blocktable* in this example, namely the outermost block, containing all the standard identifiers, and the main program block.

(c) The system puts user-declared objects in *symboltable* from entry number 32 onwards. The previous entries are occupied by the standard identifiers such as *sin*, *read*, and *maxint*.

(d) The first entry at each level has a *link* entry of 0. This is to enable the searching algorithm of *findlocinsymboltable* to recognise when it has completed searching a particular level. Contained in the *link* field of all subsequent identifiers declared at that level is the position in the symbol table of the preceding identifier declared at that level. The *indexsymtaboflastobj* field of *blocktable* contains the index in the

Table 6.2 Tables for program *first*.

identifiers	*link*	*obj*	*typ*	*ref*	*nrm*	*lev*	*adrr*
32 max	0	0	1	0	0	1	27
33 tables	32	2	5	1	0	1	27
34 table	33	1	5	1	1	1	5
35 i	34	1	1	0	1	1	32

blocks	*last*	*lpar*	*psze*	*vsze*
1	31	1	0	0
2	35	31	5	33

arrays	*xtyp*	*etyp*	*eref*	*low*	*high*	*elsz*	*size*
1	1	1	0	1	27	1	27

symbol table of the last identifier declared at that level. Thus the searching algorithm of *locinsymboltable* starts from the identifier declared last at a particular level and then chains backwards, via the *link* field, towards the identifier declared first at that level. If the identifier is not found at that level, the index to the next block to search is obtained from the *display* array. The full code of *locinsymboltable* is as follows:

```
function locinsymboltable (id : alfa) : integer;
(* if not there calls error and returns 0.
   Otherwise returns the position
   in the symbol table *)
var
   currentlevel, posinsymtable : integer;
begin
   currentlevel := level;
   (* Put identifier we are looking for into the
      bottom of the table.
      Thus the following search is guaranteed to
      find it. We can examine
      its position to determine whether it was there
      before entry to this function.
   *)
```

```
symboltable[0].name := id;
(* Start the search at the current static level
   and if not move down to the next. Continue
   until found or the bottom (global) level has
   been searched
*)
repeat
   posinsymtable := blocktable[display[currentlevel]].
      indexsymtaboflastobj;
   while symboltable[posinsymtable].name <> id do
      posinsymtable := symboltable[posinsymtable].link;
   currentlevel := currentlevel - 1;
     (*look at next block in scope*)
until (currentlevel < 0) or (posinsymtable <> 0);
if posinsymtable = 0 then
   error(0);
locinsymboltable := posinsymtable
end (*locinsymboltable*);
```

6.7.2 Example 2

As discussed earlier in this chapter, the scope of identifiers is determined by the level attribute within the symbol table, as shown in the second example.

```
program second(input,output);
var
  index0 : integer;

procedure p1(param1 : integer; var param2 : char);
  var
    index1 : integer;

  procedure p2;
    var
      index2: integer;
    begin
    end; (*p2*)

  procedure p3;
    var
      index3 : integer;
    begin
    end; (*p3*)
```

```
    begin
    end; (*p1*)

    procedure p4;
      var
        index4 : integer;
      begin
      end; (*p4*)

  begin (*main program*)
  end.
```

The compiler's tables after processing this program are given in Table 6.3.

Table 6.3 Tables for program *second*.

identifiers	*link*	*obj*	*typ*	*ref*	*nrm*	*lev*	*adrr*
32 index0	0	1	1	0	1	1	5
33 p1	32	3	0	3	1	1	2
34 param1	0	1	1	0	1	2	5
35 param2	34	1	4	0	0	2	6
36 index1	35	1	1	0	1	2	7
37 p2	36	3	0	4	1	2	0
38 index2	0	1	1	0	1	3	5
39 p3	37	3	0	5	1	2	1
40 index3	0	1	1	0	1	3	5
41 p4	33	3	0	6	1	1	3
42 index4	0	1	1	0	1	2	5

blocks	*last*	*lpar*	*psze*	*vsze*
1	31	1	0	0
2	41	31	5	6
3	39	35	7	8
4	38	37	5	6
5	40	39	5	6
6	42	41	5	6

Notes

(a) In this program there are six blocks (including the outermost one where the standard identifiers are declared). However, both *p2* and *p3* are declared at the same level so a maximum of four blocks are accessible at any point in the program. In other words, the *display* array never contains more than four elements.

(b) The identifier *p1* is declared at level 1, but the parameters to procedure *p1*, namely *param1* and *param2*, are declared at level 2. This is because the identifiers *param1* and *param2* are only accessible within *p1*, but the identifier *p1* must be accessible in the main program in order that the procedure can be called.

(c) The *normal* field of *param2* indicates that it is a variable parameter so that the code generator can generate the correct code.

(d) The existence of the *link* field in the symbol table is justified because not all the identifiers declared at the same level are contiguous within the symbol table. The identifiers *p2* and *p3* are separated by the identifiers declared within *p2* and so it is not possible to chain back by assuming that the previous identifier is declared at the same level as the current identifier.

References

International Standards Organisation, 'ISO standard: specification for the computer programming language Pascal', 7185, 1983.

Jensen, K and Wirth, N, *Pascal User Manual and Report,* Springer-Verlag, 1975.

Morris, R, 'Scatter storage techniques', *Comm. ACM,* vol. 11, pp. 38–44, 1968.

Nori, K V, Amman, U, Nageli, H H, and Jacobi, C, 'Pascal-P implementation notes', in *Pascal – The Language and Its Implementation,* ed. D W Barron, pp. 83–124, Wiley, 1981.

Chapter 7
Pascal-S Virtual Machine

7.1 The run-time environment

The Pascal-S compiler generates code for a hypothetical machine which is stack-based. This means that the hypothetical machine has no registers or accumulators in the conventional sense and so all data manipulation takes place at the top of the stack. For example, to add two items the following instruction sequence is executed:

> load value of item A to top of stack
> load value of item B to top of stack
> add two top items, replacing values with result

and the expression

$$a + b * c$$

would be translated into

> load value of *a* to top of stack
> load value of *b* to top of stack
> load value of *c* to top of stack
> multiply two top items, replacing values with result
> add two top items, replacing values with result

Thus all binary operators expect to find their operands on top of the stack. They also lower the stack by one and overwrite the first operand with their result. Pictorially the stack can be seen growing downwards as shown in Figure 7.1. How the contents of the stack alter during the evaluation of the arithmetic expression given above is illustrated in Figure 7.2. As will be seen in the following chapter, this architecture considerably simplifies code generation.

Each element on the stack can hold a variety of data. For instance, an element may hold an integer representing the value of an integer variable, an

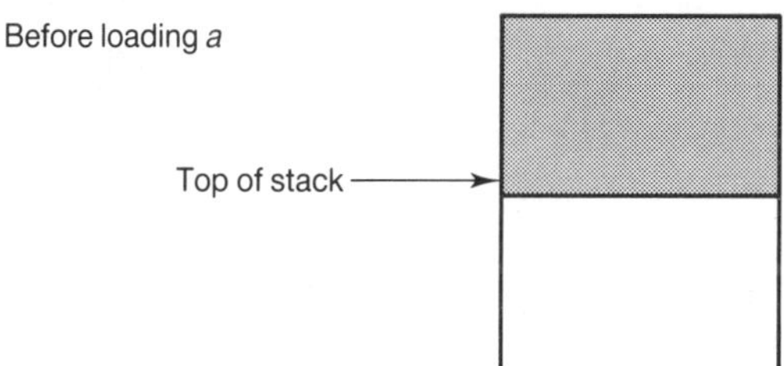

Figure 7.1 The stack contents.

address in a previous stack frame, the value returned by a function or the value of a real variable.

7.2 Stack frames

Space for all variables in a user's program is allocated on the stack. In a block-structured language, the space for the local variables of a procedure or function must be allocated at block entry (in Pascal and Pascal-S this corresponds to entry into a procedure or function). The space for local variables must stay in existence until the block has completed execution and since the code of a block may call other blocks, including itself, space allocation for variables is nested. A stack structure is therefore ideal.

Each procedure entry or function call necessitates the creation of space for parameters and local variables and this space is known as the **stack frame** or **activation record**. Recall, however, that within a particular block reference may be made to any variables declared in enclosing blocks, and to those at the level of the main program (these are known as **non-local** and **global** variables respectively). A link to the stack frames for these blocks must be preserved. This is known as the **static link** because it can be determined by inspecting the static program listing. Space for the static link must be allocated as each stack frame is created. The various static links form a backward-pointing chain through the stack until the global stack frame is reached.

The size of the stack frame varies from procedure to procedure and will depend on the number of parameters and local variables of the procedure. At procedure exit it is necessary to update the base address of the current stack frame to that of the calling procedure. A second type of link is required to record this information. This is known as the **dynamic link** as it records the dynamic calling sequence of the procedures and functions at run-time. Note that the dynamic link will always point back to the base of the previous stack frame on the stack.

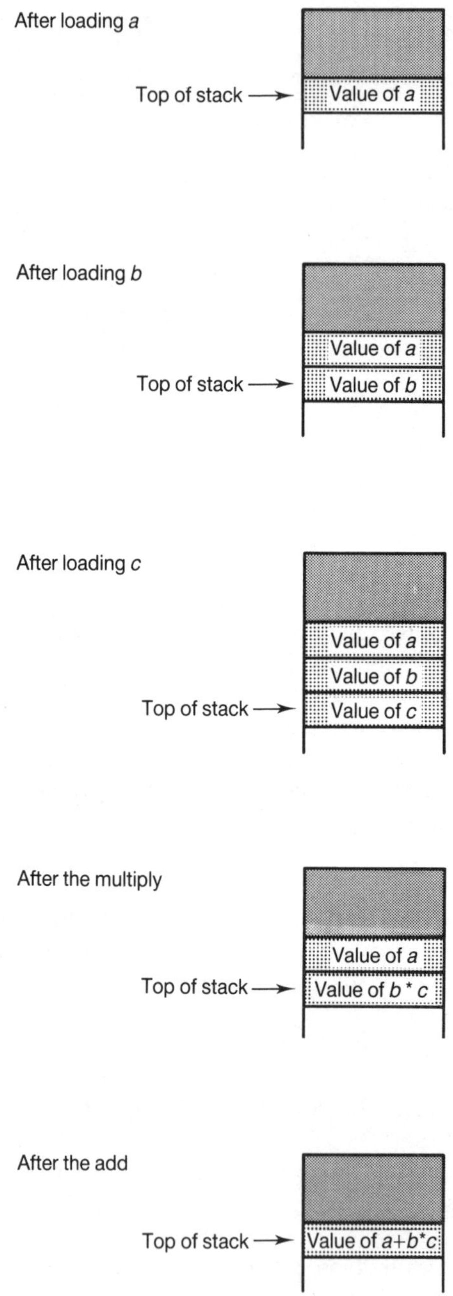

Figure 7.2 Stack contents during expression evaluation.

A third piece of housekeeping information must be stored in the stack frame – the return code address. This is the address of the instruction following the procedure or function call, and is equivalent to the return address in a subroutine call instruction at the hardware level.

For function calls only, space must be allocated in the stack frame to store the function result. To make code generation easier, this is usually the first location in the new stack frame for the function call. On return from the function, the top-of-stack pointer needs only to be incremented to leave the function result at the top of the stack. To keep stack frame allocation the same for procedure and function entry, space for the result is allocated in both cases. It is simply not used in the procedure case. In order that the Pascal-S interpreter can have access to the symbol table, a stack frame in the Pascal-S system also contains a pointer to the symbol table entry for the called procedure or function. As will be seen in Chapter 9, this enables the Pascal-S system to give useful diagnostic help when a run-time error occurs. The structure of the current stack frame is shown in Figure 7.3.

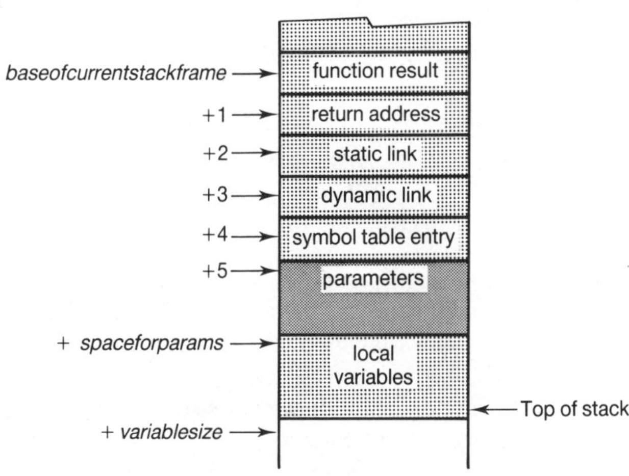

Figure 7.3 Current stack frame.

7.3 Variable access and the display

Accessing local variables is a simple offset operation from the current stack frame base, the *baseofcurrentstackframe* register. To access a non-local or global variable, however, requires the static link be followed to other stack frames, before the offset operation is performed. The number of times the link must be traversed is simply the difference in the static levels between the current block and the block in which the variable to be accessed is declared. Frequent non-local access can impose a large overhead.

Consider the sequence of procedure calls at run-time in the following program:

```
program calls;
var globals
  procedure g;
  var gvars
  begin
    ...
  end (*g*);
  procedure h;
  var hvars
    procedure i;
    var ivars
    begin
      g;
    end (*i*);
  begin
    i;
  end (*h*);
begin
  h;
end.
```

Just before the call to *g* in procedure *i*, the stack will appear as shown in Figure 7.4. After the call to *g* in *i*, the stack will be as shown in Figure 7.5. Note that only the local variables of the procedure *g* and the globals are now accessible.

To improve efficiency, an additional data structure is used to record the currently accessible frames. It is known as the **display**. Some hardware architectures have been extended so that the display can be held in special fast registers.

In Pascal-S the array named *display* holds pointers to the base of the currently accessible stack frames. The address of a variable becomes a pair of values:

(a) level number;

(b) offset from frame base.

The level number becomes the index for an element of the *display* array. The pointer so obtained has the offset added to yield the stack address of the variable. With the addition of the display, the stack frame diagram before the

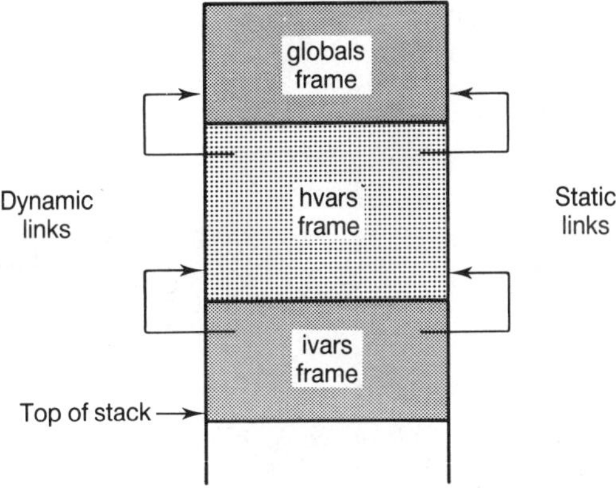

Figure 7.4 Before the call to procedure *g*.

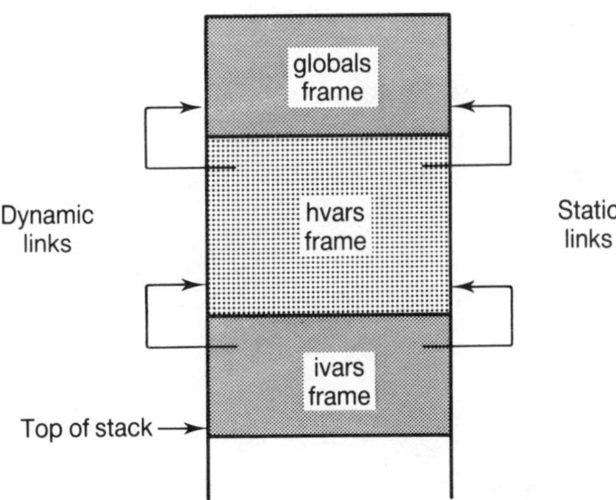

Figure 7.5 After the call to procedure *g*.

call to procedure g in procedure i is as shown in Figure 7.6. After the call to g in i, the stack will be as illustrated in Figure 7.7.

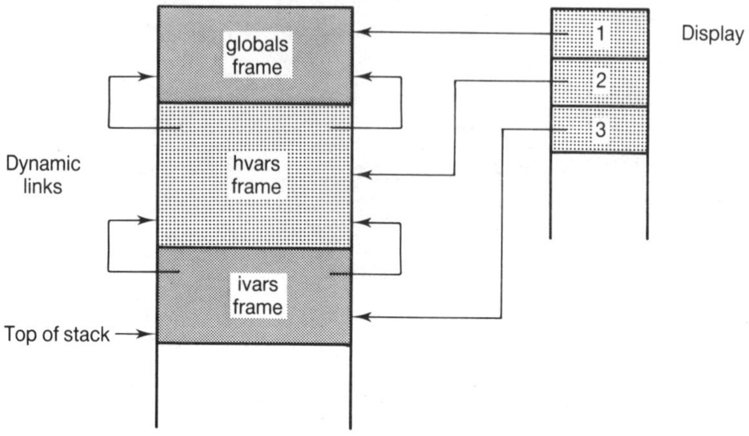

Figure 7.6 Stack and display before the call to procedure g.

In variable access, the level number becomes an index into the display, which immediately points to the base of the stack frame holding the value of the variable. This avoids following the static link chain to locate the appropriate stack frame, a technique which is usually more expensive than using the display stack to access stack frames. However, there is some overhead with using the display stack as it must be updated at block entry and exit. The Pascal-S system employs both a display stack and static links in order to take advantage of the strengths of both techniques.

For instance, consider the following program:

```
program scope(input,output);
     procedure p1;
          begin
          (* position of snapshot 2 *)
          :
          end; (*p1*)
     procedure p2;
          procedure p3;
               begin
               (* position of snapshot 4*)
               :
               p1
               end; (*p3*)
          begin (*p2*)
```

```
        (* position of snapshot 1 *)
        p1
        :
        (* position of snapshot 3 *)
        p3
        end; (*p2*)
begin (*main program*)
:
p2;
:
end.
```

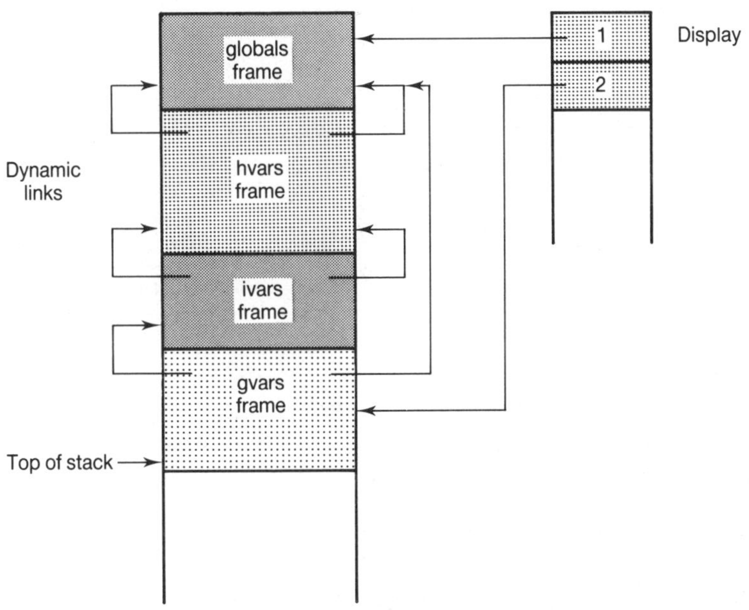

Figure 7.7 Stack and display after the call to procedure *g*.

To show the state of the display stack and the static links at various places within the program, certain points are selected where the processing is halted and the contents of the display and the static links are examined. This is known as a **snapshot**.

The program starts execution at the body of the main program and control is immediately transferred to the procedure *p2* where the first snapshot is encountered. At this point the state of the display and stack is as shown in Figure 7.8.

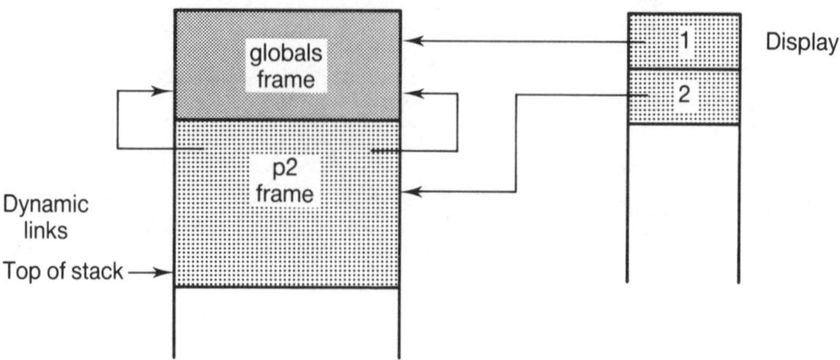

Figure 7.8 Snapshot 1.

A call to procedure *p1* then occurs and the second snapshot, shown in Figure 7.9, is located at the start of this procedure. The second element of the display stack has been overwritten by a pointer to the *p1* frame.

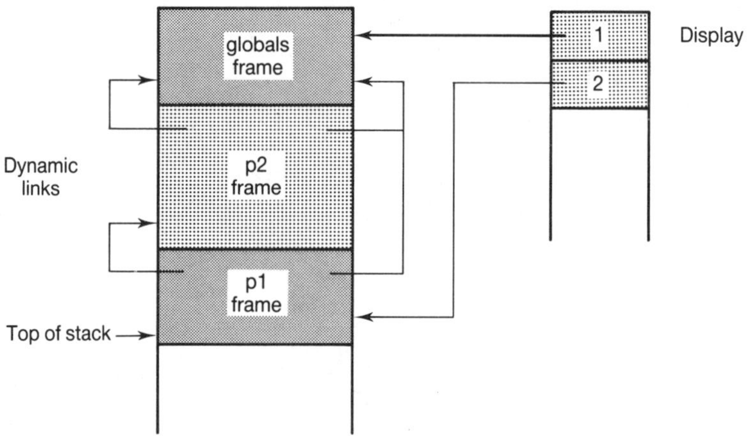

Figure 7.9 Snapshot 2.

When execution of *p1* is complete, control returns to *p2* and arrives at the position of snapshot 3. Here the state of the stack and display should be the same as in snapshot 1. Thus the second element of the display stack has been overwritten by a pointer to the frame of *p2*. This pointer can be obtained from the dynamic link from the *p1* frame back to the *p2* frame.

Snapshot 4 is positioned at the start of procedure *p3* and the situation will then be as in Figure 7.10. The *p3* procedure then calls *p1* and Figure 7.11 shows the result.

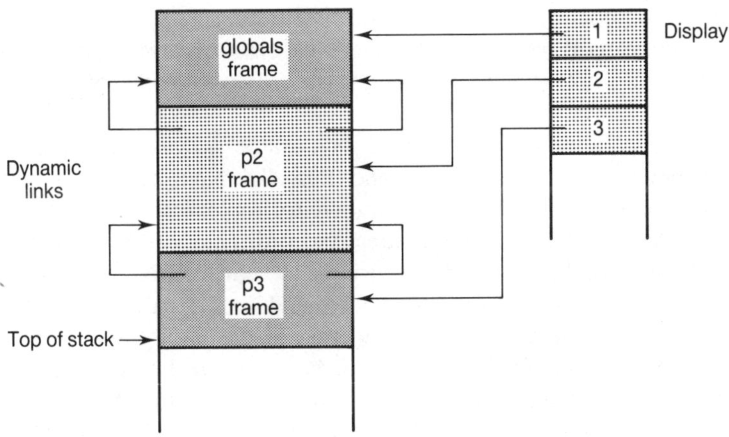

Figure 7.10 Snapshot 4.

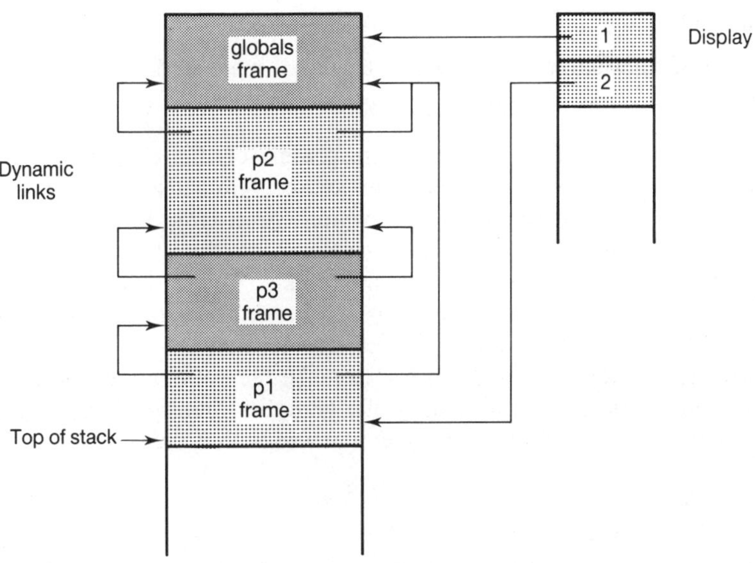

Figure 7.11 Second visit to snapshot 4.

When *p1* has completed execution the stack and display should return to that of snapshot 4. Without static links, this would have meant saving the contents of the top two elements of the display stack before the call to *p1* and restoring them once procedure *p1* completed execution.

In the Pascal-S system, which implements static links, the pointer to the *p3* frame can be obtained from the static link from *p3* to *p2*. In general, this technique can be used whatever the difference between levels, and the display stack and static link techniques, which are often thought of as mutually exclusive methods, have been combined.

There is another situation where one frame accesses another: that is, when parameters are used. Pascal and Pascal-S have only two parameter passing mechanisms, namely those required to implement value and variable parameters. With value parameters there is no difficulty as the actual parameter, which may be an expression, variable or constant, is evaluated at the point of call and stored in the space allocated in the called routine's stack frame. With a variable parameter the address in the stack frame of the actual parameter, which can only be a variable, is stored in the space allocated in the called routine's stack frame. Thus if a variable parameter is assigned a value, instructions will be required to store the assigned value into the location in the stack whose address is in the space allocated for the parameter.

7.4 Virtual machine instructions

The Pascal-S virtual machine was designed with two objectives:

(a) Ease of translation from Pascal-S to virtual machine language.

(b) The instructions should be reasonably compact.

As has been seen in the previous sections of this chapter, the virtual machine is a stack-based machine. This architecture satisfies the first objective as will be seen in the following chapter. As a large number of instructions operate on the top one or two elements on the stack, over half the instructions do not require any operands and so this architecture can also satisfy the second objective. However, the implementation of this architecture in the Pascal-S system does not take into account the different lengths of the instructions and no attempt is made to make the optimum use of space.

The instructions are inserted by the compiler into an array, *code*, with one instruction per entry. Each entry is a record with 3 fields:

opcode	operation code
field1	static level
field2	usually constant, address or offset, otherwise multi-purpose

Code entries are created by calls to the three procedures:

emit	zero-address instructions
emit1	one-operand (field2) instructions
emit2	two-operand (field1 and field2) instructions

The operation codes have been implemented as the enumeration type, *opcode*, for readability.

With a large table it is not easy to comprehend the utility of these instructions so they have been subdivided into categories. Why these instructions are useful will be seen in Chapter 8 and their implementation will be described in Chapter 9, but the functions of the instructions in the various categories will be discussed below.

7.4.1 Load and store instructions

These instructions are displayed in Table 7.1. Most instructions use elements on top of the stack, so these instructions will load the constants or the contents of variables onto the stack. The variables will have been assigned space on the stack, so loads of this kind are transfers of values from one part of the stack to another. Strictly, a stack is a data type which only permits access to its top element, so it could be argued that the object being dealt with is no longer a stack, but the term is so commonly used that we shall continue its use.

Table 7.1 Load and store instructions.

Mnemonic	*Meaning*
lodadd *x y*	load address of level *x* and offset *y*
lodval *x y*	load value from level *x*, offset *y*
lodind *x y*	load indirect (pointer at level *x*, offset *y*)
offset *y*	add *y* to value at top of stack
lodins	fetch value to top of stack, address is on top of stack
ldint *y*	load integer *y*
ldchar *y*	load character whose ordinal value is *y*
ldbool *y*	load boolean whose ordinal value is *y*
ldreal *y*	load real, *y* index to rconst
loadbl *y*	load block, *y* gives size of block
copybl *y*	copy block, *y* gives size of block
store	store top of stack into address at one below top of stack

There are separate instructions for the loading of integer, character, boolean and real constants so that each stack element can be marked with the type of element it contains. There are also instructions for loading variables whose address is in the top element of the stack. Included in this group is the *offset* instruction which is used to modify the address on top of the stack. There are only two instructions to store items from the top of the stack, *store* and *copybl,* as the only possible destination is within the stack.

7.4.2 Jump instructions

These instructions are displayed in Table 7.2. There is an unconditional jump instruction, *jump*, which transfers control to the instruction whose index in the *code* array is the operand of the instruction. Only one unconditional jump instruction, *jmpfal* which jumps if the top of the stack contains 0, is required.

Table 7.2 Jump instructions.

Mnemonic	*Meaning*
jump *y*	unconditional jump to *y*
jmpfal *y*	jump to *y* if top of stack false
halt	halt program execution

The *halt* instruction is classified in this category. Although it is not a jump instruction it does affect the flow of control.

7.4.3 Arithmetic instructions

These instructions are displayed in Table 7.3.

Table 7.3 Arithmetic instructions.

Mnemonic	*Meaning*
float	float top of stack
negate	replace integer on top of stack with its negative
add	add the two integers on top of the stack
sub	subtract top integer from integer one below top
addr	add the two reals on top of the stack
subr	subtract top real from real one below top
mult	multiply the two integers on top of stack
div	divide top integer into integer one below top
mod	modulus of top integer into integer one below top
multr	multiply top two reals
rdiv	divide top real into real one below top
negatr	negate a real

Integers and reals have their own sets of instructions for the basic operations such as addition, subtraction, multiplication and division. There is also an instruction to convert from integer to real and negate either integers or reals.

7.4.4 Boolean operations

These instructions are displayed in Table 7.4. As with arithmetic operations, there are separate sets of instructions for comparisons of reals and integers. Most of these instructions have integer or real operands and give boolean results, but there are also instructions which operate on boolean values (*and*, *or* and *not*).

Table 7.4 Boolean operations.

Mnemonic	*Meaning*
not	replace boolean on top of stack by its complement
equalr	check two reals on top of stack for equality
noteqr	check two reals on top of stack for inequality
lessr	check top real < real one below top of stack
lesser	check top real <= real one below top of stack
greal	check top real > real one below top of stack
gereal	check top real >= real one below top of stack
equal	check two integers on top of stack for equality
notequ	check two integers on top of stack for inequality
lessth	check top integer < integer one below top of stack
lesseq	check top integer <= integer one below top of stack
greatt	check top integer > integer one below top of stack
greate	check top integer >= integer one below top of stack
or	or the two booleans on top of the stack
and	and the two booleans on top of the stack

7.4.5 Routine calling instructions

These instructions are displayed in Table 7.5. Special instructions are required to handle calling procedures and functions in Pascal-S. These instructions build stack frames and ensure parameters are stored in the called parameter's stack frame. Standard routines such as *read, sin* and *chr* are treated separately from user-defined routines and have their own instruction, namely *stfunc*.

7.4.6 High-level instructions

These instructions are displayed in Table 7.6. The instructions in this category are very specialized. They are generated only when the compiler has recognized certain high-level language constructs. For instance the *forfdn* and *forsdn* instructions simulate the **downto** version of the Pascal-S **for** statement. Similarly, the *switch* instruction is the instruction which simulates the

Table 7.5 Routine calling instructions.

Mnemonic	*Meaning*
updis *x y*	update display (move down from level *y* to *x*)
stfunc *y*	execute standard function specified by *y*
markst *y*	mark stack
call *y*	call user procedure
leavep	exit procedure
leavef	exit function

case statement. The exact interpretation of these instructions is given in Chapter 9.

Table 7.6 High-Level Instructions.

Mnemonic	*Meaning*
switch *y*	jump to case table at *y* and select entry
pbreak *y*	case table entry – *y* is case value (jump address in next instruction)
forfup *y*	for-loop entry test (up case), *y* address after loop
forsup *y*	for-loop retry test (up case), *y* address of loop code
forfdn *y*	for-loop entry test (down), *y* address after loop
forsdn *y*	for-loop retry test (down), *y* address of loop code
index1 *y*	indexed fetch (element size<>1), *y* points to *arraytable*
indexm *y*	indexed fetch, *y* points to *arraytable*

7.4.7 Input and output instructions

These instructions are displayed in Table 7.7. They are generated when the *read*, *readln*, *write* and *writeln* procedure calls are encountered within a Pascal-S program. Their functions are closely related to the input/output system in Pascal-S, but each instruction only handles input and output of a single item. Hence a typical *writeln* statement in a user's program might generate several of the individual output instructions as well as the *writeln* instruction, which terminates the output line.

Table 7.7 Input and output instructions.

Mnemonic	*Meaning*
read *y*	read value, *y* indicates type
wrstrg *y*	write string, *y* gives stab entry, top of stack gives length
write *y*	write with default field widths, *y* indicates type
wr1fld *y*	write with specified field widths, *y* indicates type
wr2fld	write a real with 2 fieldwidth parameters
readln	readln
writln	writeln

7.4.8 Unimplemented instructions

Four of the instructions have not been implemented. They were intended to handle the implementation-dependent functions of *reset* and *rewrite*.

Chapter 8
Intermediate Code Generation

In a one-pass compilation system, the reading of characters, the formation of lexical units, syntax checking, semantic processing and code generation all take place at the same time. The Pascal-S system is driven by the syntax analyser, which calls the lexical analyser when it requires a token, calls a semantic routine when it requires information from the symbol table and calls the code generator when an intermediate code instruction is to be generated. Thus calls to the code generator occur throughout the syntax analysis routines.

The objective of this chapter is to give the reader an introduction to intermediate code instruction generation for given constructs in Pascal-S.

8.1 Expression evaluation

The expression analysis routines are based on the indirectly recursive grammar:

<expression> ::= *<simple expression>* |
<relational exp>
<relational exp> ::= *<simple expression>*
<relational op>
<simple expression>
<relational op> ::= = | <> | >= | > | < | <=
<simple expression> ::= *<term>* |
<signed term> |
<adding exp>
<signed term> ::= *<sign>* *<term>*
<adding exp> ::= *<term>* { *<adding op>* *<term>* }
<sign> ::= + | -
<adding op> ::= + | - | **or**
<term> ::= *<factor>*
{ *<multiplying op>* *<factor>* }
<multiplying op> ::= * | / | **div** | **mod** | **and**
<factor> ::= *<unsigned constant>* |
<variable> |

<*func call*> |
<*brack exp*> |
not <*factor*>

Section 7.1 described the architecture of the Pascal-S virtual machine, the principal component of which is the run-time stack which is used both for expression analysis and the housekeeping associated with stack frames. The virtual machine instructions use the stack and some typical instructions are:

load value of item A to top of stack
load value of item B to top of stack
add two top items, lower the stack by two and
put result on top of stack

This section will fill in the missing link by describing the code generation for the basic structures of the language.

The BNF grammar for Pascal expressions given above is parsed by four procedures, namely *expression, simpleexpression, type* and *factor*. *factor* is nested within *term, term* within *simpleexpression* and *simpleexpression* within *expression*. As the Pascal-S virtual machine is stack-based, Pascal expressions such as

b * *c*

have to be converted into the following intermediate code:

load value of *b* onto stack
load value of *c* into stack
multiply

Expressions such as *b* * *c* are parsed by *term* and the start of the code of *term* is:

```
begin (*term*)
  if tracing then
    writeln('Entering term');
  (* Get operand*)
  factor(fsys + [times, rdiv, idiv, imod, andsy],
  resultingtermitem);
  while sy in [times, rdiv, idiv, imod, andsy] do begin
    (* First operand now on stack *)
    termoperator := sy;
    insymbol;
    (* Get second operand*)
    factor(fsys + [times, rdiv, idiv, imod, andsy],
```

```
        followingfactoritem);
        (* Second operand now on stack - now for operation *)
        if termoperator = times then begin
          resultingtermitem.typ := resulttype(resultingtermitem.typ,
            followingfactoritem.typ);
          case resultingtermitem.typ of
            notyp :;
            ints : emit(MultInst);
            reals : emit(MultrInst);
          end
        :
        :
```

There is a call to *factor* which will cause the generation of the first load instruction. *term* then checks whether the next token is a multiply operator or an operator with the equivalent precedence, and if so calls *factor* a second time. This generates the second load and upon return to *term,* and after checking the types of the operands, the appropriate multiply instruction for the type is generated. *simpleexpression* and *expression* operate in the same manner to convert expressions into instructions for the stack-based virtual machine.

Expressions such as

$a + b * c$

which should generate

load the value of *a* onto stack
load the value of *b* onto stack
load the value of *c* onto stack
multiply
add

are easily handled because of the nesting of the four procedures. *expression* generates the code for the relational operators such as <=, < etc., which have the lowest priority. *simpleexpression* generates the code for the addition operators such as +, – etc. which are of the next highest priority. *term* generates the code for the multiply operators such as *, **mod** etc. *factor* only handles the **not** operator and generates code for the operands.

Consider the expression

$a < b + c * d$

and assume that the variables *a, b, c* and *d* are declared at the topmost level with addresses 5, 6, 7 and 8 respectively. The operation of the *expression* procedure on the above expression can be described by a 'code trace' as follows:

```
expression
  simpleexpression
    term
      factor                      lodval 1  5
    term
  simpleexpression
expression
  simpleexpression
    term
      factor                      lodval 1  6
    term
  simpleexpression
    term
      factor                      lodval 1  7
    term
      factor                      lodval 1  8
    term                          mult
  simpleexpression                add
expression                        lessth
```

The left-hand side is a trace of the the active procedures (indentation implies that the inner procedure is called by the previous procedure at the level one less than the current level) and the right-hand side indicates the code generated, the procedure on the left of an instruction being the generator of that instruction.

8.2 Code generation for basic structures

This section describes how code is generated for the various statements of Pascal-S. This will show the basic templates for the statement structures and why some of the instructions were included in the virtual machine's instruction set. The structures are considered in order of increasing complexity.

8.2.1 Assignment statements

The *statement* procedure calls the *assignment* procedure which, as can be seen below, commences by generating the code to load the address of the variable on the left-hand side of the statement onto the top of the stack. If this involves arrays or records then *assignment* passes on responsibility to *selector* for the generation of the offset from the base address. *assignment* then calls *expression* to generate the code for the right-hand side. At execution time this code will leave the result of the expression on the top of the stack with the address of the left-hand side beneath it. Thus *assignment* needs to generate the *store* instruction after calling *expression* in order to transfer the value of the expression into the address of the left-hand side.

```
procedure assignment (leveloflhs, offsetoflhs, posinsymtableoflhs :
                    integer);
var
  lhsitem, rhsitem : item;
  opcode : opcodes;
begin
  if tracing then
    writeln('Entering assignment');
  lhsitem.typ := symboltable[posinsymtableoflhs].typ;
  lhsitem.ref := symboltable[posinsymtableoflhs].ref;
  (* Check to see if lhs is variable parameter.
    If it is we need only load the value in that location
    in order to obtain the address on the stack.
    Otherwise load the address of the left-hand side.
  *)
  if symboltable[posinsymtableoflhs].normal then
    opcode := LodaddInst (*lodadd*)
  else opcode := LodvalInst; (*lodval*)
  emit2(opcode, leveloflhs, offsetoflhs);
  if sy in [lbrack, lparent, period] then
    selector([becomes, eql] + fsys, lhsitem);
  if sy = becomes then
    insymbol
  else begin
    error(51); (* Expected := *)
    if sy = eql then
      insymbol
  end;
  (* Analyse and generate code for right-hand side. *)
  expression(fsys, rhsitem);
  if lhsitem.typ = rhsitem.typ then
    if lhsitem.typ in stantyps then
      emit(StoreInst) (*store*)
    else if lhsitem.ref <> rhsitem.ref then
      error(46)
    else if lhsitem.typ = arrays then
      emit1(CopyblInst, arraytable[lhsitem.ref].size) (*copybl*)
    else emit1(CopyblInst, blocktable[lhsitem.ref].variablesize) (*copybl*)
  else if (lhsitem.typ = reals) and (rhsitem.typ = ints) then begin
    emit1(FloatInst, 0); (*float*)
```

```
      emit(StoreInst) (*store*)
    end
    else if (lhsitem.typ <> notyp) and (rhsitem.typ <> notyp) then
      error(46);
    if tracing then
      writeln('Leaving assignment');
  end (*assignment*);
```

Consider the example program:

```
program ex1(output);
var
  i,j : integer;
begin
  j := (i*7) + (i-4);
end.
```

The code trace for

```
j := (i*7) + (i-4);
```

is:

```
statement
  assignment                     lodadd 1   6
    expression
      simpleexpression
        term
          factor
            expression
              simpleexpression
                term
                  factor         lodval 1   5
                  factor         ldint      7
                term             mult
              simpleexpression
            expression
          factor
        term
        term
          factor
            expression
              simpleexpression
                term
                  factor         lodval 1   5
```

```
                term
                term
                  factor          ldint   4
                term
              simpleexpression    sub
            expression
          factor
        term
      simpleexpression            add
    expression
  assignment                      store
statement
```

The only other instructions generated by *assignment* are *float* and *copybl*. *float* is generated when the right-hand side has type integer and the left-hand side has type real. The *float* instruction transforms the top of stack from integer to real. The *copybl* instruction is used when the type of the left-hand and right-hand sides are either records or arrays and will store a number of items from the top of the stack into an area starting from the address *assignment* previously loaded onto the stack.

8.2.2 Repeat statement

The **repeat** statement has the form

> **repeat**
>   <statement>;
>   <statement>;
>   :
> **until** <boolean expression>

and the skeleton of the code required to implement this is:

```
label
        code for statements
        code for boolean expression
        jump to label if boolean expression is false
```

The **repeat** statement is a structured statement in the sense that it contains nested statements within it. These are handled by a call to *statement* which will generate the appropriate code for the statements between the **repeat** and **until**. Similarly code for the boolean expression following the **until** is generated by *expression* and its local procedures. The *repeatstatement* procedure is:

```
procedure repeatstatement;
var
  untilexpitem : item;
  locofrepeat : integer;
begin
  if tracing then
    writeln('Entering repeatstatement');
  locofrepeat := locationcounter;
  insymbol;
  statement([semicolon, untilsy] + fsys);
  while sy in [semicolon] + statbegsys do begin
    if sy = semicolon then
      insymbol
    else error(14);
    statement([semicolon, untilsy] + fsys)
  end;
  if sy = untilsy then begin
    insymbol;
    (* Process boolean expression. *)
    expression(fsys, untilexpitem);
    if not (untilexpitem.typ in [bools, notyp]) then
      error(17);
    emit1(JmpfalInst, locofrepeat) (*jump if false*)
  end
  else error(53);
  if tracing then
    writeln('Leaving repeatstatement')
end (*repeatstatement*);
```

This procedure is required to generate code at the end of the loop to test the result of the boolean expression following the **until**. However, it needs to record the value of the program counter at the start of the loop, so that when producing the conditional jump back to the start of the loop it can give the *jump* instruction a destination address. The local variable, *locofrepeat*, holds this information. As an example of the code generated for the repeat statement, consider the program:

```
program test(output);
var i:integer;
begin
  repeat
    i:=i+1;
  until i=7;
end.
```

It generates the code trace:

```
statement
 repeatstatement
  statement
   assignment                 0  lodadd 1  5
    expression
     simpleexpression
      term
       factor                 1  lodval 1  5
      term
     simpleexpression
      term
       factor                 2  ldint     1
      term
     simpleexpression         3  add
    expression
   assignment                 4  store
  statement
 repeatstatement
  expression
   simpleexpression
    term
     factor                   5  lodval 1  5
    term
   simpleexpression
  expression
   simpleexpression
    term
     factor                   6  ldint     7
    term
   simpleexpression
  expression                  7  equal
 repeatstatement              8  jmpfal    0
```

8.2.3 While statement

The code produced for the **while** statement, shown below, is slightly different from the **repeat** statement as the test takes place at the top of the loop rather than the bottom. Within the **while** loop the code is terminated by an unconditional jump back to the start of the code of the boolean expression. As this unconditional jump will not be produced until later, the location of the start of the code corresponding to the evaluation of the boolean expression must be saved.

```
label1
        code to evaluate boolean expression
        jump to label2 if boolean expression was false
        code for statement
        jump to label1
label2
```

The *whilestatement* procedure then calls *expression* to produce code for the boolean expression. A conditional jump is then required so that if the boolean expression is false, the next statement to be executed is the one following the **while** statement. At this point, however, the location of the code of the following statement is not known as it has yet to be encountered.

Thus *whilestatement* produces a *jmpfal* instruction with a destination address of 0 and saves the value of the location counter. It then calls *statement* to process the statement within the loop. On return from *statement*, *whilestatement* can produce the unconditional jump back to the start of the code evaluating the boolean expression and insert the current value of the location counter in the destination field of the *jmpfal* instruction. The example program:

```
program test(output);
var i:integer;
begin
  while i<>7 do
    i := i+1;
end.
```

generates the code trace below which illustrates these actions:

```
whilestatement
  expression
    simpleexpression
      term
        factor                 0  lodval  1   5
      term
    simpleexpression
  expression
    simpleexpression
      term
        factor                 1  ldint       7
      term
    simpleexpression
  expression                   2  notequ
whilestatement                 3  jmpfal      0
```

```
    statement
      assignment                      4  lodadd 1 5
        expression
          simpleexpression
            term
              factor                  5  lodval  1   5
            term
          simpleexpression
            term
              factor                  6  ldint       1
            term
          simpleexpression            7  add
        expression
      assignment                      8  store
    statement
  whilestatement                      9  jump        0
```

Fill in destination address of instruction 3 with 10

```
                                      10 halt
```

8.2.4 If ... then statement

As with the while statement, the *ifstatement* procedure is required to fill in earlier conditional jump instructions when the destination address is known. The skeleton is:

```
        code for boolean expression
        jump to label1 if boolean expression is false
        code for statement
label1
```

It is best illustrated by the example program:

program *test(output)*;
var *i* : *integer*;
begin
 if *i=7* **then**
  i:=i+1
end.

The code trace is shown below (for simplicity, the calls to local procedures within *expression* are omitted).

```
ifstatement
  expression                     0  lodval  1   5
                                 1  ldint       7
                                 2  equal
  ifstatement                    3  jmpfal  0
  statement
    assignment                   4  lodadd  1   5
      expression                 5  lodval  1   5
                                 6  ldint   1
                                 7  add
    assignment                   8  store
  statement
ifstatement

                                    Fill in destination address
                                    of instruction 3 with 9

                                 9 halt
```

8.2.5 If ... then ... else statement

The **if** ... **then** ... **else** statement is also handled by the *ifstatement* procedure. The presence of the **else** arm requires an unconditional jump at the end of the **then** arm so that the code in the **else** arm is avoided if the boolean expression evaluates to true. A conditional jump will be required to the **else** arm and so the skeleton is:

```
          code to evaluate boolean expression
          jump to label1 if boolean expression was true
          code for statements in then arm
          jump to label2
label1
          code for statements in else arm
label2
```

Both jump instructions will initially have a destination address of 0. The conditional jump destination can be filled in once the **else** is encountered. The unconditional jump can be filled in only at the end of the **else** arm. Consider the following example program:

program *test(output)*;
var *i* : *integer*;
begin
 if *i=7* **then**

```
    i:=i+1
   else
    i:=i-1
  end.
```

The code trace is:

```
ifstatement
  expression                 0  lodval  1  5
                             1  ldint      7
                             2  equal
  ifstatement                3  jmpfal  0
  statement
    assignment               4  lodadd  1  5
      expression             5  lodval  1  5
                             6  ldint  1
                             7  add
    assignment               8  store
  statement
ifstatement                  9  jump       0

                                Fill in destination address
                                of instruction 3 with 10

  statement
    assignment               10 lodadd  1  5
      expression             11 lodval  1  5
                             12 ldint  1
                             13 sub
    assignment               14 store
ifstatement

                                Fill in destination address
                                of instruction 9 with 15

                             15 halt
```

8.2.6 For statement

A **for** statement generates code quite different from any of the statements encountered so far. It should be emphasized that the values of the initial and terminating expressions are evaluated once at the start of the loop and are not re-evaluated upon subsequent iterations of the loop. These values are put onto the stack on top of the address of the control variable.

In essence a **for** statement is very similar to a **while** statement with a test for termination of the statement at the top of the loop. However, the Pascal-S system does not employ the conditional and unconditional jumps used in the code generation of **while** statements. Instead, it uses four specialized instructions *forfup, forsup, forfdn* and *forsdn.* The first two instructions are used with **for** statements containing the reserved word **to** and the remaining two instructions are used with **for** statements containing the reserved word **downto.**

The instructions *forfup* and *forfdn* are generated at the top of the loop and when executed they test whether the loop is to be executed at all by comparing the value of the initial expression with the final expression. If the loop is to be executed they also initialize the control variable whose address is underneath the value of the initial expression on the stack.

The instructions *forsup* and *forsdn* are generated after the code for the statements within the loop and test whether the loop requires another execution. If the loop requires a further iteration, they also ensure that the value of the control variable is updated.

As with the **while** statement, the start of the code within the loop must be retained by the procedure *forstatement* so that it can be inserted into the destination address of *forsup* or *forsdn.* Similarly the destination address of *forfup* or *forfdn* must also be updated after the code within the loop has been generated.

Consider the following example program incorporating a **for** statement:

```
program test(output);
var i, j : integer;
begin
 for i :=1 to 7 do
   j :=j + 1;
end.
```

Its code trace is:

```
forstatement            0  lodadd 1  5
  expression            1  ldint     1
  expression            2  ldint     7
forstatement            3  forfup    0
  statement
    assignment          4  lodadd 1  6
      expression        5  lodval 1  6
                        6  ldint     1
                        7  add
    assignment          8  store
  statement
forstatement            9  forsup    4
```

Fill in the destination address of instruction 3 with 10

10 halt

8.2.7 Case statement

The basic skeleton of the code generated for each **case** statement is:

```
            evaluate case expression
            switch <address of case table>
a1:         code to execute case arm 1;
            jump endcase
a2:         code to execute case arm 2;
            jump endcase
            :
an:         code to execute case arm n;
            jump endcase
table:      pbreak <case label value 1>
            pbreak <arm code address>
            pbreak <case label value 2>
            pbreak <arm code address>
            :
            pbreak <case label value m>
            pbreak <arm code address>
            jump 0  { end-of-table sentinel }
endcase:    :
```

Within the *casestatement* procedure, the local procedure *onecase* is called for each arm of the **case** statement. This in turn calls *caselabel* for each label encountered. The two local procedures record the case label values, code addresses for each arm, and the location of the *jump endcase* instructions. Two data structures are used for this:

```
casetable : array[1..casetablemax] of
              record
                val,          (* case label value *)
                startofcode : index; (* arm code address *)
              end;
exittab : array[1..csmax] of integer; (* address of jump instructions *)
```

The **case** table itself contains two *pbreak* instructions for each **case** label value. The instruction itself is unimportant; it is the operands of the instruction which are the useful part of these instructions. The first *pbreak* instruction holds the actual label value, and the second the corresponding address of the code to be executed for that value. As with previous forward jumps, the location of the **case** table will be inserted into the destination field of the *switch* instruction after the analysis of all the **case** arms.

An example program is:

```
program test(output);
var i,j : integer;
begin
 case i of
  1,4: j:=j+1;
  6:  j:=j-1;
 end;
end.
```

The code trace is:

```
casestatement
  expression                     0  lodval 1  5
casestatement                    1  switch    0
  statement
    assignment                   2  lodadd 1  6
      expression                 3  lodval 1  6
                                 4  ldint     1
                                 5  add
    assignment                   6  store
  statement
    casestatement                7  jump      0
  statement
   assignment                    8  lodadd 1  6
     expression                  9  lodval 1  6
                                 10 ldint     1
                                 11 sub
   assignment                    12 store
  statement
    casestatement                13 jump      0

                                    Fill in the destination address
                                    of instruction 1 with 14

                                 14 pbreak    1
                                 15 pbreak    2
                                 16 pbreak    4
                                 17 pbreak    2
```

```
18 pbreak    6
19 pbreak    8
20 jump      0
```

Fill in the destination address of instructions 7 and 13 with 21

```
21 halt
```

There are alternative methods of generating code for **case** statements. With the method described above, a linear search of the **case** labels is made. Assuming that the required label is always present, an average of *n*/2 comparisons has to be made, where *n* is the number of labels used. An alternative skeleton for the example above is:

```
           load value of i
           jump to label1
label2
           code to execute j := j + 1;
           jump endcase
label3
           code to execute j := j - 1;
           jump endcase
label1
           check if value on top of stack is
                between lowest and highest case label
           subtract off value of lowest case label minus 1
           jump to the address given in the entry in the case
                table found by adding the current location
                to the value on top of the stack
           address of code for label 1 i.e. label2
           address of error routine
           address of error routine
           address of code for label 4 i.e. label2
           address of error routine
           address of code for label 6 i.e. label3
endcase
```

In this skeleton the **case** selector is also loaded onto the stack and control transferred to the **case** table. The **case** table is made up of an entry for each possible value between the lowest and highest **case** label encountered. If the **case** label was present then the address of the appropriate **case** arm is put in the table entry. If the **case** label was not present, then the address of an error routine is put into that entry.

Instead of a linear search through the table, the lowest **case** label value, less one, is subtracted off the value on top of the stack and the remaining value is used to locate the correct entry in the **case** table and control is then directly transferred to the appropriate **case** arm. This method is likely to be much faster then the previous method, especially when there is a large number of **case** labels. If however the **case** tables are widely spaced such as in

```
case i of
        1:      ... ;
        1000:   ... ;
end; (*case*)
```

then the **case** table will take up one thousand entries with the second method, but only four with the first method.

8.3 Procedure and function entry/exit

A procedure or function call is compiled into the sequence indicated by:

18: advance the top of stack
    compile the parameters
19: call
 3: update display (if necessary)

The procedure *call* is responsible for the production of this code.

The main purpose of advancing the top of stack by five units is to create enough space for the housekeeping information of the stack frame. Parameter evaluation may be arbitrarily complex (including further function and then procedure calls), and require large amounts of stack space and this will be allocated above the new top of stack.

As described in Section 7.3, if the call is to a block on a higher level, then the calling procedure must update the contents of the display after the call is complete. This is performed by the *update display* instruction which takes two arguments

```
upddis x y
```

This is interpreted as 'update entries *display[y]* down to *display[x+1]*'.

Procedure and function exit is obtained by generating a *leavep* or a *leavef* instruction respectively, which obtains the return address from the base of the stack frame and lowers the dynamic pointer back to the base of the calling routine's stack frame.

An example program which demonstrates the code generated for procedure entry/exit is:

```
program proc;
 procedure g;
 var i,j:integer;
 begin
   i:=i+j;
 end {g};
 procedure h;
   procedure i;
   begin
     g;
   end {i};
 begin
   i;
 end {h};
begin
  h;
end.
```

The sequence of code generated is:

```
block
  procdeclaration
    block
      statement
        assignment                 0  lodadd 2  5
          expression               1  lodval 2  5
                                   2  lodval 2  6
                                   3  add
        assignment                 4  store
      statement
    block
  procdeclaration                  5  leavep
block
  procdeclaration
    block
      statement
        call                       6  markst    32
                                   7  call       4
                                   8  upddis 1  3
      statement
    block
  procdeclaration                  9  leavep
```

```
block
  procdeclaration
    block
      statement
        call                          10 markst   36
                                      11 call     4
      statement
    block
  procdeclaration                     12 leavep
block
  statement
    call                              13 markst   35
                                      14 call     4
  statement
block                                 15 halt
```

The procedure calls in the main program and in the body of procedure *h* do not need to update the display on return, because they are calls to procedures at a lower block level, which causes an additional entry in the display. However, the call to *g* in procedure *i* is to a higher (more global) level. This causes an entry on the display to be overwritten, which must be restored on return. Hence the

```
updis 1 3
```

instruction at 8.

8.4 Procedure and function parameters

As mentioned in the previous section, actual parameters may be arbitrarily complex. The example Pascal-S program listed below illustrates the code required to produce the actual parameters.

```
program params(output);
var
  i,j : integer;
 function f(k:integer) : integer;
 begin
  f := sqr(k)
 end;
 procedure copy(in:integer;
              var out:integer);
 begin
  out := in
```

```
  end;
begin
  i := f(j);
  copy(f(i),i);
end.
```

The contents of the symbol table are shown in Table 8.1.

Table 8.1 Tables for *params* program.

identifiers	*link*	*obj*	*typ*	*ref*	*nrm*	*lev*	*adrr*
32 i	0	1	1	0	1	1	5
33 j	32	1	1	0	1	1	6
34 f	33	4	1	3	1	1	0
35 k	0	1	1	0	1	2	5
36 copy	34	3	0	4	1	1	5
37 in	0	1	1	0	1	2	5
38 out	37	1	1	0	0	2	6

blocks	*last*	*lpar*	*psze*	*vsze*
1	31	1	0	0
2	36	31	5	7
3	35	35	6	6
4	38	38	7	7

The code generated is:

f := sqr(k)

```
0  lodadd 2  0
1  lodval 2  5
2  stfunc    2
3  store

4  leavef
```

out := in

```
5  lodval 2  6
6  lodval 2  5
7  store
8  leavep
```

```
i := f(j);
                9  lodadd 1   5
                10 markst    34
                11 lodval 1   6
                12 call       5
                13 store

copy(f(i),i)
                14 markst    36
                15 markst    34
                16 lodval 1   5
                17 call       5
                18 lodadd 1   5
                19 call       6

                20 halt
```

Parameters to standard functions are also loaded onto the stack as shown in the code for *f* := *sqr(k)*.

The next assignment involves the storing of the value of a value parameter into a variable parameter. The space allocated on the stack for the variable parameter contains the address of the actual parameter, so instead of the normal *lodadd* instruction the *lodval* instruction is used to get the address of the left-hand side onto the stack.

The next assignment illustrates the use of the *markst* and *call* instructions with parameters. The address of the left-hand side is placed on the stack and this is followed by the code to call the function *f*. The *markst* instruction increases the stack by five and the next instruction loads the value of *i* into the parameter space for the called function. The *call* instruction then completes the housekeeping and transfers control to the function. When this is complete, the function value is left on top of the stack and can be stored in the variable whose address is immediately beneath the top of stack.

The final assignment illustrates what happens when an actual parameter includes a function call. The initial *markst* instruction is for the *copy* procedure and the second one is for the *f* function. The parameter to the function is then loaded onto the stack and control transferred to the function with the *call* instruction. When this is complete the value returned by the function will be on top of the stack, which is also the space allocated for the value parameter of the *copy* procedure. The address of the variable parameter is then loaded and control transferred to the *copy* procedure.

8.5 Data structures

The *selector* procedure generates the code for both array and record accesses.

8.5.1 Arrays

For array accesses, *selector* relies heavily on two of the Pascal-S virtual machine instructions, namely *index1* and *indexm*. These instructions simplify the task of accessing the appropriate element of the array. The former is used if the size of the elements of the array is one and the latter otherwise. Thus when calculating the offsets of a multi-dimensional array, *indexm* is used for all the dimensions other than the last, when *index1* is used.

Consider the example program:

```
program test(output);
var
  arr1 : array [1..10] of real;
  arr2 : array [-10..0,1..10] of real;
begin
  arr1[7] := 27;
  arr2[-8,9] := arr1[7]
end.
```

The contents of the symbol tables are shown in Table 8.2. There are three entries in the array table, one for *arr1* and two for *arr2*, one for each dimension. Note also that the element type of the first dimension of *arr2*, namely *eref*, is an index into the third element of the array table which holds the details of the second dimension.

The code generated for this example is:

```
arr1[7] := 27;
  0   lodadd  1   5
  1   ldint       7
  2   index1      1
  3   ldint      27
  4   float       0
  5   store

arr2[-8,9] := arr1[7]
  6   lodadd  1  15
  7   ldint       8
  8   negate
  9   indexm      2
 10   ldint       9
 11   index1      3
```

```
12   lodadd 1   5
13   ldint      7
14   index1     1
15   lodins
16   store

17   halt
```

Table 8.2 Tables for program *test*.

identifiers	*link*	*obj*	*typ*	*ref*	*nrm*	*lev*	*adrr*
32 arr1	0	1	5	1	1	1	5
33 arr2	32	1	5	2	1	1	15

blocks	*last*	*lpar*	*psze*	*vsze*
1	31	1	0	0
2	33	31	5	125

arrays	*xtyp*	*etyp*	*eref*	*low*	*high*	*elsz*	*size*
1	1	2	0	1	10	1	10
2	1	5	3	-10	0	10	110
3	1	2	0	1	10	1	10

For the first assignment statement, the address of *arr1* is loaded onto the stack. This is followed by the index 7. The *index1* instruction subtracts the lower bound of the array, obtained from the entry in the array table, adds the result to the base address and leaves this result on top of the stack. The right-hand side is then loaded onto the stack in the usual manner.

In the second assignment statement, the base address of *arr2* is loaded onto the stack, followed by the index. The *indexm* instruction then subtracts off the lower bound, multiplies by the size of the elements in this dimension and adds this to the base of *arr2*. In this case the result left on the stack is

base address of arr2 + (–8 – (–10)) * 10

The next index is then loaded onto the stack and the *index1* instruction subtracts off the lower bound of the second dimension leaving base address of arr2 + (–8 – (–10)) * 10 + (9 – 1)

that is:

base address of arr2 + 28

8.5.2 Records

There is also a special instruction, namely *offset*, for accessing the fields of a record. When a record is encountered the base address of the record is loaded onto the stack. If the field which is accessed is not the first one an *offset* instruction is generated which when executed will add the appropriate value to the base address to obtain the correct address of the field within the record. If the field is the first one, there is no need to generate an *offset* instruction as the base address of the record will be the same as the address of the first field within that record. Consider the example program:

```
program testrec(output);
var
  arec : record
            i : integer;
            r : real
         end;
begin
  arec.i := 27;
  arec.r := arec.i
end.
```

The contents of the symbol tables are shown in Table 8.3. As described in Chapter 6, a record introduces a new level into the block table so that the field names are at a different level from the record name.

The code generated is:

```
arec.i := 27;
  0   lodadd  1   5
  1   ldint      27
  2   store

arec.r := arec.i
  3   lodadd  1   5
  4   offset      1
  5   lodadd  1   5
  6   lodins
```

```
7   float   0
8   store

9   halt
```

Table 8.3 Tables for program *testrec*.

identifiers	*link*	*obj*	*typ*	*ref*	*nrm*	*lev*	*adrr*
32 arec	0	1	6	3	1	1	5
33 i	0	1	1	0	1	2	0
34 r	33	1	2	0	1	2	1

blocks	*last*	*lpar*	*psze*	*vsze*
1	31	1	0	0
2	32	31	5	7
3	34	0	0	2

8.5.3 Arrays and records

To illustrate the use of records and arrays together, consider:

```
program data(output);
var d : array[1..3] of
        record
          c : char;
          b : boolean;
          r : real;
          a : array[5..10] of char;
        end;
    m : array[1..10,1..10] of real;
begin
  m[7,8] := 4.5;
  d[2].c := chr(7);
  d[3].b := true;
  d[1].r := 47.66 - m[5][5];
  d[2].a[6] := 'x';
end.
```

This program uses an array of records with one of the fields of the record also being an array. The contents of the symbol tables are shown in Table 8.4.

Table 8.4 Tables for program *data*.

identifiers	*link*	*obj*	*typ*	*ref*	*nrm*	*lev*	*adrr*
32 d	0	1	5	1	1	1	5
33 c	0	1	4	0	1	2	0
34 b	33	1	3	0	1	2	1
35 r	34	1	2	0	1	2	2
36 a	35	1	5	2	1	2	3
37 m	32	1	5	3	1	1	32

blocks	*last*	*lpar*	*psze*	*vsze*
1	31	1	0	0
2	37	31	5	132
3	36	0	0	9

arrays	*xtyp*	*etyp*	*eref*	*low*	*high*	*elsz*	*size*
1	1	6	3	1	3	9	27
2	1	4	0	5	10	1	6
3	1	5	4	1	10	10	100
4	1	2	0	1	10	1	10

The code generated is:

```
m[7,8]:=4.5;
  0   lodadd 1  32
  1   ldint      7
  2   indexm      3
  3   ldint      8
  4   index1      4
  5   ldreal     1
  6   store

d[2].c:=chr(7);
  7   lodadd 1   5
  8   ldint      2
  9   indexm      1
 10   ldint      7
```

```
 11   stfunc     5
 12   store

d[3].b:=true;
 13   lodadd  1  5
 14   ldint      3
 15   indexm     1
 16   offset     1
 17   ldint      1
 18   store

d[1].r := 47.66-m[5][5];
 19   lodadd  1  5
 20   ldint      1
 21   indexm     1
 22   offset     2
 23   ldreal     2
 24   lodadd  1  32
 25   ldint      5
 26   indexm     3
 27   ldint      5
 28   index1     4
 29   lodind
 30   subrea
 31   store

d[2].a[6] := 'x';
 32   lodadd  1  5
 33   ldint      2
 34   indexm     1
 35   offset     3
 36   ldint      6
 37   index1     2
 38   ldchar   120
 39   store

 40   halt
```

Chapter 9
Pascal-S Interpreter

The Pascal-S system consists of a single program containing two sections which have quite different functions. The compiler section of the program checks that a user's Pascal-S program is legal and, if it is, produces an intermediate code version of the program. The interpreter section is only executed if the compilation phase is successful and simulates the execution of the intermediate code version. It does this by examining the current intermediate code instruction and then branching to an appropriate section of code which simulates the execution of that instruction. This process is known as **interpretation.**

There are other methods apart from interpretation which would result in the intermediate code being executed. Interpretation has the advantage that no target machine dependencies are included within the system, with the exception of assumptions regarding character set ordering. Also, because the interpreter is contained within the same program as the compiler, it has access to the compiler's symbol table and is thus able to provide helpful diagnostics if a run-time error occurs.

The interpreter is designed to execute the algorithm:

set program counter to first instruction;
repeat
  access current instruction using program counter;
  jump to appropriate piece of code to simulate that instruction;
  update program counter;
until *run-time error* **or** *program execution completed normally*;

Accessing the current instruction and jumping to the appropriate section of code is implemented in the interpreter by a case statement.

The intermediate code instructions produced by the compiler are stored in the array *code*. Each element of this array is of the type:

```
instruction   = packed record
                  opcode : opcodes;
                  field1 : -maxlevel .. +maxlevel;
                  field2 : -integermax .. +integermax;
                end;
```

The *opcode* field holds a value of an enumeration type representing the intermediate code instruction. The other two fields hold parameters to the intermediate code instruction and are not always used.

9.1 Interpretation of instructions

The simulation of the intermediate code instructions is the main function of the interpreter. As part of this function, the interpreter maintains the run-time stack, which is an array of the type:

```
stack : array [1 .. stacksize] of record
            case tp : types of
              ints : (
                i : integer);
              reals : (
                r : real);
              bools : (
                b : boolean);
              chars : (
                c : char);
              notyp, arrays, records : ()
        end;
```

As each element of *stack* can hold different types the tag field *tp* is used to indicate what kind of element it currently contains.

The *stack* array will contain the values of variables, addresses for keeping track of where stack frames begin and end, temporaries for expression evaluation, pointers to the compiler's tables for debugging purposes and other useful information. Most instructions involve accessing or amending the elements of this array. For instance, consider the section of code taken from the interpreter given below which simulates the ordinal add and subtract operations.

```
currentinstruction := code[progcounter];
case currentinstruction.opcode of
     :
     :
 AddInst : (* + for ordinals*)
   begin
     topofstack := topofstack - 1;
     stack[topofstack].i := stack[topofstack].i + stack[topofstack + 1].i;
   end;
     :
     :
```

```
SubInst : (* – for ordinals*)
  begin
    topofstack := topofstack – 1;
    stack[topofstack].i := stack[topofstack].i – stack[topofstack + 1].i
  end;
   :
```

Both instructions expect to find their operands in the top two elements of the stack. The top of stack is then lowered by one and the result of the operation is placed in the top element of the stack. The value of *code[progcounter]* is copied into *currentinstruction* so that if access is required to the parameters then it can be achieved efficiently without accessing the array element more than once.

The parameters to an instruction are used for a variety of purposes. In the *lodval* instruction, for instance, they give the level and offset of the variable whose value is being loaded onto the stack. The example given below also illustrates some of the error checking which is the subject of a later section.

```
LodvalInst : (*load value*)
  begin
  topofstack := topofstack + 1;

  if topofstack > stacksize then
    programstatus := stackfullerror
   else stack[topofstack] :=
         stack[display[currentinstruction.field1] +
           currentinstruction.field2]
  end;
```

In the *func* instruction, which indicates that a standard function is being called, the *field1* is not used and *field2* is used to indicate which standard function is required. This is illustrated in:

```
StfuncInst : (*standard function*)
  case  currentinstruction.field2 of
    0 : stack[topofstack].i := abs(stack[topofstack].i);
    1 : stack[topofstack].r := abs(stack[topofstack].r);
    2 : stack[topofstack].i := sqr(stack[topofstack].i);
         :
```

In the majority of cases the simulation of the intermediate code instructions is reasonably straightforward. However, in certain cases the code to simulate the intermediate code instruction is more complicated.

Consider the following fragment of Pascal-S:

```
case i of
  1,3 : j := j + 1;
    4 : j := j - 1
end;
```

which is translated into the code:

```
 0   lodval  1   5
 1   switch     14
 2   lodadd  1   6
 3   lodval  1   6
 4   ldint       1
 5   add
 6   store
 7   jump       21
 8   lodadd  1   6
 9   lodval  1   6
10   ldint       1
11   sub
12   store
13   jump       21
14   pbreak      1
15   pbreak      2
16   pbreak      3
17   pbreak      2
18   pbreak      4
19   pbreak      8
20   jump        0
```

The code for the two assignment statements corresponds to instructions numbered 2 to 6 and 8 to 12 and the remaining instructions are the relevant ones for the implementation of a **case** statement. Instructions 14 to 20 form a jump table which is used by the interpreter to find the location of the sections of code corresponding to each **case** label. Each location in the jump table is given a *break* instruction with the final entry being given a *jump* instruction in order to mark it as the final entry. For each **case** label in the **case** statement there are two locations in the jump table. The first location contains the label itself. Thus locations 14, 16 and 18 contain the labels used in the **case** statement. The second location contains the address of the start of the code corresponding to that label. Thus locations 15 and 17 contain 2, which is the address of the code labelled by 1 and 3, and location 19 contains the address of the code labelled by 4.

The interpreter accesses all this information when it simulates the execution of the *switch* instruction. The code for this is:

```
SwitchInst : (*switch*)
  begin
    (* Get value of selector *)
    with stack[topofstack - 1] do begin
      case tp of
        ints: h1 := i;
        chars: h1 := ord(c);
        bools: h1 := ord(b)
      end;
    topofstack := topofstack - 1;
    (* Get base of case table *)
    h2 := currentinstruction.field2;
    h3 := 0;
    repeat
      (* If we are not within case table then run-time error *)
      if code[h2].numopcode <> 13 then begin
        h3 := 1;
        programstatus := nocaselabelerror
      end
      else if code[h2].field2 = h1 then begin
              (* Found value of selector in case table. Now go
                 to code attached to that label *)
              h3 := 1;
              progcounter := code[h2 + 1].field2
            end
        else h2 := h2 + 2
    until h3 <> 0
  end;
```

The first action of the interpreter is to pick up the value of the case selector which has been left on the top of the stack. In this example it is just the value of *i*, but in general it could be the result of an expression. Next the location of the jump table is taken from *field2* of the *switch* instruction. *h3* is to be used as a 'control variable' for the loop and is initialized to 0.

The purpose of the repeat loop is to search through the jump table comparing the value of the case selector, now contained in *h1*, with the labels in the case statement, which are in *field2* of the first location of each pair of entries in the jump table. If a label matching the value in *h1* is found, then the program counter is altered to become the address of the code corresponding to that label, which is found in *field2* of the following instruction. If a matching label is not found then the interpreter will come to the *jump* instruction which marks the end of the jump table. In this situation, the interpreter changes the status of the executing program so that it terminates with a run-time error.

The code generated by a **for** statement and for array accesses also requires the interpreter to simulate a non-trivial activity. Consider the following fragment of code:

```
for i := 1 to 10 do
  table[i] := 0;
```

where *table* is declared as

```
table : array [1..10] of integer;
```

With the debugging option on, it can be seen that the compiler sets up the components of the symbol table as shown in:

identifiers	*link*	*obj*	*typ*	*ref*	*nrm*	*lev*	*adrr*
32 i	0	1	1	0	1	1	5
33 table	32	1	5	1	1	1	6

blocks	*last*	*lpar*	*psze*	*vsze*
1	31	1	0	0
2	33	31	5	16

arrays	*xtyp*	*etyp*	*eref*	*low*	*high*	*elsz*	*size*
1	1	1	0	1	10	1	10

The code generated is:

```
code:
 0 lodadd 1   5
 1 ldint      1
 2 ldint     10
 3 forfup    10
 4 lodadd 1   6
 5 lodval 1   5
 6 index1     1
 7 ldint      0
 8 store
 9 forsup     4
```

The instructions in locations 4 to 8 are concerned with initializing elements of the array table, which will be considered later, and the remaining operations concern the operation of the **for** statement. The algorithm that the interpreter uses to simulate a **for** statement is as follows:

```
  put the address of the control variable on the top of the stack;
  put the value of the initial expression on the top of the stack;
  put the value of the final expression on top of the stack;
  if the value of the initial expression is greater than
     the value of the final expression
  then lower the stack by 3 and jump to label2
  else store the value of the initial expression in the control variable;
label1:
  code for statements in the loop;
  obtain the current value of the control variable;
  add 1 to this value;
  if value is less than or equal to the final expression
  then store this value into the control variable and
     jump to label1;
  lower the stack by 3;
label2:
```

The placing of the address of the control variable and the values of the expressions on the top of the stack is done explicitly by the instructions in locations 0, 1 and 2. These three elements remain on top of the stack throughout the execution of the **for** statement. The code the interpreter uses to simulate the *forfup* instruction is:

```
ForfupInst : (*for first up*)
  begin
    with stack[topofstack - 1] do
      case tp of
        ints : h1 := i;
        chars : h1 := ord(c);
        bools : h1 := ord(b);
      end;
    with stack[topofstack] do begin
      case tp of
        ints: h2 := i;
        chars: h2 := ord(c);
        bools: h2 := ord(b)
      end;
    if h1 <= h2 then
       stack[stack[topofstack - 2].i] := stack[topofstack - 1]
    else begin
       (* Loop never to be executed *)
       topofstack := topofstack - 3;
       progcounter := currentinstruction.field2
    end
  end;
```

This code obtains the value of the initial expression from the stack, compares it with the final expression, also obtained from the stack, and either initializes the control variable or prepares to leave the **for** statement. The location of *label2* is found in *field2* of the *forfup* instruction. The remainder of the algorithm is incorporated in the simulation of the *forsup* instruction, which is:

```
ForsupInst : (*for second up*)
   begin
      (* Get the address of the control
         variable *)
      h2 := stack[topofstack - 2].i;
      (* Increment the current value in the control variable *)
      with stack[h2] do
        case tp of
          ints : h1 := i + 1;
          chars : h1 := ord(c) + 1;
          bools : h1 := ord(b) + 1;
        end;
      with stack[topofstack - 1] do
        case tp of
          ints : h3 := i;
          chars : h3 := ord(c);
          bools : h3 := ord(b);
        end;
      (* Compare with the value of the final expression *)
      if h1 <= stack[topofstack].i then begin
         (* Go round loop again *)
         with stack[h2] do
           case tp of
             ints : i := h1;
             chars : c := chr(h1);
             bools : b := (h1 = 1);
           end;
         progcounter := currentinstruction.field2
      end
      else topofstack := topofstack - 3;
   end;
```

The code for *forfup* and *forsup* also illustrates the checking required to ensure that the correct type is obtained from the stack element. The control variable can be of type integer, real or boolean and the appropriate value has to be extracted from the element of *stack*.

The *forfup* and *forsup* instructions are generated by the compiler for loops where the value of the control variable increases by one each time through the loop. For statements where the value of the control variable is decreased by one, the compiler generates the *forfdn* and the *forsdn* instructions, whose simulation by the interpreter is very similar to the *forfup* and *forsup* instructions, respectively.

When accessing arrays, the compiler generates the *indexl* or *indexm* instructions, the latter only being used in the case of multi-dimensional arrays. In the example above the compiler first generates code to load what is known as the base address of the array onto the stack. The base address of an array is the address of the lowest element in the array and in the example above this will be the address of *table[1]*. This is followed by code to leave on the top of the stack the value of the index. In this case the index to the array is just a simple variable, but in general it could be an expression. The compiler then generates an *indexl* instruction with a 1 in *field2*. The code used by the interpreter to simulate an *indexl* instruction is:

```
IndexlInst : (*indexl - a one-dimensional array*)
  begin
    h1 := currentinstruction.field2; (*h1 points to arraytable*)
    h2 := arraytable[h1].low;
    with stack[topofstack] do
      case tp of
        ints : h3 := i;
        chars : h3 := ord(c);
        bools : h3 := ord(b);
      end;
    if h3 < h2 then
      programstatus := outofrangeerror
    else if h3 > arraytable[h1].high then
      programstatus := outofrangeerror
    else begin
      topofstack := topofstack - 1;
      stack[topofstack].i := stack[topofstack].i + (h3 - h2)
    end
  end;
```

field2 of the *indexl* instruction is a pointer into the array table *arraytable*, pointing to the information about the array. The interpreter then collects the value of the lowest and highest index from *arraytable* and compares the value of the index against these two values. The interpreter changes the program status to indicate a run-time error if the value of the index is not between these two limits. If the index is in the required range, it adds the difference between the index and the lowest index to the base address to give the address of the actual array element. This is kept on the stack in this example while the value of the right-hand side is evaluated and then accessed by the *store* instruction.

The other group of instructions which involve non-trivial simulation are those dealing with the calling of user-defined procedures and functions. There are four instructions in this group namely *markst, call, leavep* and *leavef.* Consider the following procedure heading

procedure *check(***var** *found:boolean; number:integer);*

and the following call to this procedure from within the main program

check(ok,10);

The code generated for this call is:

```
1   markst      33
2   lodadd  1    5
3   ldint       10
4   call         6
```

and the procedure check is terminated by the instruction *leavep.* The code to simulate *markst* is:

```
MarkstInst : (*mark stack in preparation for function or
      procedure call*)
   begin
     hl := blocktable[symboltable[currentinstruction.field2]
          .ref].variablesize;
     if topofstack + hl > stacksize then
       programstatus := stackfullerror
     else begin
       topofstack := topofstack + 5;
       (* Leave size of variables in called routine on the
          stack for call to pick up
       *)
       stack[topofstack - 1].tp := ints;
       stack[topofstack - 1].i := hl - 1;
       stack[topofstack].i := ints;
       stack[topofstack].i := currentinstruction.field2
     end
   end;
```

field2 of the *markst* instruction contains a pointer to the symbol table *symboltable* which points to the entry for the procedure or function name. The *ref* field of this entry is a pointer into the block table *blocktable* and the *variablesize* field of this entry gives the amount of space required on the stack for this procedure or function, including the space required to hold the housekeeping values such as the dynamic and static links. If there is not enough space left on the stack then the interpreter changes the program status to indicate a run-time error.

If all is well, the stack is raised by five and the element one below the top is filled with the value representing the stack space required for this procedure or function (less one for ease of calculation later). The element on the top of the stack is filled with the pointer to the symbol table and this is used if a post-mortem dump or snapshot is required (see Sections 9.5 and 9.6 respectively). The other three entries are left undefined.

Code is then generated to load the procedures parameters onto the stack, which in this example involves loading the address of the variable *ok* and the literal 10. The *topofstack* variable will now have been raised a total of 7 since the *markst* instruction has been encountered. The next instruction is *call* and its code is:

```
CallInst : (*call a procedure or function*)
  begin
    (* h1 to point to base of new stack frame*)
    h1 := topofstack - currentinstruction.field2;
    (* h2 points to symboltable *)
    h2 := stack[h1 + 4].i;
    (* Obtain static level of called routine *)
    h3 := symboltable[h2].lev;
    (* Adjust appropriate element of display *)
    display[h3 + 1] := h1;
    (* Pick up amount of space required for called routine.
       This was left on the stack by code for markst
       instruction. h4 will now be new topofstack
    *)
    h4 := stack[h1 + 3].i + h1;
    (* Put return address on stack *)
    stack[h1 + 1].tp := ints;
    stack[h1 + 1].i := progcounter;
    (* Put static link on stack *)
    stack[h1 + 2].tp := ints;
    stack[h1 + 2].i := display[h3];
    (* Put dynamic link on stack *)
    stack[h1 + 3].tp := ints;
    stack[h1 + 3].i := baseofcurrentstackframe;
    (* Initialize all variables *)
    for h3 := topofstack + 1 to h4 do begin
       stack[h3].tp := ints;
       stack[h3].i := 0
       end;
    baseofcurrentstackframe := h1;
```

```
        topofstack := h4;
        progcounter := symboltable[h2].adrr
    end;
```

The interpreter first works out the address of the base of the new stack frame which is going to be set up when the new procedure is called. It then collects the pointer to the procedures symbol table entry left by the *markst* instruction and updates the appropriate element of the display. It also collects the size of the new stack frame and puts the various housekeeping values into the base of the stack frame. It then initializes any local variables to 0 before adjusting the base of the current stack frame, top of stack and program counter.

leavep, which is encountered at the end of a procedure, first resets the top of stack to one less than the base of the current stack frame and then picks up the return address stored on the stack and the dynamic link and uses the latter to reset the base of the current stack frame. *leavef* is very similar except that the top of stack is set to the value of the base of the current stack frame to indicate that the result of the function is on the top of the stack.

9.2 Links between the compiler and interpreter

Besides the *code* array, the interpreter uses several other tables which are declared in the compiler section of the program. Some of the uses of these tables have been seen in the previous section but for completeness all these tables and their uses are summarized here:

arraytable — This is the table containing all the required information about arrays declared in the user's program. This is used when interpreting the *index1* and *indexm* instructions to check whether the array index is in bounds and to evaluate the offset of the array element from the base of the current stack frame.

blocktable — This is used to set up the stack size during the initialization phase of the interpreter and is accessed each time a new stack frame is created with the *markst* operand. It is also used to find the name of the last variable declared at a particular level. From this variable it can access the other variables declared at this level and so interpret the values on the stack in terms of their variable names. This is extremely useful when an unexpected error occurs and can lead the user to discover his error more quickly.

realconsttable — All real constants are stored in this array and when one is required to be loaded onto the stack by the *ldreal* instruction, then this array is accessed.

stringtable	All string constants are stored in this array by the compiler and, when required to be output, are obtained by the interpreter from *stringtable*.
symboltable	The main symbol table is used for the post-mortem dump, initializing the interpreter and for finding the static level of a procedure during the interpretation of the *markst* operand. This is required in order to update the appropriate element of the display.

9.3 Error checking

The interpreter uses the variable *programstatus* to indicate the current state of execution of the user's program. Under normal circumstances this variable has the value *running*, but can take other values under certain circumstances. Some examples of these circumstances were shown in Section 9.2. The other values that *programstatus* can take are:

finishwithouterrors	The user's program has completed execution.
nocaselabelerror	The value of the **case** statement selector has no corresponding label in the **case** statement.
divideby0error	An attempt has been made to divide by zero.
outofrangeerror	The value of an array index is outside the bounds of an array or a parameter to the *chr* function is outside the range which maps onto the set of characters.
stackfullerror	An attempt has been made to increase the run-time stack beyond its maximum size.
toomanylinesoutputerror	An attempt has been made to exceed the maximum number of lines that can be output. This restriction can easily be lifted by making very trivial alterations to the interpreter.
linetoolongerror	An attempt has been made to output characters or numbers beyond the maximum length of a line.
noreadingpasteoferror	When reading a character or number or performing a *readln*, the end of file condition has been detected.

If *programstatus* achieves any of these values, then execution of the user's program ceases and the user is supplied with a message such as:

```
halt at line 35 of source because of division by 0
```

There is no attempt to catch illegal input in the interpreter. Thus if the interpreter was expecting to read an integer and was supplied with a character which was not a digit, then this error would only be caught by the underlying run-time system controlling the execution of the interpreter. Hence any error which was reported might be of the form:

illegal input on line 1632

where the line number refers to the appropriate line in the interpreter rather than the user's program. This is clearly very misleading and appropriate error checking should be included in the interpreter so that errors are reported in terms of the user's program.

9.4 Post-mortem dump

If a run-time error occurs it is often useful for the user to know the values of all accessible variables. For instance, if the user has received the following run-time error message:

halt at line 35 of source because array index is out of bounds

and line 35 contains the statement:

table[index] := 27;

then it can be very useful to determine the exact value of *index* at this point. A post-mortem dump is a list of the values of all accessible variables at a particular point in the program. In this example, the user is only interested in the value of *index*, but in general he may wish to know the values of other variables as well. The post-mortem dump also produces a list of the procedures which have not finished execution and where they were called from.

The post-mortem dump obtains its information from an index to the main symbol table which is deposited on the run-time stack by the *markst* instruction. The address from which the procedure or function is called is also found on the stack. The index to the symbol table points to the name of the procedure which has been called. This entry contains an index into the block table and the corresponding entry in that table holds an index to the symbol table entry of the last variable declared in that block. Thus it is possible to find all variables declared within this procedure and using the offset addresses from the base of the stack frame which are stored with each variable entry, the values on the run-time stack can be associated with the variable names they represent.

As an example of the diagnostics produced by the post-mortem dump consider the program:

```
program runtimeerror(input,output);
const
  tablesize = 10;
type
  tables = array [1..tablesize] of integer;
var
  table : tables;

procedure readinto(var atable :tables);
  var
    index : integer;
  begin
  writeln('Type in ',tablesize:1,' entries');
  for index := 1 to tablesize do
    read(atable[index]);
  end; (*readinto*)

procedure writeout(atable :tables);
  var
    index : integer;
  begin
  writeln;
  writeln('In descending order :');
  for index := 1 to tablesize do
    writeln(atable[index])
  end; (*writeout*)

procedure sort(var atable :tables);
  var
    index : integer;

  procedure getsmallestinto(var atable :tables;
                limit :integer);
    (*ensures that the smallest entry in atable
      between 1 and limit is deposited in
      atable[limit]*)
    var
      temp,index : integer;
    begin
    (*the cause of the error is on the next line of
      code. limit should be replaced by limit-1*)
    for index := 1 to limit do
    (*the run-time error will occur on the next line*)
      if atable[index] < atable[index+1] then
        begin
```

```
            temp := atable[index];
            atable[index] := atable[index+1];
            atable[index+1] := temp
            end
        end; (*getsmallestinto*)

    begin (*sort*)
    for index := tablesize downto 2 do
        getsmallestinto(atable,index);
    end; (*sort*)

begin (*main program*)
readinto(table);
sort(table);
writeout(table)
end.
```

The diagnostics produced are:

```
halt at line 42 of source because array index is out of bounds

 getsmalles called at 83
    index          = 10
    temp           = 1
    limit          = 10

 sort       called at 91
    index          = 10
```

9.5 Snapshots

Post-mortem dumps are only obtained if the user's program contains a run-time error. A program can run to completion without any run-time errors but give incorrect results. In this situation it is often essential to know the values of key variables at certain points in the program. This usually leads to the user inserting statements like:

writeln('The value of i on entry to sort is',i);

in his program. The Pascal-S system has facilities to allow the user to obtain this type of information, but without using long-winded *writeln* statements. All that is required is the insertion of a call to the built-in procedure *pbreak* at the appropriate points in the program.

The compiler translates this procedure call into the *break* instruction. When the interpreter comes to this instruction it calls a local procedure *brake*, which prints out the values of all accessible variables at that point in the program. This is known as a *snapshot*. The difference between a snapshot and a post-mortem dump is that with a snapshot execution continues, whereas a post-mortem dump occurs when execution has already terminated.

Consider the program given below which involves recursion and which is calculating the *n*th number in the Fibonacci series (each number in this series is the sum of the previous two in the series and the first two numbers in the series are assumed to be 1 and 1).

```
program obtainfibonacci(input,output);
var
  answer, number : integer;

function fibonacci(par :integer) :integer;
  begin
  break;
  if par = 2 then
    fibonacci := 1
  else
    if par = 1 then
      fibonacci := 1
    else
      fibonacci := fibonacci(par–1) + fibonacci(par–2)
  end; (*fibonacci*)

begin (*main program*)
writeln('Which number in the fibonacci series ',
       'is required ? ');
read(number);
answer := fibonacci(number);
writeln('Answer = ',answer:1)
end.
```

The output from this program when 4 is supplied as input is:

```
Execution starting...
Which number in the fibonacci series is required ?
break at    7
 fibonacci  called at 19
    par            = 4
    number         = 4
    answer         = 0
break at    7
```

```
 fibonacci  called at 14
   par           = 3
 fibonacci  called at 19
   par           = 4
   number        = 4
   answer        = 0
break at   7
 fibonacci  called at 14
   par           = 2
 fibonacci  called at 14
   par           = 3
 fibonacci  called at 19
   par           = 4
   number        = 4
   answer        = 0
break at   7
 fibonacci  called at 15
   par           = 1
 fibonacci  called at 14
   par           = 3
 fibonacci  called at 19
   par           = 4
   number        = 4
   answer        = 0
break at   7
 fibonacci  called at 15
   par           = 2
 fibonacci  called at 19
   par           = 4
   number        = 4
   answer        = 0
 Answer = 3
 101 instructions executed
```

Chapter 10
Extending the Pascal-S System

10.1 Enumeration types

Enumeration types were included in the original definition of Pascal (Jensen and Wirth, 1975), but were not included in the definition of Pascal-S (Wirth, 1981). The reasons for this omission are not clear because the extension of the Pascal-S system to include enumeration types is relatively straightforward. This section will describe the changes required to extend the Pascal-S system to include enumeration types.

10.1.1 Use of enumeration types

Enumeration types are useful because they improve the readability of the user's program, an important factor when considering the maintenance of the program. For example, consider the fragments of a Pascal-S program given below which simulates the traffic flow at a junction controlled by traffic lights using the British system:

```
program simulate(input, output);
   :
   :
var
   colourofnorthlights : integer;
   :
   :
procedure initialize;
   begin
   colourofnorthlights := 0;
   :
   :
   end; (*initialize*)

procedure updatelight(var light : integer);
   begin
```

```
    if light = 3 then
      light := 0
    else
      light := light + 1
    end; (*updatelight*)

      :
      :
begin (*main program*)
initialize;
repeat
    outputcurrentsituation;
    lookattrafficflow;
    updatelight(colourofnorthlights);
      :
until finished
end.
```

Under the British system, traffic lights are ordered in the following sequence: red, red and yellow, green, yellow and then back to red. In the above program these conditions are represented by the integers 0, 1, 2 and 3 respectively. This is not clear from the above program because the variable *colourofnorthlights* is declared as an integer and it is not obvious what values it can take or what they represent. The program fragment given above is rewritten with *colourofnorthlights* declared as an enumeration type to give:

```
program simulate(input, output);
    :
    :
    :
type
   lightsequence = (red, redyellow, green, yellow);
    :
    :
var
   colourofnorthlights : lightsequence;
    :
    :
procedure initialize;
   begin
   colourofnorthlights := red;
    :
    :
   end; (*initialize*)
```

```
procedure updatelight(var light : lightsequence);
  begin
  if light = yellow then
    light := red
  else
    light := succ(light)
  end; (*updatelight*)

  :
  :
begin (*main program*)
initialize;
repeat
   outputcurrentsituation;
   lookattrafficflow;
   updatelight(colourofnorthlights);
     :
until finished
end.
```

10.1.2 The extent of the problem

The above fragment also illustrates some of the areas of the Pascal-S system which have to be altered in order to implement enumeration types, namely type declarations, expression evaluation, parameter passing and the *pred* and *succ* functions. There are also other areas which will require alteration. For instance, using the second of the programs as an example we must be able to detect such errors as:

```
writeln(colourofnorthlights);
  (*output of enumeration types not permitted*)

colourofnorthlights := colourofnorthlights + 1;
  (*addition of enumeration types not permitted*)

type
  colours = (red, yellow, blue, green);
  stateofmind = (happy, bored, schizophrenic, blue);
    (*same identifier declared twice*)

colourofnorthlights := succ(yellow);
  (*the definition of enumeration types does not specify
    that the last value is succeeded by the first*)
```

All these errors can be detected by the compiling phase, but in the last example, if the value *yellow* is replaced by a variable of type *lightsequence*, which happens to contain the value *yellow* when the statement is executed, then this error can only be detected by the interpreter.

An enumeration type can be named, that is declared in the type declaration part, for example:

days = (mon, tue, wed, thur, fri, sat, sun);

or can be declared anonymously, that is declared in the variable declaration part:

day : (mon, tue, wed, thur, fri, sat, sun);

Enumeration types can also occur in the definition of arrays and records. For instance, consider the following declarations (which are not part of the same program):

```
table : array[mon..fri] of integer;

table : array [days] of integer;

table : array[(red, yellow, blue)] of
            (found, notthere, stilllooking);

record1 : record
            dayofbirth :
              (mon, tue, wed, thur, fri, sat, sun);
            eyecolour  : colours
          end;
```

Variables of enumeration type can also occur as the control variables of **for** loops, selectors in **case** statements and in boolean expressions.

Enumeration types can also be used as the types returned by functions.

10.1.3 Implementation

The main symbol table will record information about any enumeration type, so the discussion of the implementation of enumeration types will commence with how the symbol table will hold this information.

As has already been seen, there is also a need to be able to distinguish between different enumeration types and the simplest way of accomplishing this is to assign each type a different number.

The implementation of enumeration types does not involve generating code which will manipulate the identifiers *mon, tue* etc. At run-time these values are replaced by their ordinal values, so in the symbol table entry the ordinal value must also be recorded.

Clearly, the list of types available in Pascal-S will also have to be extended and so the definition of *types* will be extended to

```
types = (notyp, ints, reals, bools, chars, arrays, records, enums);
```

The standard symbol table entry is an element of the record *symtabletype* which is declared as:

```
symtabletype   = packed record
                   name : alfa;
                   link : index;
                   obj : object;
                   typ : types;
                   ref : index;
                   normal : boolean;
                   adrr : integer;
                   lev : levtype;
                 end;
```

For enumeration types, the *name, link, obj* and *normal* fields will be used in the standard way as described in Chapter 6 and the *typ* field will have the value *enums*. The *adrr* field will be used to record the ordinal value of an enumeration constant. Variables of enumeration type will use the *adrr* field for the normal purpose, namely their address relative to the current stack frame. The integer representing the number of the enumeration type will also have to be stored in the symbol table. It might appear that the *ref* field is the most obvious location, but there are two arguments against this:

(a) This field is used for a variety of purposes already and further use could cause further unnecessary complication.

(b) The entry for a function name uses all the fields and as functions can return an enumeration type, space must be reserved for the number of the enumeration type.

Thus a new field *enumnumber* will be defined within *symtabletype* for this purpose.

So if, for example, a program started with

```
program first(input, output);
type
    animals = (cow, duck, hen, pig, horse);
```

then the symbol table entry for *hen* will set the *enumnumber* field to 1 and its *adrr* field set to 2 (the ordinal values of enumeration identifiers start at 0).

One of the major problems to overcome with the introduction of enumeration types is the way that the Pascal-S system passes information about types between various procedures. It considers the information on the type of an object to consist of one of the values of *types* and a value of the type *index* which is usually 0 but in the case of records and arrays is an index into the compiler's tables. In the case of enumeration types we have two pieces of information, namely that it is an enumeration type and the number of the enumeration type. This latter value can be represented by the value of type *index.* Usually the value of type *index* is obtained from the *ref* field of the symbol table entry, but in the case of an enumeration type it is required to obtain the number of the enumeration type from the field *enumnumber.* This implies some minor changes in several parts of the system.

The procedure *typ* is responsible for the analysis of all types in the user's program and will have to conform to this interface. The procedure is declared with the following heading:

```
procedure typ(fsys :symset;
              var typefound :types;
              var typereference, typesize :integer);
```

The *fsys* parameter is used to recover from syntax errors and need not concern us. *typefound* is clearly used to communicate the overall type found (i.e. record, array, integer etc.) and *typesize* is used to return the amount of space required to hold a variable of that type. *typereference,* if used at all, will contain a pointer to either the array table *arraytable* or the block table *blocktable.* In the case of an enumeration type it will be used to return the number of the enumeration type so that different enumeration types can be distinguished. For instance, if the *typ* procedure is entered with an enumeration type identifier as the current symbol then *typ* looks up the identifier found in the symbol table and copies the type found in the symbol table into *typefound* and the *ref* field of the symbol table entry into *typereference.* Clearly, the type must be checked before this assignment so that if the type is *enums* then the value of *enumnumber* in the symbol table entry should be copied into *typereference.* The processing of fields of records needs a similar alteration.

The processing of new enumeration types will obviously require more significant changes. The procedure *typ* starts with some initialization and syntax checking and then contains the line

```
if sy in typebegsys then
  begin
```

If we add *lparent* to the set *typebegsys* we can then add the statements shown below after the above two lines.

```
if sy = lparent then
   begin
   ordval := 0;
   enumerationtype;    (*see below*)
   typesize := enumsize;
   typefound := enums;
   typereference := numofenumtypes;
   maxenumvalue [typereferenece] := ordval - 1
   end;
```

ordval is used to keep track of the number of values in the enumeration type and *numofenumtypes* is used to count the number of enumeration types discovered in the user's program. The largest value of any type is also recorded in the array *maxenumvalue* for reasons that will become clear later. *enumsize* is a declared constant indicating the amount of space used up by a variable of enumeration type which is assumed to be the same amount of space taken up by a character variable. The procedure *enumerationtype* is:

```
procedure enumerationtype;

   procedure enterenumconstant;
      begin
      enter(level, konstant, id);
      symboltable[currsymtablesize].enumnumber :=
         numofenumtypes;
      symboltable[currsymtablesize].adrr := ordval;
      symboltable[currsymtablesize].typ := enums;
      ordval := ordval + 1
      end; (*enterenumconstant*)

   begin
   insymbol;
   if sy <> ident then
      begin
      skip(fsys + [rparent], 2);
      if sy = rbrack then
         insymbol
      end
   else
      begin
      numofenumtypes := numofenumtypes + 1;
      enterenumconstant;
      insymbol;
      while sy = comma do
         begin
```

```
        insymbol;
        if sy <> ident then
          error(2)
        else
          begin
          enterenumconstant;
          insymbol
          end
        end;
      if sy <> rparent then
        skip(fsys + [semicolon], 4)
      else
        insymbol
      end
    end; (*enumerationtype*)
```

The other section of *typ* requiring alteration is the processing of array declarations. Pascal-S does not include the Pascal subrange type so all array declarations are of the following kind:

```
table : array [low..high] of integer;
```

and *low..high* cannot be replaced by a type identifier. By introducing enumeration types, a type identifier could be used in this context. However, this extension, which is relatively straightforward, is left as an exercise for the interested reader.

typ calls a local procedure *arraytyp* to handle the processing of arrays and this procedure calls *constant* twice to obtain information about the upper and lower bounds of the index type. *constant* returns the information in a variable parameter of type *constantrecord* which can be altered in the way shown below to contain information about enumeration constants.

```
constantrecord = record
                   case typeofconstant :types of
                     ints, chars, bools : (i:integer);
                     enums : (ordinalvalue :integer;
                              rf :index);
                     reals : (realvalue:real);
                     notyp, arrays, records ()
                 end;
```

Thus *constant* will return the ordinal value of the constant found in *ordinalvalue* and the number of the enumeration type in *realvalue*. *constant* can obtain the required information from the symbol table entry for the identifier.

The compiler maintains a table, *arraytable*, which holds information on any arrays in the user's program. Three of the fields of an entry in this array hold information which is relevant to the index type, namely the type of the index and its upper and lower bounds. As enumeration types are now permitted as indexes to arrays, there is a need to record the integer indicating which enumeration type is being used. Thus each element of *arraytable* requires an extra field to hold this information and small changes are required to *arraytyp* to initialize this field.

The procedure *parameterlist* will also require modification to support the interface for type passing and also to record information about the types of parameters in the symbol table. *typedeclaration* and *variabledeclaration* also require modification so that the value returned from *typ* in *typereference* and *variablereference* respectively is stored in the *enumnumber* field of the symbol table entry rather than the *ref* field.

Expression analysis also involves passing type information between various procedures, so some of these procedures will require modification in order to conform to the interface. *factor* is the procedure which is responsible for operands in expressions so it will be required to look in the *enumnumber* field of the symbol table entry if it discovers a constant or variable of enumeration type and copy the value into the *ref* field of *resultingfactoritem*. *factor* passes responsibility to *selector* if it discovers an array or record access, so *selector* will require a similar modification. Variables and constants of enumeration type can be compared using the relational operators such as =, <>, >=, etc., so a modification to *expression* is required to extend the types for which this is possible. It is also required to check that the expressions being compared are of the same enumeration type.

Procedures which analyse statements such as *assignment*, *casestatement* and *forstatement* all require to analyse the type of a variable or expression and save that information so that it can be used to check that an expression or label occurring later in the statement is of the same type. If the initial variable or expression is of enumeration type the number of the enumeration type will also have to be retained. *casestatement* will also require the ordinal value of any enumeration constants used as case labels in order to construct a jump table. These can be found from the *adrr* field in the symbol table entry for those constants.

call, which handles non-standard procedure and function calls, will require similar type-checking code. The parameters of the standard functions *succ* and *pred* should be extended to include enumeration types and the code for this is in the procedure *standfct*. As explained above, the interpreter will need to check that the parameters of *succ* and *pred* are legal. The compiler could do this if the parameters were constants but this is left as an exercise for the reader. In the case of *succ*, the interpreter will need to know the maximum ordinal value of this enumeration type so this is passed as one of the operands of the *stfunc* instruction. This instruction normally has only one operand, namely an integer corresponding to the standard function which has been called. Thus a second operand is added to this instruction which implies a call to *emit2* rather than *emit1* when this instruction is generated. The interpreter will also need to know when the *succ* function has been passed an enumeration type as a parameter so that it can carry out the run-time check. When some other type has been passed this check is not required (note that the original Pascal-S system does not check for integer overflow or attempting to find the successor of the final character in the character set). Thus when an enumeration type is not a parameter, a value of −1 is passed to the *succ* function and for all other uses of *stfunc*.

The *pred* function in the original Pascal-S system also does not involve any check to see if the parameter will cause underflow. If this policy is continued then no alteration is required to support enumeration types.

Other alterations to the interpreter are relatively straightforward: in particular, defining a new run-time error to give better error reporting and amendments to the post-mortem dump routine to support enumeration types. *printtables* also requires some simple modifications in order to reflect the changing structure of the symbol table. Permitting functions to return values of enumeration type only involves altering *block* so that the appropriate fields in the symbol table entry for the function are set correctly.

10.2 Subrange types

Subrange types are another useful facility included in Pascal, but not Pascal-S. As with enumeration types, the extension of the Pascal-S system to support subrange types is relatively straightforward.

10.2.1 Use of subrange types

Subrange types have two main functions. Firstly they make the user's program more readable. Suppose a variable *day* is declared as follows:

day : *integer*;

then it is not clear from the declaration whether *day* will contain the day of the week or the day of the month or some other interpretation. If however *day* had been declared as:

day : *1..31*;

this gives the reader more information about the purpose of the variable.

Secondly the use of subrange types provides greater security. If *day* had been declared as:

day : *integer*;

it would be possible to assign any integer value to *day*, even though only the values 1 to 31 have any meaning. If day were declared as

day : *1..31*;

then any assignment of a value outside this range would be detected at compile-time, if the value was a constant, or at run-time.

10.2.2 The extent of the problem

This problem is very similar to the implementation of enumeration types discussed in the previous section. Changes will be required to the analysis of types, expression analysis, parameter passing, the interpreter and the *pred* and *succ* functions. The main differences between the implementation of subrange types and enumeration types are that input and output of variables of subrange type are permitted and that all assignments to variables of subrange type will require generation of extra code so that run-time checking can take place. The type declarations shown below should also be allowed.

type
day = *1..31*;
sunshinehours = *0..24*;
sunshinemonths = **array** *[days]* **of** *sunshinehours*;

which implies alteration of the analysis of array declarations.

As with enumeration types, subrange types can be named or anonymous, can occur in record declarations, **for** statements, or **case** statements and can be the type returned by functions.

10.2.3 Implementation

As with enumeration types, the main symbol table *symboltable* will require alteration to be able to hold information about objects of subrange type. However, besides requiring the information that an object is of subrange type it will also be necessary to obtain the upper and lower bounds of that type, the type of the host type and, if it is an enumeration type, the integer corresponding to that type. An initial strategy might be to record all the information about the subrange type in the existing fields of the symbol table. However, there is a requirement to be able to recognize that *x* and *y* in the following are not the same type:

x : *1..10*;
y : *1..10*;

Thus for ease of type checking it would be better to have a separate subrange table and a new entry in *symboltable* which referenced the appropriate entry in the subrange table. Thus the types of *x* and *y* would have separate entries in the subrange table and different indexes in *symboltable*. The subrange table could be declared as:

```
subrtable : array [1..maxnumsubrtype] of
            record
              lowbound,highbound : integer;
              case hosttype : types of
                enum : (hostenumnumber : integer);
                notyp,ints,reals,bools,chars,arrays,
                records,subrange : ()
            end;
```

A fundamental decision in the implementation of subrange types is where, if ever, in the compiler's internal structure is an object of subrange type converted into an object of the host type. For instance, if *x* and *y* are declared as follows:

```
x : 1..31;
y : 1..7;
```

then consider the assignment statement

```
x := y;
```

The procedure *assignment* will require to know that the left-hand side is a variable of subrange type in order to generate code to check that the assignment is legal. However, it does not need any other information about the right-hand side other than the type of the expression, which in this case is the type of the host type, namely integer in this example. This is true for all expressions, so the procedure which analyses operands, *factor*, can alter subrange objects into objects of the host type. Procedures which are called by *factor*, such as *selector*, can pass back the actual type providing *factor* does the necessary conversion.

As with enumeration types, alteration is also required to the way the types of objects are communicated to various procedures. Probably the easiest way of achieving this is to pass *subrange* as the appropriate type and to use the *ref* field to hold the index to the appropriate entry in the subrange table.

In the original version of the Pascal-S system the analysing of array indexes is performed by *arraytyp*. As the definition of subrange types can now occur in other contexts, it is best to centralize the analysis of subrange types and allocate this task to a single procedure. This procedure could have the form:

```
procedure subrangetype(var typ:types; var subrangeref :integer);
  var
    low,high : constantrecord;
  begin
  constant([colon,rbrack,rparent,ofsy,
              deadcolonsy]+fsys, low);
  if low.typeofconstant = reals then
    begin
    error(27);
    low.typeofconstant := ints;
    low.ordinalvalue := 0
    end ;
  if sy = deadcolonsy then insymbol else error(13);
  constant([rbrack,comma,rparent,ofsy]+fsys,high);
  if high.typofconstant <> low.typofconstant then
    begin
    error(27);
    high.ordinalvalue := low.ordinalvalue
    end ;
  if low.ordinalvalue > high.ordinalvalue then
    error(59)
  else
    with subrtable[numsubrtypes] do
       begin
       hosttype := low.typeofconstant;
       if hosttype = enums then
         begin
         lowbound := low.ordinalvalue;
         highbound := high.ordinalvalue;
         hostenumnumber := low.rf
         end
       else
         begin
         lowbound := low.ordinalvalue;
         highbound := high.ordinalvalue;
         hostenumnumber := 0
         end
       end;
  subrangeref := numsubrtypes;
  typesize := 1;
  typ := subrange
  end; (*subrangetype*)
```

This procedure can be called directly if *typ* discovers a constant as the symbol starting a type declaration. *arraytyp* would not call the above procedure but can make an indirect recursive call to *typ*. This would permit declarations of the following kind:

table : **array** *[(mon, tue, wed, thur, fri)]* **of** *integer*;

arraytyp enters information about the array being declared in the array table *arraytable*. This includes information on the index type and the upper and lower bounds. This information will be returned to *arraytyp* from *typ* in the *inxref* variable which will contain an index to the subrange table.

The method of passing type information between procedures described above implies changes to the processing of subranges as fields of records, when passing parameters, in *typedeclaration*, *variabledeclaration* and *selector*.

Type checking of value parameters in *call* becomes more complicated as the formal parameter may be a subrange type and the actual parameter could be of the host type, but otherwise the changes are straightforward.

factor requires alteration in order to convert objects of subrange type into their host type, but this has the benefit that changes that were required for enumeration types in order to permit use of *succ* and *pred* are not required for subrange types.

Only two of the procedures which analyse statements require modification, namely *assignment* and *forstatement*. If either the variable on the left-hand side of an assignment statement or the control variable of a **for** loop is of subrange type then extra code should be generated so that the interpreter can check whether the assignment is legal. (If the expression on the right-hand side of the assignment or the initial or terminating expressions of the **for** loop were constants, then this check could be carried out by the compiler, but this is left as an exercise for the interested reader.) A new instruction is required to implement this task and its two operands can be the upper and lower bounds of the subrange type which can be obtained from the subrange table. As with *call*, both these procedures need slightly more complicated code to carry out the necessary type checking.

As input and output of subrange types are permitted, changes are required to *standproc*, but only to the analysis of parameters of *read* and *readln*. This will have to generate the subrange check instruction to the interpreter in order to check that the input of values to subrange types is legal. No changes are required to the analysis of parameters of *write* or *writeln* since this code calls *expression* which passes back objects of the host type.

As with enumeration types, minor changes to *block* are required to permit functions to return results of subrange type. The interpreter requires code to implement the interpretation of the new instruction and changes to the post-mortem dump routine. Finally the *printtables* procedure, which is used for debugging purposes, requires modification to print out the extra field in *symboltable* and the subrange table.

10.3 Further extensions to the Pascal-S system

Unlike Pascal, Pascal-S has no sets, pointers, variant records or **goto** statements. Pascal also permits files other than input and output and files of more complex objects. The implementation of any of these features in the Pascal-S system would be a more difficult task than the implementation of enumeration or subrange types.

The major problem is the structure of the symbol table. The current structure is not easy to follow and the addition of enumeration and subrange has increased its complexity. Any attempt to implement pointers, sets or variant records would further increase its complexity to an unacceptable level. A major re-design is required which would have a number of extra fields dependent on the type. To ease the complexity, it would also be desirable to abandon the use of arrays as the main building block of the symbol table. The initial choice of arrays was probably taken for ease of translation into other languages. A structure based on pointers would be the best alternative and this was the method chosen for the symbol table structure of the Pascal-P compiler (Nori *et al.*, 1981) which is:

```
identptr = ^identifier;
identifier = packed record
    name : alpha; (*a packed array of characters*)
    leftlink,rightlink
        : identptr; (*symbol table is held as a binary
                      tree. These two point to the
                      following elements in the table*)
    idtype : stp; (*a pointer to a record giving
                    the structure of a type*)
    next : identptr; (*only used to link succeeding objects
                       before entry into the table*)
    case klass : identclass of
      konst : (values : valuerecord);
      vars  : (varkind : formaloractual;
               varlevel : levelrange;
               varaddress : addressrange);
      field : (fieldaddress : addressrange);
      proc,
      func  : (case procfuncdeckind : declarekind of
                 standard :
                   (key: 1..15);
                 declared :
                   (procfunclevel : levelrange;
                    procfuncname : integer;
                    case procfunckind of
                      actual :
```

```
                    (forward, extern : boolean);
                  formal :
                    ()
                )
            )
    end;
```

The *identifier* record hold the details of all standard and declared objects in the user's program. The information on the type of the object is held in a separate record and pointed to by the *idkind* field in the *identifier* record. The record recording the type information is of the form:

```
typeptr = ^structure;

structure = packed record
              size : addressrange;
              case form : structureform of
                scalar :
                  (case scalarkind  : declarekind of
                      declared :
                        (fconst : identptr);
                      standard :
                        ()
                  );
                subrange :
                  (rangetype : typeptr;
                   min,max : valuerecord);
                pointer : (elementtype : typeptr);
                power : (elementofset : typeptr); (*sets*)
                arrays : (arrayeltype,indextype : typeptr);
                files : (filetype : typeptr);
                tagfield :
                  (tagfieldptr : identptr;
                   firstvar : typeptr);
                variant :
                  (nextvar,subvar : typeptr;
                   varaintvalue : valuerecord)
              end;
```

10.4 Suggested exercises and projects

It has been our experience that it helps students' understanding of the compilation process if they participate in some practical work. There is usually not time for students, even working in teams, to produce a complete compiler, so we have given them a copy of the Pascal-S system and asked them to extend it in various ways as outlined in the earlier sections of this chapter. We invite you to try your hand at those exercises, and the ones listed below. A further benefit of such work is that is compels you to read code written by someone else, an experience you will rarely have in an educational institution, but which will be a common experience when you take up employment.

The following exercises and projects involve extensions to the Pascal-S system and increase in difficulty and complexity.

(a) The system currently prompts the user to see if debugging and tracing is required. Alter the system so that these options are taken as flags from the command line and set suitable defaults if they are not supplied.

(b) The Pascal-S system assumes that the Pascal-S source to be compiled and interpreted is to be found in a file named *source*. Alter the system so that the source file name can be taken from the command line.

(c) Adjust the lexical analyser so that the Pascal comment delimiters '{' and '}' are accepted.

(d) Implement the *reset* and *rewrite* procedures within the Pascal-S system.

(e) Currently the system gives only error numbers when reporting a compilation error. Error messages are given at the end of the listing file, but they are very terse. Revise these messages so that they are more informative. Replace the error numbers by the error messages.

(f) Pascal-S has three forms of structured looping statement – **for**, **while** and **repeat** statements. All of these entail testing the termination condition at the top or bottom of the loop. Testing in the middle of the loop is often something that is desirable. Implement such a language construct (choose your own syntax after consideration of languages which contain this construct, e.g. Ada).

(g) The interpreter currently does not perform any checks when interpreting a *pred*, *succ* or *chr* operation. Thus any errors may be caught by the underlying run-time system used to compile the Pascal-S system. Insert checks into the interpreter's code for these operations so that the interpreter signals a run-time error when an error is detected.

(h) Currently if an undeclared identifier is discovered an error is reported on every subsequent occurrence of that identifier. Design and implement a method to avoid reporting an error on all but the first occurrence.

(i) A profile gives a summary of how many times the lines of the source code are executed. Implement a profile option within the Pascal-S system.

(j) Alter the structure of the symbol table to use a hashing function to speed up searching of the symbol table.

(k) Implement the with statement of Pascal in the Pascal-S system.

(l) Peephole optimization is the process of examining the code produced by the code generator to see if it is possible to eliminate or combine some of the instructions and thus speed up execution of the user's program. Design and implement a peephole optimizer which is called before the interpreter commences execution.

(m) Implement an interactive debugger for the system. With such a system the user would be able to put break points into the program at the source level and the interpreter would suspend execution when these points are reached. The user should then be able to examine the values of variables, set or erase break points or continue execution.

(n) The Pascal-S system's symbol table is a complicated array structure. Produce a more flexible and simpler representation for the symbol table based on pointers, but maintain the same interface to the system.

References

Jensen, K and Wirth, N, *Pascal User Manual and Report,* Springer-Verlag, 1975.

Nori, K V, Amman, U, Nageli, H H, and Jacobi, C, 'Pascal-P implementation notes', in *Pascal – The Language and Its Implementation,* ed. D W Barron, pp. 83–124, Wiley, 1981.

Wirth, N, 'Pascal-S: a subset and its implementation', in *Pascal - The Language and Its Implementation,* ed. D W Barron, pp. 199–260, Wiley, 1981.

Appendix A
Pascal-S Syntax in BNF

<program> ::= program <identifier> (<identifier list>) ;
<block> .

<block> ::= <const declaration> <type declaration>
<var declaration>
{ <proc declaration> | <func declaration> }
begin <statement sequence> end

<const declaration> ::= <empty> | <const part>

<const part> ::= const <const list> { <const list> }

<const list> ::= <identifier> = <constant> ;

<type declaration> ::= <empty> | <type part>

<type part> ::= type <type list> { <type list> }

<type list> ::= <identifier> = <type> ;

<type> := <type identifier> |
<array type> |
<record type>

<array type> ::= array [<indextype>] of <type>

<record type> ::= record <field part> end

<indextype> ::= <constant> .. <constant>

<field part> ::= { <identifier list> : <type> }

<var declaration> ::= <empty> | <var part>

<var part> ::= var <var list> { <var list> }

<var list> ::= <identifier list> : <type> ;

<proc declaration> ::= procedure <identifier>

<formal parameter part>
; <block> ;

<func declaration> ::= function <identifier>
<formal parameter part>
: <type identifier> ; <block> ;

<formal parameter part> ::= <empty> |
<formal parameter list>

<formal parameter list> ::= (<parameter part>
{ ; <parameter part> })

<parameter part> ::= <parameter list> |
<var parameter list>

<var parameter list> ::= var <parameter list>

<parameter list> ::= <identifier list> :
<type identifier>

<identifier list> ::= <identifier> { , <identifier> }

<type identifier> ::= <identifier>

<identifier> ::= <letter> { <letter> | <digit> }

<statement sequence> ::= <statement> { ; <statement> }

<statement> ::= <assignment statement> |
<proc call> |
<compound statement> |
<if statement> |
<case statement> |
<while statement> |
<repeat statement> |
<for statement> |
<empty>

<assignment statement> ::= <assign dest> := <expression>

<assign dest> ::= <variable> | <func identifier>

<proc call> ::= <proc identifier>
<actual parameter part>

<proc identifier> ::= <identifier>

<actual parameter part> ::= <empty> |
<actual parameter list>

<actual parameter list> ::= (<expression> { , <expression> })

<func identifier> ::= <identifier>

<compound statement> ::= begin <statement sequence> end

<if statement> ::= <if then statement> | <if then else statement>

<if then statement> ::= if <expression> then <statement>

<if then else statement> ::= if <expression> then <statement> else <statement>

<case statement> ::= case <expression> of <case part> end

<case part> ::= <empty> | <case list>

<case list> ::= <case arm> { ; <case arm> }

<case arm> ::= <case label list> : <statement>

<case label list> ::= <constant> { , <constant> }

<while statement> ::= while <expression> do <statement>

<repeat statement> ::= repeat <statement sequence> until <expression>

<for statement> ::= for <variable identifier> := <expression> <to or downto> <expression> do <statement>

<to or downto> ::= to | downto

<variable identifier> ::= <identifier>

<expression> ::= <simple expression> | <relational exp>

<relational exp> ::= <simple expression> <relational op> <simple expression>

<relational op> ::= = | <> | >= | > | < | <=

```
<simple expression> ::= <term> |
                        <signed term> |
                        <adding exp>

<signed term> ::= <sign> <term>

<adding exp> ::= <term> { <adding op> <term> }

<sign> ::= + | –

<adding op> := + | – | or

<term> ::= <factor>
        { <multiplying op> <factor> }

<multiplying op> ::=  * | / | div | mod | and

<factor> ::= <unsigned constant> |
             <variable> |
             <func call> |
             <brack exp> |
             <not factor>

<func call> ::= <func identifier> <actual parameter part>

<brack exp> ::= ( <expression> )

<not factor> ::= not <factor>

<variable> ::= <variable identifier>
               { <array access> | <record access> }

<array access> ::= [ <index part> ]

<record access> ::= . <field identifier>

<index part> ::= <expression> { , <expression> }

<field identifier> ::= <identifier>

<constant> ::= <constant part> | <char constant>

<constant part> ::= <constant num or id> |
                    <signed const num or id>

<signed const num or id> ::= <sign>
                             <constant num or id>

<constant num or id> ::= <unsigned number> |
                         <constant identifier>
```

<constant identifier> ::= <identifier>

<char constant> ::= ' <character> '

<unsigned constant> ::= <constant identifier> |
<unsigned number> |
<char constant>

<unsigned number> ::= <unsigned integer> <real part>

<real part > ::= <empty> |
<decimal part> |
<E signed part> |
<E unsigned part>

<decimal part> ::= . <unsigned integer>

<E signed part> ::= E <sign> <unsigned integer>

<E unsigned part> ::= E <unsigned integer>

<unsigned integer> ::= <digit> { <digit> }

Appendix B
Pascal-S Compiler Source Listing

```
program pascals (input, output, source, listing);

(* The Pascal-S system was originally written by N Wirth
   of ETH Zurich. This version modified by MJ Rees and DJ Robson.
*)

label
   99;

const
   numofkeywords   = 27;
   numofsigchars   = 10;
   maxinputline    = 140;
   maxexponent     = 127;
   minexponent     = -128;
   maxnumofsigdigits = 8;
   symboltablemax  = 200;
   blocktablemax   = 30;
   arraytablemax   = 40;
   stringtablemax  = 500;
   realconstanttablemax = 30;
   casetablelemax  = 30;
   maxamountofcode = 1000;
   maxlevel        = 10;
   maxerrornumber  = 58;
   indexmax        = 32767;
   integermax      = 32767;
   outputlinelength = 80;
   maxnumofinputlines = 2000;
   stacksize       = 4000;
   ordvaloftabchar = 9;
   ordvaloffirstchar = 0;
   ordvaloflastchar = 127;

type
   symbol          = (intcon, realcon, charcon, string, notsy, plus, minus,
                      times, idiv, rdiv, imod, andsy, orsy, eql, neq, gtr, geq,
                      lss, leq, lparent, rparent, lbrack, rbrack, comma,
                      semicolon, period, colon, becomes, constsy, typesy, varsy,
```

```
                    funcsionsy, prosiduresy, arraysy, recordsy, programsy,
                    ident, beginsy, ifsy, casesy, repeatsy, whilesy, forsy,
                    endsy, elsesy, untilsy, ofsy, dosy, tosy, downtosy, thensy,
                    deadcolonsy);
    index           = -indexmax .. +indexmax;
    alfa            = packed array [1 .. numofsigchars] of char;
    object          = (konstant, variable, atype, prozedure, funktion);
    types           = (notyp, ints, reals, bools, chars, arrays, records);
    symset          = set of symbol;
    typset          = set of types;
    posint          = 0 .. maxint;
    item            = record
                        typ : types;
                        ref : index;
                      end;
    opcodes         = ( LodaddInst, LodvalInst, LodindInst, UpddisInst,
                        Reset1Inst, Reset2Inst, Rewrt1Inst, Rewrt2Inst,
                        StfuncInst, OffsetInst, JumpInst, JmpfalInst,
                        SwitchInst, PbreakInst, ForfupInst, ForsupInst,
                        ForfdnInst, ForsdnInst, MarkstInst, CallInst,
                        Index1Inst, IndexmInst, LoadblInst, CopyblInst,
                        LdintInst, LdcharInst, LdboolInst, LdrealInst,
                        FloatInst, ReadInst, WrstrgInst, WriteInst,
                        Wr1fldInst, HaltInst, LeavepInst, LeavefInst,
                        LodinsInst, NotInst, NegateInst, Wr2fldInst,
                        StoreInst, EqualrInst, NoteqrInst, LessrInst,
                        LesserInst, GrealInst, GerealInst, EqualInst,
                        NotequInst, LessthInst, LesseqInst, GreattInst,
                        GreateInst, OrInst, AddInst, SubInst,
                        AddrealInst, SubrealInst, AndInst, MultInst,
                        DivInst, ModInst, MultrInst, RdivInst,
                        ReadlnInst, WritlnInst, NegatrInst);
    instruction     = packed record
                        opcode : opcodes;
                        field1 : -maxlevel .. +maxlevel;
                        field2 : -integermax .. +integermax;
                      end;
    levtype         = 0 .. maxlevel;
    symtabletype    = packed record
                        name : alfa;
                        link : index;
                        obj : object;
                        typ : types;
                        ref : index;
                        normal : boolean;
                        adrr : integer;
                        lev : levtype;
                      end;

var
```

```

(* The following variables are all altered by insymbol. *)

   lastcharread : char;
   sy : symbol;                    (* Last symbol read by insymbol. *)
   lastidentread : alfa;
   lastintegerread : integer;
   lastrealread : real;
   ordvalofchar : integer;
   lengthoflaststring : integer;
   posinstringtable : integer;
   line : array [1 .. maxinputline] of char;
   charactercount : integer;
   locationcounter : integer;
   linecounter : integer;
   currentlinelength : integer;

(* Variables associated with error handling and syntax analysis. *)

   setofallerrors : set of 0 .. maxerrornumber;
   errpos : integer;
   progname : alfa;
   inputusedasprogparam, outputusedasprogparam : boolean;
   constbegsys, typebegsys, blockbegsys, facbegsys, statbegsys : symset;
   keyword : array [1 .. numofkeywords] of alfa;
   keywordsy : array [1 .. numofkeywords] of symbol;
   specialsymbol : array [char] of symbol; (* Special symbols. *)

(* Indices to tables. *)

   currsymtablesize, currarraytablesize, currblocktablesize,
   lastcharinstringtable, currrealconsttablesize : integer;
   stantyps : typset;
   display : array [0 .. maxlevel] of integer;
   symboltable : array [0 .. symboltablemax] of symtabletype;
   arraytable : array [1 .. arraytablemax] of packed record
                 inxtyp, eltyp : types;
                 elref, low, high, elsize, size : index;
              end;
   blocktable : array [1 .. blocktablemax] of packed record
                 indexsymtaboflastobj, indexsymtablastparam, spaceforparams,
                 variablesize : index
              end;
   stringtable : packed array [0 .. stringtablemax] of char;
   realconsttable : array [1 .. realconstanttablemax] of real;
   code : array [0 .. maxamountofcode] of instruction;
   linerror, profile : array [0 .. maxamountofcode] of integer;
   linewrittentoscreen : boolean;
   errcount : 0 .. maxint;
   tracing, debugging : boolean;
```

```
    source, listing : text;
    swalloweddeadcolon : boolean;

    procedure errormsg;

(* Printing of these very brief error messages is only undertaken
   on completion of parsing the entire program. Messages are not
   sent to the standard output, only into the file associated
   with the listing file variable.
*)

    var
      errornum : 0 .. maxerrornumber;
      msg : array [0 .. maxerrornumber] of alfa;

    begin
      writeln(listing);
      msg[0] := 'undef id  ';
      msg[1] := 'multi def ';
      msg[2] := 'identifier';
      msg[3] := 'program   ';
      msg[4] := ')         ';
      msg[5] := ':         ';
      msg[6] := 'syntax    ';
      msg[7] := 'ident, var';
      msg[8] := 'of        ';
      msg[9] := '(         ';
      msg[10] := 'id, array ';
      msg[11] := '[         ';
      msg[12] := ']         ';
      msg[13] := '..        ';
      msg[14] := ';         ';
      msg[15] := 'func. type';
      msg[16] := '=         ';
      msg[17] := 'boolean   ';
      msg[18] := 'convar typ';
      msg[19] := 'type      ';
      msg[20] := 'prog.param';
      msg[21] := 'too big   ';
      msg[22] := '.         ';
      msg[23] := 'typ (case)';
      msg[24] := 'character ';
      msg[25] := 'const id  ';
      msg[26] := 'index type';
      msg[27] := 'indexbound';
      msg[28] := 'no array  ';
      msg[29] := 'type id   ';
      msg[30] := 'undef type';
      msg[31] := 'no record ';
      msg[32] := 'boole type';
```

```
      msg[33] := 'arith type';
      msg[34] := 'integer   ';
      msg[35] := 'types     ';
      msg[36] := 'param type';
      msg[37] := 'variab id ';
      msg[38] := 'string    ';
      msg[39] := 'no.of pars';
      msg[40] := 'type      ';
      msg[41] := 'type      ';
      msg[42] := 'real type ';
      msg[43] := 'integer   ';
      msg[44] := 'var, const';
      msg[45] := 'var, proc ';
      msg[46] := 'types (:=)';
      msg[47] := 'typ (case)';
      msg[48] := 'type      ';
      msg[49] := 'store ovfl';
      msg[50] := 'constant  ';
      msg[51] := ':=        ';
      msg[52] := 'then      ';
      msg[53] := 'until     ';
      msg[54] := 'do        ';
      msg[55] := 'to downto ';
      msg[56] := 'begin     ';
      msg[57] := 'end       ';
      msg[58] := 'factor    ';
      errornum := 0;

      while setofallerrors <> [] do begin
         while not (errornum in setofallerrors) do
            errornum := errornum + 1;

         writeln(listing, errornum, ' ', msg[errornum]);
         setofallerrors := setofallerrors - [errornum]
      end
   end (*errormsg*);

   procedure error (n : integer);

(* Prints error numbers under the point of detection of the error,
   both on the standard output and in the file associated with the
   listing file variable.
*)

   var
      i : integer;

   begin
      errcount := errcount + 1;
```

```
      if not linewrittentoscreen then begin
         write(linecounter : 4, ' ', locationcounter : 5, ' ');

         (* Write out the current source line. *)
         for i := 1 to currentlinelength do
            write(line[i]);

         writeln;
         write(' ' : 9);
         write(listing, ' ' : 9);
         linewrittentoscreen := true
      end;

      if charactercount <= errpos then begin
         writeln;
         writeln(listing);
         write(' ' : 9);
         write(listing, ' ' : 9);
         errpos := 0;
      end;

      write(' ' : charactercount - errpos, '^', n : 2);
      write(listing, ' ' : charactercount - errpos, '^', n : 2);
      errpos := charactercount + 3;
      setofallerrors := setofallerrors + [n]
   end (*error*);

   procedure fatal (messagenum : integer);

(* Only called if compiler's tables are full. *)

   var
      msg : array [1 .. 7] of alfa;

   begin
      writeln;
      msg[1] := 'identifier';
      msg[2] := 'procedures';
      msg[3] := 'reals     ';
      msg[4] := 'arrays    ';
      msg[5] := 'levels    ';
      msg[6] := 'code      ';
      msg[7] := 'strings   ';
      writeln(' compiler table for ', msg[messagenum], ' is too small');
      writeln(' compilation terminated');
      goto 99 (*terminate program*)
   end (*fatal*);

   procedure nextch;
```

```
(* Read the next character from the source, deal with eof and ignore eoln. *)

   begin

      (* First check to see whether we have processed all the characters in
         the array line.
      *)
      if charactercount = currentlinelength then begin
         (* We have processed all the characters in the array line. *)
         if eof(source) then begin
            writeln;
            writeln('program incomplete');
            errormsg;
            goto 99 (*terminate program*)
         end;

         (* Check to see if the previous line has errors. If so, terminate
            those lines both on standard output and in the file associated
            with the file variable listing.
         *)
         if errpos <> 0 then begin
            writeln;
            writeln(listing);
            errpos := 0
         end;

         (* As we read the next line of input into the array line, put it
            straight out to the file associated with listing.
         *)
         write(listing, linecounter : 4, ' ', locationcounter : 5, ' ');
         currentlinelength := 0;
         linecounter := linecounter + 1;
         linewrittentoscreen := false;
         charactercount := 0;

         while (currentlinelength < maxinputline - 1)
               and (not eoln(source)) do begin
            currentlinelength := currentlinelength + 1;
            read(source, lastcharread);
            write(listing, lastcharread);
            line[currentlinelength] := lastcharread
         end;

         writeln(listing);
         if eoln(source) then begin
           readln(source);
           (* Replace end-of-line with space *)
           currentlinelength := currentlinelength + 1;
           line[currentlinelength] := ' ';
         end;
```

```
      end;

      (* The array line contains unread characters, the first of which can
         be returned to insymbol.
      *)

      charactercount := charactercount + 1;
      lastcharread := line[charactercount]
    end; (* nextch *)

(*-------------------------------------------------------insymbol-*)

    procedure insymbol;

(* Returns the next symbol in the input stream. Calls nextch to
    obtain the next character.
*)

    var
      lower, middle, upper, count, numofintegerdigits, exponent,
      stringlength : integer;
      symbolfound : boolean;

      procedure readscale;

(*    Calculates the value after the exponent in a real constant.
      Read character by character, formed into an integer and added into
      exponent.
*)

      var
        valueafterE, sign : integer;

      begin
        nextch;
        sign := 1;
        valueafterE := 0;

        if lastcharread = '+' then
          nextch
        else if lastcharread = '–' then begin
          nextch;
          sign := –1
        end;

        while lastcharread in ['0' .. '9'] do begin
          valueafterE := 10 * valueafterE + ord(lastcharread) – ord('0');
          nextch
        end;

```

```
      exponent := valueafterE * sign + exponent
   end (*readscale*);

   procedure adjustscale;

(* Calculate actual multiplying factor from number of digits before the
   decimal dot and the number following the E or e.
*)

   var
      power : integer;
      scaler, multiplyingfactor : real;

   begin
      if numofintegerdigits + exponent > maxexponent then
         error(21) (*Exponent too big*)
      else if numofintegerdigits + exponent < minexponent then
         lastrealread := 0
      else begin
         power := abs(exponent);
         multiplyingfactor := 1.0;
         scaler := 10.0;

         (* The only way to understand the following is to get pencil
            and paper and trace it through.
         *)
         repeat
            while not odd(power) do begin
               power := power div 2;
               scaler := sqr(scaler)
            end;

            power := power - 1;
            multiplyingfactor := scaler * multiplyingfactor
         until power = 0;

         if exponent >= 0 then
            lastrealread := lastrealread * multiplyingfactor
         else lastrealread := lastrealread / multiplyingfactor
      end
   end (*adjustscale*);

   function endofstring : boolean;

(* Check for single quote to end string.
   Allow adjacent single quotes through. *)

   begin
      nextch;
      if lastcharread = '''' then begin
```

```
          nextch;
          endofstring := lastcharread <> '''';
        end
        else endofstring := false;
      end (*endofstring*);

    begin (*insymbol*)
      if tracing then
        writeln('entering insymbol');

      repeat
        symbolfound := true;
        (* Catch control characters except tab (note ascii dependency). *)
        while (lastcharread < ' ') and
                (lastcharread <> chr(ordvaloftabchar)) do
        begin
          nextch;
          error(24)
        end;
        (* Ignore spaces or tabs (note ascii dependency). *)
        while (lastcharread = ' ') or (lastcharread = chr(ordvaloftabchar)) do
          nextch;

        (* The deadcolon symbol is .. When processing something like 3..10
          and having read the 3. you have to guess whether you're getting
          a real number or an integer 3 followed by a deadcolon symbol.
          Pascal-S assumes it is the former. If it is the latter the
          following piece of code sorts it out.
        *)
        if swalloweddeadcolon then begin
          swalloweddeadcolon := false;
          sy := deadcolonsy;
          nextch
        end
        else begin
          if lastcharread in ['A' .. 'Z', 'a' .. 'z'] then begin

            (* Identifier or keyword. Build it up in the array lastidentread.
              Only the first numsigchars are put into the array. The
              rest are ignored.
             *)

            count := 0;
            lastidentread := '          ';

            repeat
              if count < numofsigchars then begin
                count := count + 1;

                if lastcharread in ['A' .. 'Z'] then
```

```
                lastcharread := chr(ord(lastcharread) - ord('A') +
                                        ord('a'));

              lastidentread[count] := lastcharread
            end;

            nextch
          until not (lastcharread in ['A' .. 'Z', '0' .. '9', 'a' .. 'z']);

          (* Check to see if the identifier is a keyword. *)
          (* Binary search. *)
          lower := 1;
          upper := numofkeywords;
          repeat
            middle := (lower + upper) div 2;
            if lastidentread <= keyword[middle] then upper := middle - 1;
            if lastidentread >= keyword[middle] then lower := middle + 1
          until lower > upper;

          if lower - 1 > upper then
            sy := keywordsy[middle]
          else sy := ident
        end
        else if lastcharread in ['0' .. '9'] then begin
          (* Number *)
          numofintegerdigits := 0;
          lastintegerread := 0;
          sy := intcon;

          (* Build up the integer character by character. *)
          repeat
            lastintegerread := lastintegerread * 10 +
                                 ord(lastcharread) - ord('0');
            numofintegerdigits := numofintegerdigits + 1;
            nextch
          until not (lastcharread in ['0' .. '9']);

          if (numofintegerdigits > maxnumofsigdigits) or (lastintegerread >
          integermax) then begin
            error(21); (* Too big *)
            lastintegerread := 0;
            numofintegerdigits := 0
          end;

          (* Check to see if real number or a dead colon (..). *)
          if lastcharread = '.' then begin
            nextch;

            if lastcharread = '.' then
              swalloweddeadcolon := true
```

```
                else begin
                    (* Have a real number of the form 3.3 or 3.3e-2. *)
                    sy := realcon;
                    lastrealread := lastintegerread;
                    exponent := 0;

                    (* Build up part following decimal point, but before
                      the exponent.
                    *)
                    while lastcharread in ['0' .. '9'] do begin
                        exponent := exponent - 1;
                        lastrealread := 10.0 * lastrealread +
                                (ord(lastcharread) - ord('0'));
                        nextch
                    end;

                    if (lastcharread = 'E') or (lastcharread = 'e') then
                        readscale;

                    if exponent <> 0 then
                        adjustscale
                end
            end
            else if (lastcharread = 'e') or (lastcharread = 'E') then begin
                (* Have a real number of the form 3e3. *)
                sy := realcon;
                lastrealread := lastintegerread;
                exponent := 0;
                readscale;
                if exponent <> 0 then
                    adjustscale
            end;
        end
        else
            (* Characters which can be simply formed into symbols. *)
            case lastcharread of
                ':' :
                    begin
                        nextch;
                        (* Check for the assignment operator :=. *)
                        if lastcharread = '=' then begin
                            sy := becomes;
                            nextch
                        end
                        else sy := colon
                    end;
                '<' :
                    begin
                        nextch;
                        if lastcharread = '=' then begin
```

```
                    sy := leq;
                    nextch
                  end
                  else if lastcharread = '>' then begin
                    sy := neq;
                    nextch
                  end
                  else sy := lss
                end;
              '>' :
                begin
                  nextch;

                  if lastcharread = '=' then begin
                    sy := geq;
                    nextch
                  end
                  else sy := gtr
                end;
              '.' :
                begin
                  nextch;

                  if lastcharread = '.' then begin
                    sy := deadcolonsy;
                    nextch
                  end
                  else sy := period
                end;
              '''' :
                begin
                  (* Start of string or character constant. All strings
                     are stored contiguously in stringtable, with their
                     starting position and length passed back to
                     insymbol's caller.
                  *)
                  stringlength := 0;

                  while not endofstring do begin

                    if lastcharinstringtable + stringlength =
                                                      stringtablemax
                    then
                      fatal(7);

                    stringtable[lastcharinstringtable + stringlength] :=
                      lastcharread;
                    stringlength := stringlength + 1;

                    if charactercount = currentlinelength then
```

```
                    (*end of line*)
                    stringlength := stringlength - 1;
                end; (* while *)

                (* Have now put all characters of string into
                  stringtable. Check to see if only character constant.
                *)
                if stringlength = 1 then begin
                  sy := charcon;
                  ordvalofchar := ord(stringtable
                                  [lastcharinstringtable])
                end
                else if stringlength = 0 then begin
                  error(38); (* Null string not permitted. *)
                  sy := charcon;
                  posinstringtable := 0
                end
                else begin
                  sy := string;
                  posinstringtable := lastcharinstringtable;
                  lengthoflaststring := stringlength;
                  lastcharinstringtable := lastcharinstringtable +
                    stringlength
                end
              end;
            '(' :
              begin
                nextch;

                if lastcharread <> '*' then
                  sy := lparent
                else begin (* Comment. *)
                  nextch;

                  repeat
                    while lastcharread <> '*' do
                      nextch;

                    nextch
                  until lastcharread = ')';

                  nextch;
                  symbolfound := false; (* Try for another symbol. *)
                end
              end;
            '+', '-', '*', '/', ')', '=', ',', '[', ']', ';' :
              begin
                sy := specialsymbol[lastcharread];
                nextch
              end;
```

```
                '$', '%', '@', '^', '_', '?', '&', '{', '}',
                '\', '~', '`', '"', '#', '!', '|' :
                  begin
                    nextch;
                    error(24); (* These characters not permitted. *)
                    symbolfound := false;
                  end
              end; (*case*)
          end
        until symbolfound;
      end (*insymbol*);

      procedure enterarray (tp : types;
                            lowindex, highindex : integer);

    (* Enter details of a user declared array into the arraytable. *)

      begin
        if lowindex > highindex then
          error(27);

        if (abs(lowindex) > indexmax) or (abs(highindex) > indexmax) then begin
          error(27); (* Array indices out of range. *)
          lowindex := 0;
          highindex := 0;
        end;

        if currarraytablesize = arraytablemax then
          fatal(4)
        else begin
          currarraytablesize := currarraytablesize + 1;

          with arraytable[currarraytablesize] do begin
            inxtyp := tp;
            low := lowindex;
            high := highindex
          end
        end
      end (*enterarray*);

      procedure enterblock;

    (* Initialize entry of blocktable. *)

      begin
        if tracing then
          writeln('entering enterblock');

        if currblocktablesize = blocktablemax then
          fatal(2)
```

```
      else begin
        currblocktablesize := currblocktablesize + 1;
        blocktable[currblocktablesize].indexsymtaboflastobj := 0;
        blocktable[currblocktablesize].indexsymtablastparam := 0
      end
  end (*enterblock*);

  procedure enterreal (x : real;
                       var posintable : integer);

(* Enter a real number into realconsttable. *)
  var
    step : integer;

  begin
    if currrealconsttablesize = realconstanttablemax - 1 then
      fatal(3)
    else begin
      realconsttable[currrealconsttablesize + 1] := x;
      step := 1;

      while realconsttable[step] <> x do
        step := step + 1;

      if step > currrealconsttablesize then
        currrealconsttablesize := step;

      posintable := step
    end
  end (*enterreal*);

  procedure emit (instr : opcodes);

(* Put an intermediate code instruction without any arguments into
  the array code.
*)

  begin
    if locationcounter >= maxamountofcode then
      fatal(6);

    linerror[locationcounter] := linecounter;
    code[locationcounter].opcode := instr;
    locationcounter := locationcounter + 1
  end (*emit*);

  procedure emit1 (instr : opcodes; arg2 : integer);

(* Put an intermediate code instruction with one argument into the
 array code.
```

```
*)

  begin
    if locationcounter >= maxamountofcode then
      fatal(6);

    linerror[locationcounter] := linecounter;

    with code[locationcounter] do begin
      opcode := instr;
      field2 := arg2
    end;

    locationcounter := locationcounter + 1
  end (*emit1*);

  procedure emit2 (instr : opcodes; arg1, arg2 : integer);

(* Put an intermediate code instruction with two arguments into the
  array code.
*)

  begin
    if locationcounter >= maxamountofcode then
      fatal(6);

    linerror[locationcounter] := linecounter;

    with code[locationcounter] do begin
      opcode := instr;
      field1 := arg1;
      field2 := arg2
    end;

    locationcounter := locationcounter + 1
  end; (*emit2*)

(*----------------------------------------------------------block--*)

  procedure block (fsys : symset;
                  isfunction : boolean;
                  level : integer);

(* The procedure which deals with the declarations and the body of each
  program. It is called recursively to deal with the declarations and
  body of any procedure or function.
*)

  type
    constantrecord = record
```

```
                    case typeofconstant : types of
                      ints, chars, bools : (
                        ordinalvalue : integer);
                      reals : (
                        realvalue : real);
                      notyp, arrays, records : ()
                  end;

  var
    spaceforlocals : posint;
    symtabindexatentry : integer;
    blocktabindexatentry : integer;
    posinsymboltable : integer;

    procedure skip (fsys : symset;
                errornum : integer);

(*  Report error and skip over symbols looking for any symbol
    contained in fsys (the set of legal following symbols).
*)

    begin
      error(errornum);

      while not (sy in fsys) do
        insymbol;
    end (*skip*);

    procedure test (legalsymbols, legalfollowingsymbols : symset;
                errornum : integer);

(*  Test to see if current symbol is in a set of legal symbols and
    call skip if it is not.
*)

    begin
      if not (sy in legalsymbols) then
        skip(legalsymbols + legalfollowingsymbols, errornum);
    end (*test*);

    procedure testsemicolon (fsys : symset);

    begin
      if sy = semicolon then
        insymbol
      else begin
        error(14);

        if sy in [comma, colon] then
          insymbol
```

```
      end;

      test([ident] + blockbegsys, fsys, 6)
   end (*testsemicolon*);

   procedure enter (objdescription : object;
                    id : alfa);

(* Check to see if an identifier is in the main symbol table at this
   level and if not enter it and its description.
*)

   var
      posinsymtable, indexoffirstsyminblock : integer;

   begin
      if currsymtablesize = symboltablemax then
         fatal(1)
      else begin
         (* Put the identifier into the bottom of the symbol table so
            that the following search is guaranteed to find it. We can
            then look at its position to determine whether it is already
            there.
         *)
         symboltable[0].name := id;
         (* Find out where to search from. *)
         posinsymtable := blocktable[display[level]].indexsymtaboflastobj;
         indexoffirstsyminblock := posinsymtable;

         while symboltable[posinsymtable].name <> id do
            posinsymtable := symboltable[posinsymtable].link;

         if posinsymtable <> 0 then (*i.e. already in symbol table*)
            error(1)
         else begin
            currsymtablesize := currsymtablesize + 1;

            with symboltable[currsymtablesize] do begin
               name := id;
               link := indexoffirstsyminblock;
               obj := objdescription;
               typ := notyp;
               ref := 0;
               lev := level;
               adrr := 0
            end;

            blocktable[display[level]].indexsymtaboflastobj :=
               currsymtablesize
         end
```

```
    end
  end (*enter*);

  function locinsymboltable (id : alfa) : integer;

(* If not there calls error and returns 0. Otherwise returns the position
  in the symbol table. *)

  var
    currentlevel, posinsymtable : integer;

  begin
    currentlevel := level;
    (* Put identifier we are looking for into the bottom of the table.
      Thus the following search is guaranteed to find it. We can examine
      its position to determine whether its was there before entry
      to this function.
    *)
    symboltable[0].name := id;

    (* Start the search at the current static level and if not there
      move down to the next level. Continue until found or the
      bottom (global) level has been searched.
    *)
    repeat
      posinsymtable := blocktable[display[currentlevel]].
        indexsymtaboflastobj;

      while symboltable[posinsymtable].name <> id do
        posinsymtable := symboltable[posinsymtable].link;

      currentlevel := currentlevel - 1; (*look at next block in scope*)
    until (currentlevel < 0) or (posinsymtable <> 0);

    if posinsymtable = 0 then
      error(0);

    locinsymboltable := posinsymtable
  end (*locinsymboltable*);

  procedure entervariable;

  begin
    if sy = ident then begin
      enter(variable, lastidentread);
      insymbol
    end
    else error(2)
  end (*entervariable*);
```

```
      procedure constant (fsys : symset;
                    var theconstant : constantrecord);

(*    Process all constants, whether they be numbers or identifiers,
      and whether they are found on the rhs of a constant declaration
      or as the lower or upper bound of an array declaration.
*)


      var
        posinsymboltable, sign : integer;

      begin
        theconstant.typeofconstant := notyp;
        theconstant.ordinalvalue := 0;
        test(constbegsys, fsys, 50);

        if sy in constbegsys then begin
          if sy = charcon then begin
            theconstant.typeofconstant := chars;
            theconstant.ordinalvalue := ordvalofchar;
            insymbol
          end
          else begin
            sign := 1;

            if sy in [plus, minus] then begin
              if sy = minus then
                sign := -1;

              insymbol
            end;

            if sy = ident then begin
              posinsymboltable := locinsymboltable(lastidentread);

              if posinsymboltable <> 0 then
                if symboltable[posinsymboltable].obj <> konstant then
                  error(25) (* expected a constant *)
                else begin
                  theconstant.typeofconstant := symboltable[
                    posinsymboltable].typ;

                  (* Get value from symbol table entry. *)
                  if theconstant.typeofconstant = reals then
                    theconstant.realvalue := sign * realconsttable[
                      symboltable[posinsymboltable].adrr]
                  else theconstant.ordinalvalue := sign * symboltable[
                      posinsymboltable].adrr
                end;

```

```
                insymbol
             end
             else if sy = intcon then begin
                theconstant.typeofconstant := ints;
                theconstant.ordinalvalue := sign * lastintegerread;
                insymbol
             end
             else if sy = realcon then begin
                theconstant.typeofconstant := reals;
                theconstant.realvalue := sign * lastrealread;
                insymbol
             end
             else skip(fsys, 50)
          end;

          test(fsys, [], 6) (* Do we now have a legal symbol? *)
       end
    end (*constant*);

    procedure typ (fsys : symset;
                   var typefound : types;
                   var typereference, typesize : integer);

(*  Processes all instances involving types, whether they be in a
    type declaration or variable declaration.
*)

    var
       posinsymboltable : integer;
       fieldtype : types;
       fieldreference : integer;
       fieldsize, offset, startoffieldsinsymtable, endoffieldsinsymtable :
                                              integer;

       procedure arraytyp (var arrayreference, arraysize : integer);

(*     Handles processing of array declarations. Does a recursive call of
       arraytyp to handle multi-dimensional arrays.
       Note that Pascal-S does not permit the following:
         type r = 1..10;
             arr = array [r] of integer;
       only
         type arr = array [1..10] of integer;
*)

       var
          elementtype : types;
          low, high : constantrecord;
          elementreference, elementsize : integer;

```

```
      begin
        if tracing then
          writeln('Entering arraytyp');

        constant([colon, rbrack, rparent, ofsy, deadcolonsy] + fsys, low);

        if low.typeofconstant = reals then begin
          error(27); (* Index type cannot be real *)
          low.typeofconstant := ints;
          low.ordinalvalue := 0
        end;

        if sy = deadcolonsy then
          insymbol
        else error(13);

        constant([rbrack, comma, rparent, ofsy] + fsys, high);

        if high.typeofconstant <> low.typeofconstant then begin
          error(27); (* Incompatible types *)
          high.ordinalvalue := low.ordinalvalue
        end;

        (* Initialize entry in arraytable. *)
        enterarray(low.typeofconstant, low.ordinalvalue, high.ordinalvalue);
        arrayreference := currarraytablesize;

        if sy = comma then begin
          insymbol;
          elementtype := arrays;
          arraytyp(elementreference, elementsize)
        end
        else begin
          if sy = rbrack then
            insymbol
          else begin
            error(12);

            if sy = rparent then
              insymbol
          end;

          if sy = ofsy then
            insymbol
          else error(8);

          (* Analyse type of elements of the array. *)
          typ(fsys, elementtype, elementreference, elementsize)
        end;
```

```
    (* Fill in arraytable. *)
    with arraytable[arrayreference] do begin
      arraysize := (high - low + 1) * elementsize;
      if arraysize > indexmax then
        error(21)
      else
        size := arraysize;
      eltyp := elementtype;
      elref := elementreference;
      elsize := elementsize
    end;

    if tracing then
      writeln('Leaving arraytyp');
  end (*arraytyp*);

begin (*typ*)
  if tracing then
    writeln('Entering typ');

  typefound := notyp;
  typereference := 0;
  typesize := 0;
  test(typebegsys, fsys, 10);

  if sy in typebegsys then begin
    if sy = ident then begin
      (* Have we come across this before? *)
      posinsymboltable := locinsymboltable(lastidentread);

      if posinsymboltable <> 0 then
        with symboltable[posinsymboltable] do
          if obj <> atype then
            error(29) (* Expecting a type *)
          else begin
            typefound := typ;
            typereference := ref;
            typesize := adrr;

            if typefound = notyp then
              error(30) (* Undefined type *)
          end;

      insymbol
    end
    else if sy = arraysy then begin
      insymbol;

      if sy = lbrack then
        insymbol
```

```
                    else begin
                        error(11);

                        if sy = lparent then
                            insymbol
                    end;

                    typefound := arrays;
                    arraytyp(typereference, typesize)
                end
                else begin (* Records *)
                    insymbol;
                    enterblock;
                    typefound := records;
                    typereference := currblocktablesize;

                    if level = maxlevel then
                        fatal(5);

                    level := level + 1;
                    display[level] := currblocktablesize;
                    offset := 0;

                    (* Process fields of record. *)
                    while sy = ident do begin
                        startoffieldsinsymtable := currsymtablesize;
                        entervariable;

                        while sy = comma do begin
                            insymbol;
                            entervariable
                        end;

                        if sy = colon then
                            insymbol
                        else error(5);

                        endoffieldsinsymtable := currsymtablesize;

                        (* Analyse type of field. *)
                        typ(fsys + [semicolon, endsy, comma, ident], fieldtype,
                        fieldreference, fieldsize);

                        (* Fill in details of type in field entry in symboltable. *)
                        while startoffieldsinsymtable < endoffieldsinsymtable do
                        begin
                            startoffieldsinsymtable := startoffieldsinsymtable + 1;

                            with symboltable[startoffieldsinsymtable] do begin
                                typ := fieldtype;
```

```
                  ref := fieldreference;
                  normal := true;
                  adrr := offset;
                  offset := offset + fieldsize;
                  if offset > indexmax then begin
                     error(21); (*too big*)
                     offset := 0
                     end
               end
            end;

            if sy <> endsy then begin
               if sy = semicolon then
                  insymbol
               else begin
                  error(14);

                  if sy = comma then
                     insymbol
               end;

               test([ident, endsy, semicolon], fsys, 6)
            end
         end;

         if sy <> endsy then
            error(57); (*end expected*)

         blocktable[typereference].variablesize := offset;
         typesize := offset;
         blocktable[typereference].spaceforparams := 0;
         insymbol;
         level := level - 1
      end; (*records*)

      test(fsys, [], 6)
   end;

   if tracing then
      writeln('Leaving typ');
end (*typ*);

procedure parameterlist;

(*  Analyse parameter list of a procedure or function. *)

var
   parametertype : types;
   parameterreference, parametersize, posinsymboltable,
   indextoparamsinsymboltable : integer;
```

```
      valpar : boolean;

    begin
      if tracing then
        writeln('Entering parameterlist');

      insymbol;
      parametertype := notyp;
      parameterreference := 0;
      parametersize := 0;
      test([ident, varsy], fsys + [rparent], 7);

      while sy in [ident, varsy] do begin

        (* Check to see if variable parameter. *)
        if sy <> varsy then
          valpar := true
        else begin
          insymbol;
          valpar := false
        end;

        indextoparamsinsymboltable := currsymtablesize;
        entervariable;

        while sy = comma do begin
          insymbol;
          entervariable;
        end;

        if sy = colon then begin
          insymbol;

          if sy <> ident then
            error(2) (* Must have a type name *)
          else begin
            posinsymboltable := locinsymboltable(lastidentread);
            insymbol;

            if posinsymboltable <> 0 then
              with symboltable[posinsymboltable] do
                if obj <> atype then
                  error(29)
                else begin
                  parametertype := typ;
                  parameterreference := ref;

                  if valpar then
                    parametersize := adrr
                  else parametersize := 1
```

```
                  end;
         end;

         test([semicolon, rparent], [comma, ident] + fsys, 14)
      end
      else error(5);

      (* Fill in details of type in parameter entry in the
         symbol table.
      *)
      while indextoparamsinsymboltable < currsymtablesize do begin
         indextoparamsinsymboltable := indextoparamsinsymboltable + 1;

         with symboltable[indextoparamsinsymboltable] do begin
            typ := parametertype;
            ref := parameterreference;
            normal := valpar;
            adrr := spaceforlocals;
            lev := level;
            spaceforlocals := spaceforlocals + parametersize;
            if spaceforlocals > indexmax then begin
               error(21); (*too big*)
               spaceforlocals := 0
               end
         end
      end;

      if sy <> rparent then begin
         if sy = semicolon then
            insymbol
         else begin
            error(14);

            if sy = comma then
               insymbol
         end;

         test([ident, varsy], [rparent] + fsys, 6)
      end
   end (*while*);

   if sy = rparent then begin
      insymbol;
      test([semicolon, colon], fsys, 6)
   end
   else error(4);

   if tracing then
      writeln('Leaving parameterlist');
end (*parameterlist*);
```

```
      procedure constntdeclaration;

(*    Processes all declarations following the keyword const. *)

      var
        valofconstant : constantrecord;
        posinrealtable : integer;

      begin
        if tracing then
          writeln('Entering constntdeclaration');

        insymbol;
        test([ident], blockbegsys, 2);

        while sy = ident do begin
          enter(konstant, lastidentread);
          insymbol;

          if sy = eql then
            insymbol
          else begin
            error(16);

            if sy = becomes then
              insymbol
          end;

          (* Get value and type. *)
          constant([semicolon, comma, ident] + fsys, valofconstant);

          (* Fill in symbol table entry. *)
          symboltable[currsymtablesize].typ := valofconstant.typeofconstant;
          symboltable[currsymtablesize].ref := 0;
          symboltable[currsymtablesize].normal := false;

          if valofconstant.typeofconstant = reals then begin
            enterreal(valofconstant.realvalue, posinrealtable);
            symboltable[currsymtablesize].adrr := posinrealtable
          end
          else symboltable[currsymtablesize].adrr := valofconstant.
              ordinalvalue;

          testsemicolon(fsys)
        end;

        if tracing then
          writeln('Leaving constntdeclaration');
      end (*constntdeclaration*);
```

```
    procedure typedeclaration;

(*  Handles type declarations. Main work done by typ. *)

    var
      typefound : types;
      typereference, typesize, indexinsymtableoftype : integer;

    begin
      if tracing then
        writeln('Entering typedeclaration');

      insymbol;
      test([ident], blockbegsys, 2);

      while sy = ident do begin
        enter(atype, lastidentread);
        indexinsymtableoftype := currsymtablesize;
        insymbol;

        if sy = eql then
          insymbol
        else begin
          error(16);

          if sy = becomes then
            insymbol
        end;

        typ([semicolon, comma, ident] + fsys, typefound, typereference,
        typesize);

        with symboltable[indexinsymtableoftype] do begin
          typ := typefound;
          ref := typereference;
          adrr := typesize;
          normal := false
        end;

        testsemicolon(fsys)
      end;

      if tracing then
        writeln('Leaving typedeclaration');
    end (*typedeclaration*);

    procedure variabldeclaration;

(*  Handles variable declarations. Main work done by typ. *)
```

```
    var
      indexinsymtable, indexinsymtableoflastvar, variablereference,
      variablesize : integer;
      variabletype : types;

    begin
      if tracing then
        writeln('Entering variabledeclaration');

      insymbol;

      while sy = ident do begin
        indexinsymtable := currsymtablesize;
        entervariable;

        while sy = comma do begin
          insymbol;
          entervariable;
        end;

        if sy = colon then
          insymbol
        else error(5);

        indexinsymtableoflastvar := currsymtablesize;
        typ([semicolon, comma, ident] + fsys, variabletype,
        variablereference, variablesize);

        (* Fill in type info. in variables symbol table entry. *)
        while indexinsymtable < indexinsymtableoflastvar do begin
          indexinsymtable := indexinsymtable + 1;

          with symboltable[indexinsymtable] do begin
            typ := variabletype;
            ref := variablereference;
            lev := level;
            adrr := spaceforlocals;
            normal := true;
            spaceforlocals := spaceforlocals + variablesize;
            if spaceforlocals > indexmax then begin
              error(21); (*too big*)
              spaceforlocals := 0
              end
          end
        end;

        testsemicolon(fsys)
      end;
```

```
      if tracing then
        writeln('Leaving variabledeclaration')
    end (*variabledeclaration*);

    procedure procdeclaration;

(*  Handles procedure and function declarations by recursively calling
    block.
*)

    var
      isfunction : boolean;

    begin
      if tracing then
        writeln('Entering procdeclaration');

      isfunction := sy = funcsionsy;
      insymbol;

      if sy <> ident then begin
        error(2);
        lastidentread := '          '
      end;

      if isfunction then
        enter(funktion, lastidentread)
      else enter(prozedure, lastidentread);

      symboltable[currsymtablesize].normal := true;
      insymbol;
      block([semicolon] + fsys, isfunction, level + 1);

      if sy = semicolon then
        insymbol
      else error(14);

      if isfunction then
       emit(LeavefInst)
      else
       emit(LeavepInst);

      if tracing then
        writeln('Leaving procdeclaration')
    end (*proceduredeclaration*);

    procedure statement (fsys : symset);

(*  Handles processing of all statements. *)
```

```
      var
        posinsymtable : integer;

        procedure expression (fsys : symset;
                              var resultingexpitem : item);
        forward;

        procedure selector (fsys : symset;
                            var lastitem : item);

(*      Handles the selection of array indexes and fields of records when
        used either in expressions or say on the left-hand side of an
        assignment statement.
*)

        var
          expressionitem : item;
          offsetinstackframe, posinarraytable, posinsymtable : integer;

        begin (*sy in [lparent, lbrack, period]*)
          if tracing then
            writeln('Entering selector');

          repeat
            if sy = period then begin
              insymbol; (* Field selector *)

              if sy <> ident then
                error(2)
              else begin
                if lastitem.typ <> records then
                  error(31)
                else begin (* Search for field identifier *)
                  posinsymtable := blocktable[lastitem.ref].
                    indexsymtaboflastobj;
                  symboltable[0].name := lastidentread;

                  while symboltable[posinsymtable].name <> lastidentread
                  do
                    posinsymtable := symboltable[posinsymtable].link;

                  if posinsymtable = 0 then
                    error(0); (* can't find this field *)

                  lastitem.typ := symboltable[posinsymtable].typ;
                  lastitem.ref := symboltable[posinsymtable].ref;
                  offsetinstackframe := symboltable[posinsymtable].adrr;

                  if offsetinstackframe <> 0 then
                    emit1(OffsetInst, offsetinstackframe)
```

```
            end;

            insymbol
         end
      end
      else begin (* Array selector *)
         if sy <> lbrack then
            error(11); (* Expecting [ *)

         (* May be multi-dimensional. *)
         repeat
            insymbol;
            expression(fsys + [comma, rbrack], expressionitem);

            if lastitem.typ <> arrays then
               error(28)
            else begin
               posinarraytable := lastitem.ref;

               if arraytable[posinarraytable].inxtyp <> expressionitem.
               typ then
                  error(26) (* Wrong type found *)
               else if arraytable[posinarraytable].elsize = 1 then
                  emit1(Index1Inst, posinarraytable) (*index1*)
               else emit1(IndexmInst, posinarraytable); (*indexm*)

               lastitem.typ := arraytable[posinarraytable].eltyp;
               lastitem.ref := arraytable[posinarraytable].elref
            end
         until sy <> comma;

         if sy = rbrack then
            insymbol
         else begin
            error(12);

            if sy = rparent then
               insymbol
         end
      end
   until not (sy in [lbrack, lparent, period]);

   test(fsys, [], 6);

   if tracing then
      writeln('Leaving selector')
end (*selector*);

procedure call (fsys : symset;
               locofcalledroutine : integer);
```

```
(*      Handles all procedure and function calls with the exception
        of standard routines.
*)

        var
          expressionitem : item;
          locoflastparam, locofcurrentparam, locofactualparam : integer;

        begin
          if tracing then
            writeln('Entering call');

          emit1(MarkstInst, locofcalledroutine); (* mark stack *)
          locoflastparam := blocktable[symboltable[locofcalledroutine].ref].
            indexsymtablastparam;
          locofcurrentparam := locofcalledroutine;

          if sy = lparent then begin (* Actual parameter list *)
            repeat
              insymbol;

              if locofcurrentparam >= locoflastparam then
                error(39)
              else begin
                locofcurrentparam := locofcurrentparam + 1;

                if symboltable[locofcurrentparam].normal then begin

                  (* Value parameter. *)
                  expression(fsys + [comma, colon, rparent],
                  expressionitem);

                  (* Check type of actual parameter against
                    formal parameter type.
                   *)
                  if expressionitem.typ = symboltable[locofcurrentparam].
                  typ then begin
                    if expressionitem.ref <> symboltable[
                    locofcurrentparam].ref then
                      error(36)
                    else if expressionitem.typ = arrays then
                      emit1(LoadblInst,
                            arraytable[expressionitem.ref].size)
                    else if expressionitem.typ = records then
                      emit1(LoadblInst, blocktable[expressionitem.ref].
                      variablesize) (*load block*)
                  end
                  else if (expressionitem.typ = ints) and (symboltable[
                  locofcurrentparam].typ = reals) then
```

```
          emit1(FloatInst, 0) (*float*)
        else if expressionitem.typ <> notyp then
          error(36); (*bad type*)
      end
      else begin (* Variable parameter *)
        if sy <> ident then
          error(2)
        else begin
          locofactualparam := locinsymboltable(lastidentread);
          insymbol;

          if locofactualparam <> 0 then begin
            if symboltable[locofactualparam].obj <> variable
            then
              error(37); (* has to be a variable *)

            expressionitem.typ := symboltable[locofactualparam
              ].typ;
            expressionitem.ref := symboltable[locofactualparam
              ].ref;

            if symboltable[locofactualparam].normal then
              emit2(LodaddInst,
                  symboltable[locofactualparam].lev,
                  symboltable[locofactualparam].adrr)
            else emit2(LodvalInst,
                 symboltable[locofactualparam].lev,
                 symboltable[locofactualparam].adrr);

            if sy in [lbrack, lparent, period] then
              selector(fsys + [comma, colon, rparent],
              expressionitem);

            if (expressionitem.typ <> symboltable[
            locofcurrentparam].typ) or (expressionitem.ref <>
            symboltable[locofcurrentparam].ref) then
              error(36) (* Type incompatibility *)
          end
        end
      end
    end;

    test([comma, rparent], fsys, 6)
  until sy <> comma;

  if sy = rparent then
    insymbol
  else error(4)
end;
```

```
      if locofcurrentparam < locoflastparam then
        error(39); (* Too few actual parameters *)

      emit1(CallInst, blocktable[symboltable[locofcalledroutine].ref].
      spaceforparams - 1); (*call*)

      if symboltable[locofcalledroutine].lev < level then
        emit2(UpddisInst, symboltable[locofcalledroutine].lev, level);
        (*load indirect*)

      if tracing then
        writeln('Leaving call');
    end (*call*);

    function resulttype (operand1, operand2 : types) : types;

(*  If the types are identical this will return this type.
    If the types can be converted to be compatible, this function
      will return the resulting type.
    Otherwise it will signal an error and return notyp.
*)

    begin
      if (operand1 > reals) or (operand2 > reals) then begin
        error(33);
        resulttype := notyp
      end
      else if (operand1 = notyp) or (operand2 = notyp) then
        resulttype := notyp
      else if operand1 = ints then
        if operand2 = ints then
          resulttype := ints
        else begin
          resulttype := reals;
          emit1(FloatInst, 1)
        end
      else begin
        resulttype := reals;

        if operand2 = ints then
          emit1(FloatInst, 0)
      end
    end (*resulttype*);

    procedure expression;

(*  Controls analysis of all expressions. Generates code for
    relational operators.
*)

```

```
    var
      followingsimexpitem : item;
      expoperator : symbol;

      procedure simpleexpression (fsys : symset;
                                  var resultingsimexpitem : item);

(*        Generates code for: + - or operators. *)

      var
        followingtermitem : item;
        simexpoperator : symbol;

        procedure term (fsys : symset;
                        var resultingtermitem : item);

(*          Generates code for: and * div mod / operators. *)

        var
          followingfactoritem : item;
          termoperator : symbol;

          procedure factor (fsys : symset;
                            var resultingfactoritem : item);

(*            Analyses actual operands. *)

          var
            posinsymtable : integer;
            opcode : opcodes;
            posinrealtable : integer;

            procedure standfunct (standfunctnum : integer;
                                  posinsymtableoffunc : integer);

(*              Processes all standard functions. *)

            var
              allowabletypes : typset;

            begin
              if sy = lparent then
                insymbol
              else error(9);

              if standfunctnum < 17 then begin
                expression(fsys + [rparent], resultingfactoritem);

                case standfunctnum of

```

```
            0, 2 : (*abs, sqr*)
               begin
                  allowabletypes := [ints, reals];
                  symboltable[posinsymtableoffunc].typ :=
                     resultingfactoritem.typ;

                  if resultingfactoritem.typ = reals then
                     standfunctnum := standfunctnum + 1
               end;


            4, 5 : (*odd, chr*)
               allowabletypes := [ints];

            6 : (*ord*)
               allowabletypes := [ints, bools, chars];

            7, 8 : (*succ, pred*)
               begin
                  allowabletypes := [ints, bools, chars];
                  symboltable[posinsymtableoffunc].typ :=
                     resultingfactoritem.typ
               end;

            9, 10, 11, 12, 13, 14, 15, 16 :
               (*round, trunc, sin, cos,...*)
               begin
                  allowabletypes := [ints, reals];

                  if resultingfactoritem.typ = ints then
                     emit1(FloatInst, 0)
               end;
         end;

         if resultingfactoritem.typ in allowabletypes then
            emit1(StfuncInst, standfunctnum)
         else if resultingfactoritem.typ <> notyp then
            error(48);
      end
      else
      begin (*standfunctnum in [17,18]*) (*eoln, eof*)
         if sy <> ident then
            error(2)
         else if lastidentread <> 'input      ' then
            error(0)
         else insymbol;

         emit1(StfuncInst, standfunctnum);
      end;
```

```
            resultingfactoritem.typ := symboltable[
              posinsymtableoffunc].typ;

            if sy = rparent then
              insymbol
            else error(4)
          end (*standfct*);

      begin (*factor*)
        if tracing then
          writeln('Entering factor');

        resultingfactoritem.typ := notyp;
        resultingfactoritem.ref := 0;
        test(facbegsys, fsys, 58);

        while sy in facbegsys do begin
          if sy = ident then begin
            posinsymtable := locinsymboltable(lastidentread);
            insymbol;

            with symboltable[posinsymtable] do
              case obj of
                konstant :
                  begin
                    resultingfactoritem.typ := typ;
                    resultingfactoritem.ref := 0;

                    case typ of
                      ints: emit1(LdintInst, adrr);
                      chars: emit1(LdcharInst, adrr);
                      bools: emit1(LdboolInst, adrr);
                      reals: emit1(LdrealInst, adrr);
                    end;
                  end;
                variable :
                  begin
                    resultingfactoritem.typ := typ;
                    resultingfactoritem.ref := ref;

                    if sy in [lbrack, lparent, period] then
                    begin
                      if normal then
                        opcode := LodaddInst
                      else opcode := LodvalInst;

                      emit2(opcode, lev, adrr);
                      selector(fsys, resultingfactoritem);

                      if resultingfactoritem.typ in stantyps
```

```
                                then
                                   emit(LodinsInst) (*load value whose
                                         address is on top of the
                                         stack*)
                             end
                             else begin
                                if resultingfactoritem.typ in stantyps
                                then
                                   if normal then
                                      opcode := LodvalInst
                                   else opcode := LodindInst
                                     (*load indirect
                                       where address is known at
                                       compile-time*)
                                else if normal then
                                   opcode := LodaddInst
                                else opcode := LodvalInst;

                                emit2(opcode, lev, adrr)
                             end
                          end;

                       atype, prozedure : error(44);
                          (* Not allowed here *)

                       funktion :
                          begin
                             resultingfactoritem.typ := typ;

                             if lev <> 0 then
                                call(fsys, posinsymtable)
                             else standfunct(adrr, posinsymtable)
                          end
                    end (*case,with*)
              end
              else if sy in [charcon, intcon, realcon] then begin
                 if sy = realcon then begin
                    resultingfactoritem.typ := reals;
                    enterreal(lastrealread, posinrealtable);
                    emit1(LdrealInst, posinrealtable) (*load real*)
                 end
                 else begin
                    if sy = charcon then begin
                       resultingfactoritem.typ := chars;
                       emit1(LdcharInst, ordvalofchar)
                    end
                    else begin
                       resultingfactoritem.typ := ints;
                       emit1(LdintInst, lastintegerread)
                    end
```

```
                end;

                resultingfactoritem.ref := 0;
                insymbol
             end
             else if sy = lparent then begin
                (* We have a sub-expression enclosed in ( ). *)
                insymbol;
                expression(fsys + [rparent], resultingfactoritem);

                if sy = rparent then
                   insymbol
                else error(4)
             end
             else if sy = notsy then begin
                insymbol;
                factor(fsys, resultingfactoritem);

                if resultingfactoritem.typ = bools then
                   emit(NotInst)
                else if resultingfactoritem.typ <> notyp then
                   error(32)
             end;

             test(fsys, facbegsys, 6)
          end; (*while*)

          if tracing then
             writeln('Leaving factor');
       end (*factor*);

    begin (*term*)
       if tracing then
          writeln('Entering term');

       (* Get operand. *)
       factor(fsys + [times, rdiv, idiv, imod, andsy],
       resultingtermitem);

       while sy in [times, rdiv, idiv, imod, andsy] do begin
          (* First operand now on stack. *)
          termoperator := sy;
          insymbol;
          (* Get second operand. *)
          factor(fsys + [times, rdiv, idiv, imod, andsy],
          followingfactoritem);

          (* Second operand now on stack - now for operation. *)
          if termoperator = times then begin
             resultingtermitem.typ := resulttype(resultingtermitem.
```

```
            typ, followingfactoritem.typ);

          case resultingtermitem.typ of
            notyp :;
            ints : emit(MultInst);
            reals : emit(MultrInst);
          end
        end
        else if termoperator = rdiv then begin
          if resultingtermitem.typ = ints then begin
            emit1(FloatInst, 1);
            resultingtermitem.typ := reals
          end;

          if followingfactoritem.typ = ints then begin
            emit1(FloatInst, 0);
            followingfactoritem.typ := reals
          end;

          if (resultingtermitem.typ = reals) and (
          followingfactoritem.typ = reals) then
            emit(RdivInst)
          else begin
            if (resultingtermitem.typ <> notyp) and (
            followingfactoritem.typ <> notyp) then
              error(33);

            resultingtermitem.typ := notyp
          end
        end
        else if termoperator = andsy then begin
          if (resultingtermitem.typ = bools) and (
          followingfactoritem.typ = bools) then
            emit(AndInst)
          else begin
            if (resultingtermitem.typ <> notyp) and (
            followingfactoritem.typ <> notyp) then
              error(32);

            resultingtermitem.typ := notyp
          end
        end
        else begin (*termoperator in [idiv,imod]*)
          if (resultingtermitem.typ = ints) and (
          followingfactoritem.typ = ints) then
            if termoperator = idiv then
              emit(DivInst)
            else emit(ModInst)
          else begin
            if (resultingtermitem.typ <> notyp) and (
```

```
                    followingfactoritem.typ <> notyp) then
                      error(34);

                    resultingtermitem.typ := notyp
                  end
                end
              end;

              if tracing then
                writeln('Leaving term');
            end (*term*);

          begin (*simpleexpression*)
            if tracing then
              writeln('Entering simpleexpression');

            (* Deal with unary - or +. *)
            if sy in [plus, minus] then begin
              simexpoperator := sy;
              insymbol;
              term(fsys + [plus, minus], resultingsimexpitem);

              if resultingsimexpitem.typ > reals then
                error(33)
              else if simexpoperator = minus then
                    if resultingsimexpitem.typ = reals then
                      emit(NegatrInst) (*negate a real*)
                    else
                      emit(NegateInst) (*negate an integer*)
            end
            else (* Get operand *)
              term(fsys + [plus, minus, orsy], resultingsimexpitem);

            while sy in [plus, minus, orsy] do begin
              (* First operand now on stack. *)
              simexpoperator := sy;
              insymbol;

              (* Get second operand. *)
              term(fsys + [plus, minus, orsy], followingtermitem);

              if simexpoperator = orsy then begin
              (* Second operand now on stack. Now for operator. *)
                if (resultingsimexpitem.typ = bools) and (followingtermitem
                .typ = bools) then
                  emit(OrInst)
                else begin
                  if (resultingsimexpitem.typ <> notyp) and (
                  followingtermitem.typ <> notyp) then
                    error(32);
```

```

                  resultingsimexpitem.typ := notyp
               end
            end
            else begin
               resultingsimexpitem.typ := resulttype(resultingsimexpitem.
                  typ, followingtermitem.typ);

               case resultingsimexpitem.typ of
                  notyp :;
                  ints :
                     if simexpoperator = plus then
                        emit(AddInst)
                     else emit(SubInst);
                  reals :
                     if simexpoperator = plus then
                        emit(AddrealInst)
                     else emit(SubrealInst)
               end
            end
         end;

         if tracing then
            writeln('Leaving simpleexpression');
      end (*simpleexpression*);

   begin (*expression*)
      if tracing then
         writeln('Entering expression');

      (* Get operand. *)
      simpleexpression(fsys + [eql, neq, lss, leq, gtr, geq],
      resultingexpitem);

      if sy in [eql, neq, lss, leq, gtr, geq] then begin
         (* First operand now on stack. *)
         expoperator := sy;
         insymbol;

         (* Get second operand. *)
         simpleexpression(fsys, followingsimexpitem);

         (* Second operand on stack. Now for operator. *)
         if (resultingexpitem.typ in [notyp, ints, bools, chars]) and (
         resultingexpitem.typ = followingsimexpitem.typ) then
            case expoperator of
               eql : emit(EqualInst);
               neq : emit(NotequInst);
               lss : emit(LessthInst);
               leq : emit(LesseqInst);
```

```
                gtr : emit(GreattInst);
                geq : emit(GreateInst);
             end
          else begin
             if resultingexpitem.typ = ints then begin
                resultingexpitem.typ := reals;
                emit1(FloatInst, 1)
             end
             else if followingsimexpitem.typ = ints then begin
                followingsimexpitem.typ := reals;
                emit1(FloatInst, 0)
             end;

             if (resultingexpitem.typ = reals) and (followingsimexpitem.typ
             = reals) then
                case expoperator of
                   eql : emit(EqualrInst);
                   neq : emit(NoteqrInst);
                   lss : emit(LessrInst);
                   leq : emit(LesserInst);
                   gtr : emit(GreallInst);
                   geq : emit(GerealInst);
                end
             else error(35)
          end;

          resultingexpitem.typ := bools
       end;

       if tracing then
          writeln('Leaving expression')
    end (*expression*);

    procedure assignment (leveloflhs, offsetoflhs, posinsymtableoflhs :
                          integer);

    var
       lhsitem, rhsitem : item;
       opcode : opcodes;

    begin
       if tracing then
          writeln('Entering assignment');

       lhsitem.typ := symboltable[posinsymtableoflhs].typ;
       lhsitem.ref := symboltable[posinsymtableoflhs].ref;

       (* Check to see if lhs is variable parameter.
          If it is we need only load the value in that location
          in order to obtain the address on the stack
```

```
        otherwise load the address of the left-hand side.
    *)

    if symboltable[posinsymtableoflhs].normal then
        opcode := LodaddInst (*lodadd*)
    else opcode := LodvalInst; (*lodval*)

    emit2(opcode, leveloflhs, offsetoflhs);

    if sy in [lbrack, lparent, period] then
        selector([becomes, eql] + fsys, lhsitem);

    if sy = becomes then
        insymbol
    else begin
        error(51); (* Expected := *)

        if sy = eql then
            insymbol
    end;

    (* Analyse and generate code for right-hand side. *)
    expression(fsys, rhsitem);

    if lhsitem.typ = rhsitem.typ then
        if lhsitem.typ in stantyps then
            emit(StoreInst) (*store*)
        else if lhsitem.ref <> rhsitem.ref then
            error(46)
        else if lhsitem.typ = arrays then
            emit1(CopyblInst, arraytable[lhsitem.ref].size) (*copybl*)
        else emit1(CopyblInst, blocktable[lhsitem.ref].variablesize)
    else if (lhsitem.typ = reals) and (rhsitem.typ = ints) then begin
        emit1(FloatInst, 0); (*float*)
        emit(StoreInst) (*store*)
    end
    else if (lhsitem.typ <> notyp) and (rhsitem.typ <> notyp) then
        error(46);

    if tracing then
        writeln('Leaving assignment');
end (*assignment*);

procedure compoundstatement;

begin
    if tracing then
        writeln('Entering compoundstatement');

    insymbol;
```

```
      statement([semicolon, endsy] + fsys);

      while sy in [semicolon] + statbegsys do begin
         if sy = semicolon then
            insymbol
         else error(14);

         statement([semicolon, endsy] + fsys)
      end;

      if sy = endsy then
         insymbol
      else error(57); (*end expected*)

      if tracing then
         writeln('Leaving compoundstatement');
   end (*compoundstatement*);

   procedure ifstatement;

   var
      boolexpitem : item;
      locofjumptoelseorend, locofjumptoend : integer;

   begin
      if tracing then
         writeln('Entering ifstatement');

      insymbol;

      (* Analyse boolean expression. *)
      expression(fsys + [thensy, dosy], boolexpitem);

      if not (boolexpitem.typ in [bools, notyp]) then
         error(17);

      locofjumptoelseorend := locationcounter;
      emit(Jmpfallnst);
        (* Jump if false to else (if present) or end of if statement. *)

      if sy = thensy then
         insymbol
      else begin
         error(52);

         if sy = dosy then
            insymbol
      end;

      statement(fsys + [elsesy]);
```

```

      if sy = elsesy then begin
         insymbol;
         locofjumptoend := locationcounter;
         emit(JumpInst); (*jump to end of if statement*)
         code[locofjumptoelseorend].field2 := locationcounter;
         statement(fsys);
         code[locofjumptoend].field2 := locationcounter
      end
      else code[locofjumptoelseorend].field2 := locationcounter;

      if tracing then
         writeln('Leaving ifstatement');
   end (*ifstatement*);

   procedure casestatement;

(*    Generates code and analyses a case statement.
      Sets up a case table of maximum size casetablemax.
      If a label appears an entry is put in the table (in the order of
      appearance) together with the current location counter.
      The table is dumped into the intermediate code on completion of
      analysis of the entire case statement.
*)

   var
      caseselectoritem : item;
      numoflabels, numofpaths, count, locofjumptocasetable : integer;
      casetable : array [1 .. casetablelemax] of record
                     val, startofcode : index
                  end;
      exittab : array [1 .. casetablelemax] of integer;

      procedure caselabel;

(*       Analyses an single case label. *)

      var
         lab : constantrecord;
         indextocasetable : integer;

      begin
         (* Get label. *)
         constant(fsys + [comma, colon], lab);

         if lab.typeofconstant <> caseselectoritem.typ then
            error(47) (* Wrong type *)
         else if numoflabels = casetablelemax then
            fatal(6)
         else begin
```

```
            numoflabels := numoflabels + 1;
            indextocasetable := 0;
            casetable[numoflabels].val := lab.ordinalvalue;
            casetable[numoflabels].startofcode := locationcounter;

            repeat
               indextocasetable := indextocasetable + 1
            until casetable[indextocasetable].val = lab.ordinalvalue;

            if indextocasetable < numoflabels then
               error(1); (* Multiple definition of label *)
         end
      end (*caselabel*);

      procedure onecase;

(*    Analyse all labels attached to a particular section of code. *)

      begin
         if sy in constbegsys then begin
            caselabel;

            while sy = comma do begin
               insymbol;
               caselabel
            end;

            if sy = colon then
               insymbol
            else error(5);

            (* Analyse statement (could be compound) following
               label(s).
            *)
            statement([semicolon, endsy] + fsys);
            numofpaths := numofpaths + 1;
            exittab[numofpaths] := locationcounter;
            emit(JumpInst)
         end
      end (*onecase*);

   begin
      if tracing then
         writeln('Entering casestatement');

      insymbol;
      numoflabels := 0;
      numofpaths := 0;

      (* Analyse case selector. *)
```

```
    expression(fsys + [ofsy, comma, colon], caseselectoritem);

    if not (caseselectoritem.typ in [ints, bools, chars, notyp]) then
      error(23);

    locofjumptocasetable := locationcounter;
    emit(SwitchInst); (* Switch - jump to appropriate entry in
      case table will fill in address of table later. *)

    if sy = ofsy then
      insymbol
    else error(8);

    onecase;

    while sy = semicolon do begin
      insymbol;
      onecase
    end;

    (* Fill in address of casetable in switch instruction. *)
    code[locofjumptocasetable].field2 := locationcounter;

    (* Now dump the table. *)
    for count := 1 to numoflabels do begin
      emit1(PbreakInst, casetable[count].val);
        (*pbreak - unexecutable*)
      emit1(PbreakInst, casetable[count].startofcode)
        (*pbreak - unexecutable*)
    end;

    emit1(JumpInst, 0); (*jump - this acts as a sentinel*)

    (* Go back and fill in address of start of next statement in
      the jump instruction which is generated at the end of each
      arm of the case statement.
     *)
    for count := 1 to numofpaths do
      code[exittab[count]].field2 := locationcounter;

    if sy = endsy then
      insymbol
    else error(57); (*end expected*)

    if tracing then
      writeln('Leaving casestatement');
  end (*casestatement*);

  procedure repeatstatement;
```

```
        var
          untilexpitem : item;
          locofrepeat : integer;

        begin
          if tracing then
            writeln('Entering repeatstatement');

          locofrepeat := locationcounter;
          insymbol;
          statement([semicolon, untilsy] + fsys);

          while sy in [semicolon] + statbegsys do begin
            if sy = semicolon then
              insymbol
            else error(14);

            statement([semicolon, untilsy] + fsys)
          end;

          if sy = untilsy then begin
            insymbol;
            (* Process boolean expression. *)
            expression(fsys, untilexpitem);

            if not (untilexpitem.typ in [bools, notyp]) then
              error(17);

            emit1(JmpfalInst, locofrepeat) (*jump if false*)
          end
          else error(53);

          if tracing then
            writeln('Leaving repeatstatement')
        end (*repeatstatement*);

        procedure whilestatement;

        var
          whileexpitem : item;
          locoftest, locofjumptoend : integer;

        begin
          if tracing then
            writeln('Entering whilestatement');

          insymbol;
          locoftest := locationcounter;

          (* Process boolean expression. *)
```

```
            expression(fsys + [dosy], whileexpitem);

            if not (whileexpitem.typ in [bools, notyp]) then
               error(17); (* Boolean type expected *)

            locofjumptoend := locationcounter;
            emit(JmpfalInst); (*jump if false. i.e. terminate loop*)

            if sy = dosy then
               insymbol
            else error(54);

            statement(fsys);
            emit1(JumpInst, locoftest); (*jump to test*)
            code[locofjumptoend].field2 := locationcounter;

            if tracing then
               writeln('Leaving whilestatement');
         end (*whilestatement*);

         procedure forstatement;

(*       Analyses for statements. Generates either forfup and forsup or
         forfdn and forsdn instructions depending on whether to or
         downto is used. Assuming to is used, forfup is generated after
         code has been generated to put the initial and final expressions
         on the stack. This instruction is executed only at the start of the
         loop to see if the loop is to be executed at all. forsup is generated
         at the end of the loop and is executed on completion of each
         iteration of the loop (the value of the final expression remains on
         the stack throughout). Thus the interpreter's code for forsup
         does all the hard work.
*)

         var
            controlvartype : types;
            expitem : item;
            opcode : opcodes;
            posinsymtable, locofcodetojumpout, locoffirststatinfor :
                                                   integer;

         begin
            if tracing then
               writeln('Entering forstatement');

            insymbol;

            if sy = ident then begin
               posinsymtable := locinsymboltable(lastidentread);
               insymbol;
```

```
            if posinsymtable = 0 then
               controlvartype := ints
            else if symboltable[posinsymtable].obj = variable then begin
               controlvartype := symboltable[posinsymtable].typ;

               if not symboltable[posinsymtable].normal then
                  error(37) (* Can't have var param as control var. *)
               else emit2(LodaddInst, symboltable[posinsymtable].lev,
                  symboltable[posinsymtable].adrr);
                     (* Load address of control variable.*)

               if not (controlvartype in [notyp, ints, bools, chars]) then
                  error(18) (* Must be one of above types *)
            end
            else begin
               error(37); (* Must have ident as control variable *)
               controlvartype := ints
            end
         end
         else skip([becomes, tosy, downtosy, dosy] + fsys, 2);

         if sy = becomes then begin
            insymbol;
            (* Process initial expression. *)
            expression([tosy, downtosy, dosy] + fsys, expitem);

            if expitem.typ <> controlvartype then
               error(19);
         end
         else skip([tosy, downtosy, dosy] + fsys, 51);

         opcode := ForfupInst; (*forfup*)

         if sy in [tosy, downtosy] then begin
            if sy = downtosy then
               opcode := ForfdnInst; (*forfdn*)

            insymbol;
            (* Analyse final expression. *)
            expression([dosy] + fsys, expitem);

            if expitem.typ <> controlvartype then
               error(19)
         end
         else skip([dosy] + fsys, 55);

         (* Will fill in jump out of loop later. *)
         locofcodetojumpout := locationcounter;
         emit(opcode);
```

```

      if sy = dosy then
        insymbol
      else error(54);

      (* Note start of code in loop. *)
      locoffirststatinfor := locationcounter;
      statement(fsys);
      (* Generates forsup or forfdn. *)
      if opcode = ForfupInst then
       emit1(ForsupInst, locoffirststatinfor)
      else
       emit1(ForsdnInst, locoffirststatinfor);
      (* Fill in jump out instruction. *)
      code[locofcodetojumpout].field2 := locationcounter;

      if tracing then
        writeln('Leaving forstatement')
    end (*forstatement*);

    procedure standproc (stanprocnum : integer);

(*  Deals with read, readln, write, writeln, reset and readln. Latter
    two not implemented in the interpreter.
*)

    var
      posinsymtable : integer;
      opcode : opcodes;
      mainparamitem, fieldwidthitem : item;

    begin
      if tracing then
        writeln('Entering stanproc');

      case stanprocnum of
        1, 2 :
          begin (*read or readln*)
            if not inputusedasprogparam then begin
              error(20); (* Can't do any reading if input not listed
                           in program parameter list. *)
              inputusedasprogparam := true
            end;

            if sy = lparent then begin
              repeat
                insymbol;

                if sy <> ident then
                  error(2)
```

```
            else begin
               posinsymtable := locinsymboltable(lastidentread);
               insymbol;

               if posinsymtable <> 0 then
                  if symboltable[posinsymtable].obj <> variable
                  then
                     error(37) (* Can only read into variables *)
                  else begin
                     mainparamitem.typ := symboltable[
                        posinsymtable].typ;
                     mainparamitem.ref := symboltable[
                        posinsymtable].ref;

                     if symboltable[posinsymtable].normal then
                        opcode := LodaddInst (*load address*)
                     else opcode := LodvalInst; (*load value*)

                     emit2(opcode, symboltable[posinsymtable].lev
                     , symboltable[posinsymtable].adrr);

                     if sy in [lbrack, lparent, period] then
                        selector(fsys + [comma, rparent],
                        (* Reading into a field of a record or
                           an array element. *)
                        mainparamitem);

                     if mainparamitem.typ in [ints, reals, chars,
                     notyp] then
                        emit1(ReadInst, ord(mainparamitem.typ))
                              (*read*)
                     else error(40)
                  end
            end;

            test([comma, rparent], fsys, 6);
         until sy <> comma;

         if sy = rparent then
            insymbol
         else error(4)
      end;

      if stanprocnum = 2 then
         emit(ReadlnInst) (*readln*)
   end;
3, 4 :
   begin (*write or writeln*)
      if sy = lparent then begin
         repeat
```

```
            insymbol;

            if sy = string then begin
              emit1(LdintInst, lengthoflaststring);
              emit1(WrstrgInst, posinstringtable);
              insymbol
            end
            else begin
              (* Process expression to be output. *)
              expression(fsys + [comma, colon, rparent],
              mainparamitem);

              if not (mainparamitem.typ in stantyps) then
                error(41);

              if sy = colon then begin
                insymbol;

                (* Process first fieldwidth. *)
                expression(fsys + [comma, colon, rparent],
                fieldwidthitem);

                if fieldwidthitem.typ <> ints then
                  error(43);

                if sy = colon then begin
                  if mainparamitem.typ <> reals then
                    error(42);

                  insymbol;

                  (* Process second fieldwidth parameter. *)
                  expression(fsys + [comma, rparent],
                  fieldwidthitem);

                  if fieldwidthitem.typ <> ints then
                    error(43);

                  emit(Wr2fldInst)
                    (* Write with 2 fieldwidth parameters. *)
                end
                else emit1(Wr1fldInst, ord(mainparamitem.typ))
                 (* Write with 1 fieldwidth parameter. *)
              end
              else emit1(WriteInst, ord(mainparamitem.typ))
                (* Write with no fieldwidth parameters. *)
            end
          until sy <> comma;

          if sy = rparent then
```

```
                     insymbol
                  else error(4)
               end;

               if stanprocnum = 4 then
                  emit(WritlnInst) (*writeln*)
            end;
         5 :
            begin (* reset *)
               repeat
                  insymbol
               until sy = rparent;

               if line[charactercount - 3] = 'y' then
                  emit(Reset1Inst) (*NOT IMPLEMENTED*)
               else emit(Reset2Inst); (*NOT IMPLEMENTED*)

               insymbol;
            end;
         6 :
            begin (* rewrite *)
               repeat
                  insymbol
               until sy = rparent;

               if line[charactercount - 3] = 'y' then
                  emit(Rewrt1Inst) (*NOT IMPLEMENTED*)
               else emit(Rewrt2Inst); (*NOT IMPLEMENTED*)

               insymbol;
            end;
         7 :
            begin
               emit(PbreakInst);
            end;
      end; (*case*)

      if tracing then
         writeln('Leaving standproc')
   end (*standproc*);

begin (*statement*)
   if tracing then
      writeln('Entering statement');

   if sy in statbegsys + [ident] then
      case sy of
         ident :
            (* Could be assignment or procedure call. *)
            begin
```

```
                    posinsymtable := locinsymboltable(lastidentread);
                    insymbol;

                    if posinsymtable <> 0 then
                       case symboltable[posinsymtable].obj of
                          konstant, atype : error(45);
                          variable : assignment(symboltable[posinsymtable].lev,
                             symboltable[posinsymtable].adrr, posinsymtable);
                          prozedure :
                             if symboltable[posinsymtable].lev <> 0 then
                                call(fsys, posinsymtable)
                             else standproc(symboltable[posinsymtable].adrr);
                          funktion :
                             if symboltable[posinsymtable].ref = display[level]
                             then
                                assignment(symboltable[posinsymtable].lev + 1,
                                0, posinsymtable)
                             else error(45)
                       end
                 end;
              beginsy : compoundstatement;
              ifsy : ifstatement;
              casesy : casestatement;
              whilesy : whilestatement;
              repeatsy : repeatstatement;
              forsy : forstatement;
           end;

        test(fsys, [], 14);

        if tracing then
           writeln('Leaving statement');
     end (*statement*);

  begin (*block*)
     if tracing then
        writeln('Entering block');

     spaceforlocals := 5; (* 5 locations used for houskeeping. See
          declaration of stack in interpret for uses of these locations. *)
     symtabindexatentry := currsymtablesize;

     if level > maxlevel then
        fatal(5);

     test([lparent, colon, semicolon], fsys, 14);
     enterblock;
     display[level] := currblocktablesize;
     blocktabindexatentry := currblocktablesize;
     symboltable[symtabindexatentry].typ := notyp;
```

```
symboltable[symtabindexatentry].ref := blocktabindexatentry;

if (sy = lparent) and (level > 1) then
  parameterlist;

blocktable[blocktabindexatentry].indexsymtablastparam := currsymtablesize;
blocktable[blocktabindexatentry].spaceforparams := spaceforlocals;

if isfunction then
  if sy = colon then begin
    insymbol; (*function type*)

    if sy = ident then begin
      posinsymboltable := locinsymboltable(lastidentread);
      insymbol;

      if posinsymboltable <> 0 then
        if symboltable[posinsymboltable].obj <> atype then
          error(29) (* Must be a type *)
        else if symboltable[posinsymboltable].typ in stantyps then
          symboltable[symtabindexatentry].typ := symboltable[
            posinsymboltable].typ
        else error(15)
    end
    else skip([semicolon] + fsys, 2)
  end
  else error(5);

if sy = semicolon then
  insymbol
else error(14);


repeat
  if sy = constsy then
    constntdeclaration;

  if sy = typesy then
    typedeclaration;

  if sy = varsy then
    variabldeclaration;

  blocktable[blocktabindexatentry].variablesize := spaceforlocals;

  while sy in [prosedurésy, funcsionsy] do
    procdeclaration;

  test([beginsy], blockbegsys + statbegsys, 56)
until sy in statbegsys;
```

```

      symboltable[symtabindexatentry].adrr := locationcounter;
      insymbol;
      statement([semicolon, endsy] + fsys);

      while sy in [semicolon] + statbegsys do begin
        if sy = semicolon then
          insymbol
        else error(14);

        statement([semicolon, endsy] + fsys)
      end;

      if sy = endsy then
        insymbol
      else error(57); (*end expected*)

      test(fsys + [period], [], 6);

      if tracing then
        writeln('Leaving block');
    end; (*block*)

(*------------------------------------------------------------interpret--*)

    procedure interpret;

(*  Intermediate code interpreter. Called only once and only if
    the user's program has no errors.
    Global:   code, symboltable, blocktable
*)

    var
      currentinstruction : instruction; (*instruction buffer*)
      progcounter : integer;            (*program counter*)
      programstatus : (running, finishwithouterrors, nocaselabelerror,
                       dividebyOerror, outofrangeerror, stackfullerror,
                       toomanylinesoutputerror, linetoolongerror,
                       noreadingpasteoferror);
      topofstack : integer;             (*top stack index*)
      baseofcurrentstackframe : integer; (*base index*)
      countofnumofinputlines, numofinstrsexecuted, numofcharsoutputoncurrentline
      : integer;                        (*counters*)
      h1, h2, h3, h4 : integer;
                     (* These can be regarded as local variables
                        to each arm of the case statement, i.e. they
                        do not retain values between iterations of the
                        repeat loop. *)
      linenumber : integer;
      defaultfieldwidths : array [1 .. 4] of integer;
```

```
    display : array [1 .. maxlevel] of integer;
    stack : array [1 .. stacksize] of record
            case tp : types of
              ints : (i : integer);
              reals : (r : real);
              bools : (b : boolean);
              chars : (c : char);
              notyp, arrays, records : ()
          end;

    procedure dump;

(*  Print contents of all stack frames. *)

      var
        baseofstackframe, indexofblockinsymboltable, indextovar,
        actuallocation : integer;

      begin

      baseofstackframe := baseofcurrentstackframe;

      repeat
        writeln;
        (* Pick up reference to symboltable. *)
        indexofblockinsymboltable := stack[baseofstackframe + 4].i;

        if baseofstackframe > 0 then
          writeln(' ', symboltable[indexofblockinsymboltable].name,
                ' called at', stack[baseofstackframe + 1].i : 5);

        indextovar := blocktable[symboltable[indexofblockinsymboltable].
                  ref].indexsymtaboflastobj;

        while indextovar <> 0 do
          with symboltable[indextovar] do begin
            if obj = variable then
              if typ in stantyps then begin
                write(' ' : 4, name, ' = ');

                if normal then (*i.e. not a variable param*)
                  actuallocation := baseofstackframe + adrr
                else actuallocation := stack[baseofstackframe + adrr].i;

                case typ of
                  ints : writeln(stack[actuallocation].i);
                  reals : writeln(stack[actuallocation].r);
                  bools : writeln(stack[actuallocation].b);
                  chars : writeln(stack[actuallocation].c)
                end; (*case*)
```

```
                    end;

                (* Get reference to next variable at this level. *)
                indextovar := link
              end;

            (* Pick up dynamic link. *)
            baseofstackframe := stack[baseofstackframe + 3].i;
          until baseofstackframe < 0
          end; (*dump*)

    begin (*interpret*)
      for linenumber := 0 to linecounter do
        profile[linenumber] := 0;

      (* Do initialization of variables and stack. *)
      stack[1].tp := ints;
      stack[1].i := 0;
      stack[2].tp := ints;
      stack[2].i := 0;
      stack[3].tp := ints;
      stack[3].i := -1;
      stack[4].tp := ints;
      stack[4].i := blocktable[1].indexsymtaboflastobj;
      baseofcurrentstackframe := 0;
      display[1] := 0;
      topofstack := blocktable[2].variablesize - 1;
      progcounter := symboltable[stack[4].i].adrr;
      programstatus := running;
      countofnumofinputlines := 0;
      numofinstrsexecuted := 0;
      numofcharsoutputoncurrentline := 0;
      defaultfieldwidths[1] := 10;
      defaultfieldwidths[2] := 22;
      defaultfieldwidths[3] := 10;
      defaultfieldwidths[4] := 1;

      (* Start of main interpreter loop. *)
      repeat
        currentinstruction := code[progcounter];
        numofinstrsexecuted := numofinstrsexecuted + 1;
        profile[linerror[progcounter]] := profile[linerror[progcounter]] + 1;
        progcounter := progcounter + 1;

        case currentinstruction.opcode of
          LodaddInst : (*load address*)
            begin
              topofstack := topofstack + 1;

              if topofstack > stacksize then
```

```
                    programstatus := stackfullerror
                 else with stack[topofstack] do begin
                    tp := ints;
                    i := display[currentinstruction.field1]
                          + currentinstruction.field2;
                 end;
              end;
           LodvalInst : (*load value*)
              begin
                 topofstack := topofstack + 1;

                 if topofstack > stacksize then
                    programstatus := stackfullerror
                 else stack[topofstack] := stack[display[currentinstruction.
                       field1] + currentinstruction.field2]
              end;
           LodindInst : (*load indirect, where address is given in
                          the two fields*)
              begin
                 topofstack := topofstack + 1;

                 if topofstack > stacksize then
                    programstatus := stackfullerror
                 else stack[topofstack] :=
                          stack[stack[display[currentinstruction.field1] +
                             currentinstruction.field2].i]
              end;
           UpddisInst : (*update display*)
              begin
                 h1 := currentinstruction.field2;
                 h2 := currentinstruction.field1;
                 h3 := baseofcurrentstackframe;

                 repeat
                    display[h1] := h3;
                    h1 := h1 - 1;
                    h3 := stack[h3 + 2].i
                 until h1 = h2
              end;

(*         Reset1Inst:reset(input)
           Reset2Inst:reset(input)
           Rewrt1Inst:rewrite(output)
           Rewrt2Inst:rewrite(output) *)

           StfuncInst : (*standard function*)
              case currentinstruction.field2 of
                 0 : stack[topofstack].i := abs(stack[topofstack].i);
                 1 : stack[topofstack].r := abs(stack[topofstack].r);
                 2 : stack[topofstack].i := sqr(stack[topofstack].i);
```

```
        3 : stack[topofstack].r := sqr(stack[topofstack].r);
        4 : with stack[topofstack] do begin
              tp := bools;
              b := odd(i);
            end;
        5 : with stack[topofstack] do
              if (i < ordvaloffirstchar) or
                 (i > ordvaloflastchar) then
                 programstatus := outofrangeerror
              else begin
                tp := chars;
                c := chr(i);
              end;
        6 : with stack[topofstack] do begin
              case tp of
                ints: (* empty *);
                chars: i := ord(c);
                bools: i := ord(b);
              end;
              tp := ints;
            end;
        7 : with stack[topofstack] do
              case tp of
                ints: i := succ(i);
                chars: c := succ(c);
                bools: b := succ(b);
              end;
        8 : with stack[topofstack] do
              case tp of
                ints: i := pred(i);
                chars: c := pred(c);
                bools: b := pred(b);
              end;
        9 : with stack[topofstack] do begin
              tp := ints;
              i := round(r);
            end;
        10 : with stack[topofstack] do begin
              tp := ints;
              i := trunc(r);
            end;
        11 : stack[topofstack].r := sin(stack[topofstack].r);
        12 : stack[topofstack].r := cos(stack[topofstack].r);
        13 : stack[topofstack].r := exp(stack[topofstack].r);
        14 : stack[topofstack].r := ln(stack[topofstack].r);
        15 : stack[topofstack].r := sqrt(stack[topofstack].r);
        16 : stack[topofstack].r := arctan(stack[topofstack].r);
        17 : (*eof*)
            begin
              topofstack := topofstack + 1;
```

```
                    if topofstack > stacksize then
                       programstatus := stackfullerror
                    else with stack[topofstack] do begin
                       tp := bools;
                       b := eof(input);
                    end;
                 end;
              18 : (*eoln*)
                 begin
                    topofstack := topofstack + 1;

                    if topofstack > stacksize then
                       programstatus := stackfullerror
                    else with stack[topofstack] do begin
                       tp := bools;
                       b := eoln(input);
                    end;
                 end;
           end;
        OffsetInst : (*offset*)
          stack[topofstack].i := stack[topofstack].i + currentinstruction.
             field2;
        JumpInst : (*jump*)
           progcounter := currentinstruction.field2;
        JmpfalInst : (*jump if false*)
           begin
              if not stack[topofstack].b then
                 progcounter := currentinstruction.field2;

              topofstack := topofstack - 1
           end;
        SwitchInst : (*switch*)
           begin
              (* Get value of selector. *)
              with stack[topofstack] do
                case tp of
                  ints: h1 := i;
                  chars: h1 := ord(c);
                  bools: h1 := ord(b)
                end;
              topofstack := topofstack - 1;

              (* Get base of case table. *)
              h2 := currentinstruction.field2;
              h3 := 0;

              repeat
                 (* If not within case table then run-time error. *)
                 if code[h2].opcode <> PbreakInst then begin
```

```
                  h3 := 1;
                  programstatus := nocaselabelerror
                end
                else if code[h2].field2 = h1 then begin
                  (* Found value of selector in case table. Now go
                     to code attached to that label. *)
                  h3 := 1;
                  progcounter := code[h2 + 1].field2
                end
                else h2 := h2 + 2
              until h3 <> 0
            end;
          PbreakInst : (*pbreak*)
            begin
              write('break at', linerror[progcounter] - 1 : 5);
              dump
            end;
          ForfupInst : (*for first up*)
            begin
              with stack[topofstack - 1] do
                case tp of
                  ints: h1 := i;
                  chars: h1 := ord(c);
                  bools: h1 := ord(b);
                end;

              with stack[topofstack] do
                case tp of
                  ints: h2 := i;
                  chars: h2 := ord(c);
                  bools: h2 := ord(b);
                end;

              if h1 <= h2 then
                stack[stack[topofstack - 2].i] := stack[topofstack - 1]
              else begin
                (* Loop never to be executed. *)
                topofstack := topofstack - 3;
                progcounter := currentinstruction.field2
              end
            end;
          ForsupInst : (*for second up*)
            begin
              (* Get the address of the control
                 variable. *)
              h2 := stack[topofstack - 2].i;

              (* Increment the current value in the control variable. *)
              with stack[h2] do
                case tp of
```

```
            ints: h1 := i + 1;
            chars: h1 := ord(c) + 1;
            bools: h1 := ord(b) + 1;
          end;

        with stack[topofstack] do
          case tp of
            ints: h3 := i;
            chars: h3 := ord(c);
            bools: h3 := ord(b);
          end;

        (* Compare with the value of the final expression. *)
        if h1 <= h3 then begin
          (* Go round loop again. *)
          with stack[h2] do
            case tp of
              ints: i := h1;
              chars: c := chr(h1);
              bools: b := (h1 = 1);
            end;
          progcounter := currentinstruction.field2
        end
        else topofstack := topofstack - 3;
      end;
    ForfdnInst : (*for first down*)
      begin
        with stack[topofstack - 1] do
          case tp of
            ints: h1 := i;
            chars: h1 := ord(c);
            bools: h1 := ord(b);
          end;

        with stack[topofstack] do
          case tp of
            ints: h2 := i;
            chars: h2 := ord(c);
            bools: h2 := ord(b);
          end;

        if h1 >= h2 then
          stack[stack[topofstack - 2].i] := stack[topofstack - 1]
        else begin
          (* Loop never to be executed. *)
          progcounter := currentinstruction.field2;
          topofstack := topofstack - 3
        end
      end;
    ForsdnInst : (*for second down*)
```

```
            begin
              h2 := stack[topofstack - 2].i;
              with stack[h2] do
                case tp of
                  ints: h1 := i - 1;
                  chars: h1 := ord(c) - 1;
                  bools: h1 := ord(b) - 1;
                end;

              with stack[topofstack] do
                case tp of
                  ints: h3 := i;
                  chars: h3 := ord(c);
                  bools: h3 := ord(b);
                end;

              if h1 >= h3 then begin
                (* Go round loop again. *)
                with stack[h2] do
                  case tp of
                    ints: i := h1;
                    chars: c := chr(h1);
                    bools: b := (h1 = 1);
                  end;
                progcounter := currentinstruction.field2
              end
              else topofstack := topofstack - 3;
            end;
          MarkstInst : (*mark stack in preparation for function or
                        procedure call*)
            begin
              h1 := blocktable[symboltable[currentinstruction.field2].ref].
                variablesize;

              if topofstack + h1 > stacksize then
                programstatus := stackfullerror
              else begin
                topofstack := topofstack + 5;

                (* Leave size of variables in called routine on the
                   stack for call to pick up.
                *)
                stack[topofstack - 1].tp := ints;
                stack[topofstack - 1].i := h1 - 1;
                stack[topofstack].tp := ints;
                stack[topofstack].i := currentinstruction.field2
              end
            end;
          CallInst : (*call a procedure or function*)
            begin
```

```
                (* h1 to point to base of new stack frame. *)
                h1 := topofstack - currentinstruction.field2;

                (* h2 points to symboltable. *)
                h2 := stack[h1 + 4].i;

                (* Obtain static level of called routine. *)
                h3 := symboltable[h2].lev;

                (* Adjust appropriate element of display. *)
                display[h3 + 1] := h1;

                (* Pick up amount of space required for called routine.
                   This was left on the stack by code for markst instruction.
                   h4 will now be new topofstack.
                *)
                h4 := stack[h1 + 3].i + h1;

                (* Put return address on stack. *)
                stack[h1 + 1].tp := ints;
                stack[h1 + 1].i := progcounter;

                (* Put static link on stack. *)
                stack[h1 + 2].tp := ints;
                stack[h1 + 2].i := display[h3];

                (* Put dynamic link on stack. *)
                stack[h1 + 3].tp := ints;
                stack[h1 + 3].i := baseofcurrentstackframe;

                (* Initialize all variables. *)
                for h3 := topofstack + 1 to h4 do begin
                   stack[h3].tp := ints;
                   stack[h3].i := 0;
                end;

                baseofcurrentstackframe := h1;
                topofstack := h4;
                progcounter := symboltable[h2].adrr
             end;
          Index1Inst : (*index1 - a one-dimensional array*)
             begin
                h1 := currentinstruction.field2; (*h1 points to arraytable*)
                h2 := arraytable[h1].low;
                with stack[topofstack] do
                  case tp of
                    ints: h3 := i;
                    chars: h3 := ord(c);
                    bools: h3 := ord(b)
                  end;
```

```

        if h3 < h2 then
          programstatus := outofrangeerror
        else if h3 > arraytable[h1].high then
          programstatus := outofrangeerror
        else begin
          topofstack := topofstack - 1;
          stack[topofstack].i := stack[topofstack].i + (h3 - h2)
        end
      end;
    IndexmInst : (*indexm - a multi-dimensional array*)
      begin
        (*h1 points to arraytable*)
        h1 := currentinstruction.field2;
        h2 := arraytable[h1].low;
        with stack[topofstack] do
          case tp of
            ints: h3 := i;
            chars: h3 := ord(c);
            bools: h3 := ord(b)
          end;

        if h3 < h2 then
          programstatus := outofrangeerror
        else if h3 > arraytable[h1].high then
          programstatus := outofrangeerror
        else begin
          topofstack := topofstack - 1;
          stack[topofstack].i := stack[topofstack].i + (h3 - h2) *
            arraytable[h1].elsize
        end
      end;
    LoadblInst : (*load block*)
      begin
        h1 := stack[topofstack].i;
        topofstack := topofstack - 1;
        h2 := currentinstruction.field2 + topofstack;

        if h2 > stacksize then
          programstatus := stackfullerror
        else
          while topofstack < h2 do begin
            topofstack := topofstack + 1;
            stack[topofstack] := stack[h1];
            h1 := h1 + 1
          end
      end;
    CopyblInst : (*copy block*)
      begin
        h1 := stack[topofstack - 1].i;
```

```
                h2 := stack[topofstack].i;
                h3 := h1 + currentinstruction.field2;

                while h1 < h3 do begin
                   stack[h1] := stack[h2];
                   h1 := h1 + 1;
                   h2 := h2 + 1
                end;

                topofstack := topofstack - 2
             end;
          LdintInst : (*load integer onto stack*)
             begin
                topofstack := topofstack + 1;

                if topofstack > stacksize then
                   programstatus := stackfullerror
                else with stack[topofstack] do begin
                   tp := ints;
                   i := currentinstruction.field2;
                end;
             end;
          LdcharInst : (*load character onto stack*)
             begin
                topofstack := topofstack + 1;

                if topofstack > stacksize then
                   programstatus := stackfullerror
                else with stack[topofstack] do begin
                   tp := chars;
                   c := chr(currentinstruction.field2);
                end;
             end;
          LdboolInst : (*load boolean onto stack*)
             begin
                topofstack := topofstack + 1;

                if topofstack > stacksize then
                   programstatus := stackfullerror
                else with stack[topofstack] do begin
                   tp := bools;
                   b := (currentinstruction.field2 = 1);
                end;
             end;
          LdrealInst : (*load real onto stack*)
             begin
                topofstack := topofstack + 1;

                if topofstack > stacksize then
                   programstatus := stackfullerror
```

```
      else with stack[topofstack] do begin
        tp := reals;
        r := realconsttable[currentinstruction.field2];
      end;
    end;
  FloatInst : (*float*)
    begin
      h1 := topofstack - currentinstruction.field2;
      with stack[h1] do begin
        tp := reals;
        r := i;
      end;
    end;
  ReadInst : (*read*)
    begin
      if eof(input) then programstatus := noreadingpasteoferror
      else
        with stack[stack[topofstack].i] do
          case currentinstruction.field2 of
            1 : begin
                  tp := ints;
                  read(i);
                end;
            2 : begin
                  tp := reals;
                  read(r);
                end;
            4 : begin
                  tp := chars;
                  read(c);
                end;
          end;

      topofstack := topofstack - 1
    end;
  WrstrgInst : (*write string*)
    begin
      h1 := stack[topofstack].i;
      h2 := currentinstruction.field2:
      topofstack := topofstack - 1;
      numofcharsoutputoncurrentline := numofcharsoutputoncurrentline
        + h1;

      if numofcharsoutputoncurrentline > outputlinelength then
        programstatus := linetoolongerror;

      repeat
        write(stringtable[h2]);
        h1 := h1 - 1;
        h2 := h2 + 1
```

```
            until hl = 0
         end;
      WriteInst : (*write - no fieldwidth parameter*)
         begin
            numofcharsoutputoncurrentline := numofcharsoutputoncurrentline
               + defaultfieldwidths[currentinstruction.field2];
            if numofcharsoutputoncurrentline > outputlinelength then
               programstatus := linetoolongerror
            else
               case currentinstruction.field2 of
                  1 : write(stack[topofstack].i : defaultfieldwidths[1]);
                  2 : write(stack[topofstack].r : defaultfieldwidths[2]);
                  3 : write(stack[topofstack].b : defaultfieldwidths[3]);
                  4 : write(stack[topofstack].c);
               end;
            topofstack := topofstack - 1;
         end;
      Wr1fldInst : (*write with one fieldwidth parameter*)
         begin
            numofcharsoutputoncurrentline := numofcharsoutputoncurrentline
               + stack[topofstack].i;
            if numofcharsoutputoncurrentline > outputlinelength then
               programstatus := linetoolongerror
            else
               case currentinstruction.field2 of
                  1 : write(stack[topofstack - 1].i : stack[topofstack].i)
                     ;
                  2 : write(stack[topofstack - 1].r : stack[topofstack].i)
                     ;
                  3 : write(stack[topofstack - 1].b : stack[topofstack].i)
                     ;
                  4 : write(stack[topofstack - 1].c : stack[topofstack].i)
                     ;
               end; (*case*)
            topofstack := topofstack - 2
         end;
      HaltInst : (*halt*)
         programstatus := finishwithouterrors;
      LeavepInst : (*exit procedure*)
         begin
            topofstack := baseofcurrentstackframe - 1;
            progcounter := stack[baseofcurrentstackframe + 1].i;
            baseofcurrentstackframe := stack[baseofcurrentstackframe + 3].
               i
         end;
      LeavefInst : (*exit function*)
```

```
        begin
          topofstack := baseofcurrentstackframe;
          progcounter := stack[baseofcurrentstackframe + 1].i;
          baseofcurrentstackframe := stack[baseofcurrentstackframe + 3].
            i
        end;
      LodinsInst : (*load indirect, where address is on top of the stack*)
        stack[topofstack] := stack[stack[topofstack].i];
      NotInst : (*not*)
        stack[topofstack].b := not stack[topofstack].b;
      NegateInst : (*negate*)
        stack[topofstack].i := -stack[topofstack].i;
      Wr2fldInst : (*write a real with 2 fieldwidth parameters*)
        begin
          numofcharsoutputoncurrentline := numofcharsoutputoncurrentline
            + stack[topofstack - 1].i;
          if numofcharsoutputoncurrentline > outputlinelength then
            programstatus := linetoolongerror
          else write(stack[topofstack - 2].r : stack[topofstack - 1].i :
            stack[topofstack].i);

          topofstack := topofstack - 3
        end;
      StoreInst : (*store*)
        begin
          stack[stack[topofstack - 1].i] := stack[topofstack];
          topofstack := topofstack - 2
        end;
      EqualrInst : (*equality of reals*)
        begin
          topofstack := topofstack - 1;
          with stack[topofstack] do begin
            tp := bools;
            b := r = stack[topofstack + 1].r;
          end;
        end;
      NoteqrInst : (*inequality of reals*)
        begin
          topofstack := topofstack - 1;
          with stack[topofstack] do begin
            tp := bools;
            b := r <> stack[topofstack + 1].r;
          end;
        end;
      LessrInst : (*less than for reals*)
        begin
          topofstack := topofstack - 1;
          with stack[topofstack] do begin
            tp := bools;
            b := r < stack[topofstack + 1].r;
```

```
            end;
         end;
      LesserInst : (*less then or equal to for reals*)
         begin
            topofstack := topofstack - 1;
            with stack[topofstack] do begin
              tp := bools;
              b := r <= stack[topofstack + 1].r;
            end;
         end;
      GrealInst : (*greater than for reals*)
         begin
            topofstack := topofstack - 1;
            with stack[topofstack] do begin
              tp := bools;
              b := r > stack[topofstack + 1].r;
            end;
         end;
      GerealInst : (*greater than or equal to for reals*)
         begin
            topofstack := topofstack - 1;
            with stack[topofstack] do begin
              tp := bools;
              b := r >= stack[topofstack + 1].r;
            end;
         end;
      EqualInst : (*equality of ordinals*)
         begin
            topofstack := topofstack - 1;
            with stack[topofstack] do begin
              case tp of
                ints: b := i = stack[topofstack + 1].i;
                chars: b := c = stack[topofstack + 1].c;
                bools: b := b = stack[topofstack + 1].b;
              end;
              tp := bools;
            end;
         end;
      NotequInst : (*inequality of ordinals*)
         begin
            topofstack := topofstack - 1;
            with stack[topofstack] do begin
              case tp of
                ints: b := i <> stack[topofstack + 1].i;
                chars: b := c <> stack[topofstack + 1].c;
                bools: b := b <> stack[topofstack + 1].b;
              end;
              tp := bools;
            end;
         end;
```

```
LessthInst : (*less than for ordinals*)
    begin
        topofstack := topofstack - 1;
        with stack[topofstack] do begin
            case tp of
                ints: b := i < stack[topofstack + 1].i;
                chars: b := c < stack[topofstack + 1].c;
                bools: b := b < stack[topofstack + 1].b;
            end;
            tp := bools;
        end;
    end;
LesseqInst : (*less than or equal to for ordinals*)
    begin
        topofstack := topofstack - 1;
        with stack[topofstack] do begin
            case tp of
                ints: b := i <= stack[topofstack + 1].i;
                chars: b := c <= stack[topofstack + 1].c;
                bools: b := b <= stack[topofstack + 1].b;
            end;
            tp := bools;
        end;
    end;
GreatlInst : (*greater than for ordinals*)
    begin
        topofstack := topofstack - 1;
        with stack[topofstack] do begin
            case tp of
                ints: b := i > stack[topofstack + 1].i;
                chars: b := c > stack[topofstack + 1].c;
                bools: b := b > stack[topofstack + 1].b;
            end;
            tp := bools;
        end;
    end;
GreateInst : (*greater than or equal to for ordinals*)
    begin
        topofstack := topofstack - 1;
        with stack[topofstack] do begin
            case tp of
                ints: b := i >= stack[topofstack + 1].i;
                chars: b := c >= stack[topofstack + 1].c;
                bools: b := b >= stack[topofstack + 1].b;
            end;
            tp := bools;
        end;
    end;
OrInst : (*or*)
    begin
```

```
                topofstack := topofstack - 1;
                stack[topofstack].b := stack[topofstack].b or stack[topofstack
                   + 1].b
             end;
          AddInst : (* + for ordinals*)
             begin
                topofstack := topofstack - 1;
                stack[topofstack].i := stack[topofstack].i + stack[topofstack
                   + 1].i;
             end;
          SubInst : (* - for ordinals*)
             begin
                topofstack := topofstack - 1;
                stack[topofstack].i := stack[topofstack].i - stack[topofstack
                   + 1].i
             end;
          AddrealInst : (* + for reals*)
             begin
                topofstack := topofstack - 1;
                stack[topofstack].r := stack[topofstack].r + stack[topofstack
                   + 1].r;
             end;
          SubrealInst : (* - for reals*)
             begin
                topofstack := topofstack - 1;
                stack[topofstack].r := stack[topofstack].r - stack[topofstack
                   + 1].r;
             end;
          AndInst : (*and*)
             begin
                topofstack := topofstack - 1;
                stack[topofstack].b := stack[topofstack].b and stack[
                   topofstack + 1].b
             end;
          MultInst : (* * for ordinals*)
             begin
                topofstack := topofstack - 1;
                stack[topofstack].i := stack[topofstack].i * stack[topofstack
                   + 1].i
             end;
          DivInst : (*div*)
             begin
                topofstack := topofstack - 1;

                if stack[topofstack + 1].i = 0 then
                   programstatus := divideby0error
                else stack[topofstack].i := stack[topofstack].i div stack[
                      topofstack + 1].i
             end;
          ModInst : (*mod*)
```

```
                begin
                    topofstack := topofstack - 1;

                    if stack[topofstack + 1].i = 0 then
                        programstatus := divideby0error
                    else stack[topofstack].i := stack[topofstack].i mod stack[
                            topofstack + 1].i
                end;
            MultrInst : (* * for reals*)
                begin
                    topofstack := topofstack - 1;
                    stack[topofstack].r := stack[topofstack].r * stack[topofstack
                        + 1].r;
                end;
            RdivInst : (* / for reals*)
                begin
                    topofstack := topofstack - 1;

                    if stack[topofstack + 1].r = 0 then
                        programstatus := divideby0error
                    else
                        stack[topofstack].r := stack[topofstack].r /
                            stack[topofstack + 1].r;
                end;
            ReadlnInst : (*readln*)
                if eof(input) then
                    programstatus := noreadingpasteoferror
                else readln;
            WritlnInst : (*writeln*)
                begin
                    writeln;
                    countofnumofinputlines := countofnumofinputlines + 1;
                    numofcharsoutputoncurrentline := 0;

                    if countofnumofinputlines > maxnumofinputlines then
                        programstatus := toomanylinesoutputerror
                end;
            NegatrInst : (*negate a real*)
                    stack[topofstack].r := -stack[topofstack].r;
        end (*case*);
    until programstatus <> running;

    if programstatus <> finishwithouterrors then begin
        writeln;
        write('halt at line ', linerror[progcounter] - 1 : 1,
        ' of source because of ');

        case programstatus of
            nocaselabelerror : writeln('no label for this case value');
            divideby0error : writeln('division by 0');
```

```
            outofrangeerror : writeln('index is out of bounds');
            stackfullerror :
               writeln('interpreter''s stack is not large enough');
            toomanylinesoutputerror : writeln('too much output');
            linetoolongerror : writeln('line too long');
            noreadingpasteoferror :
               writeln('attempt to read passed end of file');
         end;
         writeln;
         writeln('Post-Mortem Dump');
         writeln('****************');
         dump
      end;

      writeln(numofinstrsexecuted : 1, ' instructions executed');
   end (*interpret*);

   procedure printtables;

(* Used as a diagnostic aid. Prints out copies of all tables
   including the intermediate code. The latter is stored as
   integers in a record, but here is translated into suitable
   mnemonics.
*)

   var
      count : integer;
      currentinstr : instruction;
      instr : array [opcodes] of packed array [1 .. 6] of char;

      procedure initinstructions;

      begin
         instr[LodaddInst] := 'lodadd';
         instr[LodvalInst] := 'lodval';
         instr[LodindInst] := 'lodind';
         instr[UpddisInst] := 'upddis';
         instr[Reset1Inst] := 'NOTIMP';
         instr[Reset2Inst] := 'NOTIMP';
         instr[Rewrt1Inst] := 'NOTIMP';
         instr[Rewrt2Inst] := 'NOTIMP';
         instr[StfuncInst] := 'stfunc';
         instr[OffsetInst] := 'offset';
         instr[JumpInst] := 'jump  ';
         instr[JmpfalInst] := 'jmpfal';
         instr[SwitchInst] := 'switch';
         instr[PbreakInst] := 'pbreak';
         instr[ForfupInst] := 'forfup';
         instr[ForsupInst] := 'forsup';
         instr[ForfdnInst] := 'forfdn';
```

```
instr[ForsdnInst] := 'forsdn';
instr[MarkstInst] := 'markst';
instr[CallInst] := 'call  ';
instr[Index1Inst] := 'index1';
instr[IndexmInst] := 'indexm';
instr[LoadblInst] := 'loadbl';
instr[CopyblInst] := 'copybl';
instr[LdintInst] := 'ldint ';
instr[LdcharInst] := 'ldchar';
instr[LdboolInst] := 'ldbool';
instr[LdrealInst] := 'ldreal';
instr[FloatInst] := 'float ';
instr[ReadInst] := 'read  ';
instr[WrstrgInst] := 'wrstrg';
instr[WriteInst] := 'write ';
instr[Wr1fldInst] := 'wr1fld';
instr[HaltInst] := 'halt  ';
instr[LeavepInst] := 'leavep';
instr[LeavefInst] := 'leavef';
instr[LodinsInst] := 'lodins';
instr[NotInst] := 'not   ';
instr[NegateInst] := 'negate';
instr[Wr2fldInst] := 'wr2fld';
instr[StoreInst] := 'store ';
instr[EqualrInst] := 'equalr';
instr[NoteqrInst] := 'noteqr';
instr[LessrInst] := 'lessr ';
instr[LesserInst] := 'lesser';
instr[GrealInst] := 'greal ';
instr[GerealInst] := 'gereal';
instr[EqualInst] := 'equal ';
instr[NotequInst] := 'notequ';
instr[LessthInst] := 'lessth';
instr[LesseqInst] := 'lesseq';
instr[GreattInst] := 'greatt';
instr[GreateInst] := 'greate';
instr[OrInst] := 'or    ';
instr[AddInst] := 'add   ';
instr[SubInst] := 'sub   ';
instr[AddreaInst] := 'addrea';
instr[SubreaInst] := 'subrea';
instr[AndInst] := 'and   ';
instr[MultInst] := 'mult  ';
instr[DivInst] := 'div   ';
instr[ModInst] := 'mod   ';
instr[MultrInst] := 'multr ';
instr[RdivInst] := 'rdiv  ';
instr[ReadlnInst] := 'readln';
instr[WritlnInst] := 'writln';
instr[NegatrInst] := 'negatr';
```

```
    end; (*initinstructions*)

  begin
    initinstructions;
    writeln('Tables for program named ', progname);
    writeln;
    writeln(' identifiers', '          link', ' obj  typ  ref',
    ' nrm  lev  adrr');

    for count := blocktable[1].indexsymtaboflastobj + 1 to currsymtablesize do
      with symboltable[count] do
        writeln(count, ' ', name, link : 5, ord(obj) : 5, ord(typ) : 5, ref
        : 5, ord(normal) : 5, lev : 5, adrr : 5);

    writeln(' blocks     last', ' lpar psze vsze');

    for count := 1 to currblocktablesize do
      with blocktable[count] do
        writeln(count, indexsymtaboflastobj : 5, indexsymtablastparam : 5,
        spaceforparams : 5, variablesize : 5);

    writeln(' arrays     xtyp', ' etyp eref  low', ' high elsz size');

    for count := 1 to currarraytablesize do
      with arraytable[count] do
        writeln(count, ord(inxtyp) : 5, ord(eltyp) : 5, elref : 5, low : 5,
        high : 5, elsize : 5, size : 5);

    writeln(' code:');

    for count := 0 to locationcounter - 1 do begin
      write(count : 4, ' ');
      currentinstr := code[count];
      write(instr[currentinstr.opcode], ' ');

      if currentinstr.opcode < HaltInst then
        if currentinstr.opcode < Reset1Inst then
          write(currentinstr.field1 : 2, currentinstr.field2 : 5)
        else write(currentinstr.field2 : 7)
      else write('       ');

      writeln
    end;

    writeln
  end (*printtables*);

  procedure enterstandident (x1 : object;
                             x2 : types;
                             x3 : integer;
```

```
                 x0 : alfa);

(* Enters all standard identifiers into level 0 of the symbol table. *)

  begin
    currsymtablesize := currsymtablesize + 1;

    with symboltable[currsymtablesize] do begin
      name := x0;
      link := currsymtablesize - 1;
      obj := x1;
      typ := x2;
      ref := 0;
      normal := true;
      lev := 0;
      adrr := x3
    end
  end (*enterstandident*);

  procedure setup;

(* Initialization of arrays used by insymbol and various global variables. *)

    procedure setflags;
    var
      ch : char;
    begin
      write('Debugging (y/n) ? ');
      readln(ch);
      debugging := ch = 'y';
      write('Tracing (y/n) ? ');
      readln(ch);
      tracing := ch = 'y';
    end;

  begin
    keyword[1] := 'and       ';
    keyword[2] := 'array     ';
    keyword[3] := 'begin     ';
    keyword[4] := 'case      ';
    keyword[5] := 'const     ';
    keyword[6] := 'div       ';
    keyword[7] := 'do        ';
    keyword[8] := 'downto    ';
    keyword[9] := 'else      ';
    keyword[10] := 'end       ';
    keyword[11] := 'for       ';
    keyword[12] := 'function  ';
    keyword[13] := 'if        ';
    keyword[14] := 'mod       ';
```

```
keyword[15] := 'not       ';
keyword[16] := 'of        ';
keyword[17] := 'or        ';
keyword[18] := 'procedure ';
keyword[19] := 'program   ';
keyword[20] := 'record    ';
keyword[21] := 'repeat    ';
keyword[22] := 'then      ';
keyword[23] := 'to        ';
keyword[24] := 'type      ';
keyword[25] := 'until     ';
keyword[26] := 'var       ';
keyword[27] := 'while     ';
keywordsy[1] := andsy;
keywordsy[2] := arraysy;
keywordsy[3] := beginsy;
keywordsy[4] := casesy;
keywordsy[5] := constsy;
keywordsy[6] := idiv;
keywordsy[7] := dosy;
keywordsy[8] := downtosy;
keywordsy[9] := elsesy;
keywordsy[10] := endsy;
keywordsy[11] := forsy;
keywordsy[12] := funcsionsy;
keywordsy[13] := ifsy;
keywordsy[14] := imod;
keywordsy[15] := notsy;
keywordsy[16] := ofsy;
keywordsy[17] := orsy;
keywordsy[18] := prosedurесy;
keywordsy[19] := programsy;
keywordsy[20] := recordsy;
keywordsy[21] := repeatsy;
keywordsy[22] := thensy;
keywordsy[23] := tosy;
keywordsy[24] := typesy;
keywordsy[25] := untilsy;
keywordsy[26] := varsy;
keywordsy[27] := whilesy;
specialsymbol['+'] := plus;
specialsymbol['-'] := minus;
specialsymbol['*'] := times;
specialsymbol['/'] := rdiv;
specialsymbol['('] := lparent;
specialsymbol[')'] := rparent;
specialsymbol['='] := eql;
specialsymbol[','] := comma;
specialsymbol['['] := lbrack;
specialsymbol[']'] := rbrack;
```

```
    specialsymbol['"'] := neq;
    specialsymbol['&'] := andsy;
    specialsymbol[';'] := semicolon;
    constbegsys := [plus, minus, intcon, realcon, charcon, ident];
    typebegsys := [ident, arraysy, recordsy];
    blockbegsys := [constsy, typesy, varsy, proseduresy, funcsionsy, beginsy];
    facbegsys := [intcon, realcon, charcon, ident, lparent, notsy];
    statbegsys := [beginsy, ifsy, whilesy, repeatsy, forsy, casesy];
    stantyps := [notyp, ints, reals, bools, chars];
    swalloweddeadcolon := false;
    debugging := false;
    tracing := false;
    setflags;
    lastcharread := ' ';
    reset(source);
    rewrite(listing);
    writeln;
    linecounter := 1;
    locationcounter := 0;
    currentlinelength := 0;
    charactercount := 0;
    errpos := 0;
    setofallerrors := [];
    errcount := 0;
    currsymtablesize := -1;
    currarraytablesize := 0;
    currblocktablesize := 1;
    lastcharinstringtable := 0;
    currrealconsttablesize := 0;
    display[0] := 1;
    inputusedasprogparam := false;
    outputusedasprogparam := false;
    linewrittentoscreen := false;
end; (*setup*)

procedure enterids;

begin
    enterstandident(variable, notyp, 0, '          '); (*sentinel*)
    enterstandident(konstant, bools, 0, 'false     ');
    enterstandident(konstant, bools, 1, 'true      ');
    enterstandident(atype, reals, 1, 'real      ');
    enterstandident(atype, chars, 1, 'char      ');
    enterstandident(atype, bools, 1, 'boolean   ');
    enterstandident(atype, ints, 1, 'integer   ');
    enterstandident(funktion, reals, 0, 'abs       ');
    enterstandident(funktion, reals, 2, 'sqr       ');
    enterstandident(funktion, bools, 4, 'odd       ');
    enterstandident(funktion, chars, 5, 'chr       ');
    enterstandident(funktion, ints, 6, 'ord       ');
```

```
      enterstandident(funktion, chars, 7, 'succ      ');
      enterstandident(funktion, chars, 8, 'pred      ');
      enterstandident(funktion, ints, 9, 'round     ');
      enterstandident(funktion, ints, 10, 'trunc     ');
      enterstandident(funktion, reals, 11, 'sin       ');
      enterstandident(funktion, reals, 12, 'cos       ');
      enterstandident(funktion, reals, 13, 'exp       ');
      enterstandident(funktion, reals, 14, 'ln        ');
      enterstandident(funktion, reals, 15, 'sqrt      ');
      enterstandident(funktion, reals, 16, 'arctan    ');
      enterstandident(funktion, bools, 17, 'eof       ');
      enterstandident(funktion, bools, 18, 'eoln      ');
      enterstandident(prozedure, notyp, 1, 'read      ');
      enterstandident(prozedure, notyp, 2, 'readln    ');
      enterstandident(prozedure, notyp, 3, 'write     ');
      enterstandident(prozedure, notyp, 4, 'writeln   ');
      enterstandident(prozedure, notyp, 5, 'reset     ');
      enterstandident(prozedure, notyp, 6, 'rewrite   ');

      (* The following is not a standard procedure, but is used to give a
         snapshot of the state of the run-time stack.
      *)
      enterstandident(prozedure, notyp, 7, 'break     ');
      enterstandident(prozedure, notyp, 0, '          ');

      with blocktable[1] do begin
         indexsymtaboflastobj := currsymtablesize;
         indexsymtablastparam := 1;
         spaceforparams := 0;
         variablesize := 0
      end;
   end; (*enterids*)

begin (*main program*)
   setup;
   insymbol;

   if sy <> programsy then
      error(3) (*program symbol expected*)
   else begin
      insymbol;

      if sy <> ident then
         error(2) (*program identifier expected*)
      else begin
         progname := lastidentread;
         insymbol;

         if sy <> lparent then
            error(9)
```

```
        else
          repeat
            insymbol;

            if sy <> ident then
              error(2)
            else begin
              if lastidentread = 'input      ' then
                inputusedasprogparam := true
              else if lastidentread = 'output     ' then
                outputusedasprogparam := true
              else error(0); (* Must have one or the other. In fact
                                must have output - see 10 lines down. *)

              insymbol
            end
          until sy <> comma;

        if sy = rparent then
          insymbol
        else error(4);

        if not outputusedasprogparam then
          error(20)
      end
    end;

    enterids;
    block(blockbegsys + statbegsys, false, 1);
    emit(HaltInst); (*halt at end of program*)

    if blocktable[2].variablesize > stacksize then
      error(49);

    if debugging then
      printtables;

    if tracing then
      writeln;

    if setofallerrors = [] then begin
      writeln('Execution starting...');
      interpret
    end
    else begin
      writeln;
      write(errcount : 1, ' error');

      if errcount > 1 then
        write('s');
```

```
        writeln(' (Pascal–S Version $Revision: 4.6 $)');
        errormsg
    end;

99 :
end.
```

Appendix C
Identifier Index

A list of all the identifiers used in the Pascal-S compiler source is presented in this appendix. The identifiers appear in alphabetical order. Within the list, numbers identify the lines of source text given in Appendix B.

Four pieces of information are given for each identifier.

1. The lexical context in which the identifier is declared – each level is separated from the next by a '-'. *pascals* is the top (global) level.
2. The classification of the identifier.
3. The line number at which the identifier is declared.
4. A list of line numbers on which the identifier is referenced. If more than one reference appears on a line the number of references appears in parentheses following the line number.

99 in *-pascals*, declared on 8, used on 285, 303, 4345.

actuallocation in *-pascals-interpret-dump*, class = var, declared on 3056, used on 3081, 3082, 3085, 3086, 3087, 3088.

AddInst in *-pascals*, class = enumeration, declared on 68, used on 2202, 3844, 4027.

AddrealInst in *-pascals*, class = enumeration, declared on 69, used on 2206, 3856, 4029.

adjustscale in *-pascals-insymbol*, class = procedure, declared on 393, used on 560, 570.

adrr in *-pascals*, class = field in *-pascals-symtabletype*, declared on 85, used on 934, 1177, 1242, 1338, 1357, 1476, 1527, 1969, 1970, 1971, 1972, 1986, 2008, 2021, 3081, 3082, 4052, 4105.

alfa in *-pascals*, class = type, declared on 45, used on 79, 95, 111, 114, 153, 272, 896, 943, 4090.

allowabletypes in *-pascals-block-statement-expression-simpleexpression-term-factor-standfunct*, class = var, declared on 1878, used on 1892, 1902, 1905, 1909, 1917, 1924.

AndInst in *-pascals*, class = enumeration, declared on 69, used on 2123, 3868, 4031.

andsy in *-pascals*, class = enumeration, declared on 37, used on 2076, 2079, 2084, 2120, 4153, 4191.

arg1 in *-pascals-emit2*, class = value parameter, declared on 806, used on 820.

arg2 in *-pascals-emit2*, class = value parameter, declared on 806, used on 821.

arg2 in *-pascals-emit1*, class = value parameter, declared on 786, used on 800.

arrayreference in *-pascals-block-typ-arraytyp*, class = var parameter, declared on 1074, used on 1115, 1141.

arrays in *-pascals*, class = enumeration, declared on 47, used on 845, 1119, 1197, 1654, 1731, 2319, 3047.

arraysize in *-pascals-block-typ-arraytyp*, class = var parameter, declared on 1074, used on 1142, 1143, 1146.

arraysy in *-pascals*, class = enumeration, declared on 40, used on 1185, 4154, 4194.

arraytable in *-pascals*, class = var, declared on 125, used on 722, 1141, 1659, 1662, 1666, 1667, 1733, 2320, 3483, 3493, 3504, 3514, 3519, 4064.

arraytablemax in *-pascals*, class = constant, declared on 19, used on 125, 717.

arraytyp in *-pascals-block-typ*, class = procedure, declared on 1074, used on 1120, 1198.

assignment in *-pascals-block-statement*, class = procedure, declared on 2273, used on 2896, 2905.

atype in *-pascals*, class = enumeration, declared on 46, used on 1172, 1331, 1457, 2012, 2895, 2957, 4231, 4232, 4233, 4234.

b in *-pascals-interpret*, class = field in anonymous record, declared on 3045, used on 3193, 3207, 3215(2), 3221(2), 3245, 3256, 3279, 3313, 3320, 3342, 3349, 3359, 3371, 3378, 3396, 3403, 3412, 3488, 3509, 3581, 3723, 3731, 3739, 3747, 3755, 3763, 3771, 3772, 3773(2), 3783, 3784, 3785(2), 3795, 3796, 3797(2), 3807, 3808, 3809(2), 3819, 3820, 3821(2), 3831, 3832, 3833(2).

baseofcurrentstackframe in *-pascals-interpret*, class = var, declared on 3030, used on 3060, 3114, 3171, 3468, 3476, 3684, 3685, 3686(2), 3691, 3692, 3693(2).

baseofstackframe in *-pascals-interpret-dump*, class = var, declared on 3055, used on 3060, 3065, 3067, 3069, 3081, 3082, 3097(2), 3098.

becomes in *-pascals*, class = enumeration, declared on 39, used on 581, 1415, 1466, 2300, 2302, 2660, 2662.

beginsy in *-pascals*, class = enumeration, declared on 41, used on 2910, 2988, 4155, 4195, 4197.

block in *-pascals*, class = procedure, declared on 829, used on 1571, 4318.

blockbegsys in *-pascals*, class = var, declared on 113, used on 892, 1404, 1454, 2988, 4195, 4318.

blocktabindexatentry in *-pascals-block*, class = var, declared on 851, used on 2938, 2940, 2945, 2946, 2983.

blocktable in *-pascals*, class = var, declared on 129, used on 742, 743, 916, 937, 965, 1268, 1270, 1623, 1704, 1735, 1793, 2321, 2945, 2946, 2983, 3071, 3113, 3116, 3421, 4049, 4057, 4265, 4321.

blocktablemax in *-pascals*, class = constant, declared on 18, used on 129, 738.

boolexpitem in *-pascals-block-statement-ifstatement*, class = var, declared on 2361, used on 2371, 2373.

bools in *-pascals*, class = enumeration, declared on 47, used on 841, 1905, 1909, 1971, 2058, 2121, 2122, 2183, 2184, 2233, 2266, 2373, 2492, 2565, 2592, 2652, 3045, 3087, 3192, 3207, 3215, 3221, 3244, 3255, 3279, 3313, 3320, 3342, 3349, 3359, 3371, 3378, 3396, 3403, 3412, 3488, 3509, 3580, 3722, 3730, 3738, 3746, 3754, 3762, 3773, 3775, 3785, 3787, 3797, 3799, 3809, 3811, 3821, 3823, 3833, 3835, 4198, 4229, 4230, 4233, 4237, 4250, 4251.

c in *-pascals-interpret*, class = field in anonymous record, declared on 3046, used on 3201, 3206, 3214(2), 3220(2), 3278, 3312, 3319, 3341, 3348, 3358, 3370, 3377, 3395, 3402, 3411, 3487, 3508, 3570, 3619, 3772, 3784, 3796, 3808, 3820, 3832.

call in *-pascals-block-statement*, class = procedure, declared on 1688, used on 2020, 2900.

CallInst in *-pascals*, class = enumeration, declared on 59, used on 1793, 3438, 3992.

caselabel in *-pascals-block-statement-casestatement*, class = procedure, declared on 2423, used on 2460, 2464.
caseselectoritem in *-pascals-block-statement-casestatement*, class = var, declared on 2416, used on 2435, 2490, 2492.
casestatement in *-pascals-block-statement*, class = procedure, declared on 2405, used on 2912.
casesy in *-pascals*, class = enumeration, declared on 41, used on 2912, 4156, 4197.
casetable in *-pascals-block-statement-casestatement*, class = var, declared on 2418, used on 2442, 2443, 2447, 2515, 2517.
casetablelemax in *-pascals*, class = constant, declared on 22, used on 2418, 2421, 2437.
ch in *-pascals-setup-setflags*, class = var, declared on 4115, used on 4118, 4119, 4121, 4122.
charactercount in *-pascals*, class = var, declared on 102, used on 253, 261, 262, 263, 297, 323, 346(2), 347, 639, 2853, 2865, 4210.
charcon in *-pascals*, class = enumeration, declared on 36, used on 648, 654, 1007, 2025, 2032, 4193, 4196.
chars in *-pascals*, class = enumeration, declared on 47, used on 841, 1008, 1905, 1909, 1970, 2033, 2233, 2492, 2652, 2767, 3046, 3088, 3200, 3206, 3214, 3220, 3278, 3312, 3319, 3341, 3348, 3358, 3370, 3377, 3395, 3402, 3411, 3487, 3508, 3569, 3618, 3772, 3784, 3796, 3808, 3820, 3832, 4198, 4232, 4238, 4240, 4241.
code in *-pascals*, class = var, declared on 135, used on 782, 798, 818, 2395, 2397, 2399, 2511, 2528, 2604, 2704, 3129, 3289, 3293, 3297, 4072.
colon in *-pascals*, class = enumeration, declared on 39, used on 584, 888, 1094, 1223, 1320, 1383, 1511, 1720, 1770, 2433, 2467, 2490, 2799, 2805, 2809, 2815, 2935, 2949.
comma in *-pascals*, class = enumeration, declared on 38, used on 888, 1106, 1117, 1218, 1230, 1257, 1315, 1343, 1373, 1420, 1470, 1506, 1516, 1652, 1669, 1720, 1770, 1782, 1783, 2433, 2462, 2490, 2762, 2775, 2776, 2799, 2809, 2822, 2837, 4187, 4306.
compoundstatement in *-pascals-block-statement*, class = procedure, declared on 2333, used on 2910.
constant in *-pascals-block*, class = procedure, declared on 990, used on 1094, 1106, 1420, 2433.
constantrecord in *-pascals-block*, class = type, declared on 839, used on 991, 1087, 1396, 2428.
constbegsys in *-pascals*, class = var, declared on 113, used on 1004, 1006, 2459, 4193.
constntdeclaration in *-pascals-block*, class = procedure, declared on 1391, used on 2975.
constsy in *-pascals*, class = enumeration, declared on 39, used on 2974, 4157, 4195.
controlvartype in *-pascals-block-statement-forstatement*, class = var, declared on 2625, used on 2642, 2644, 2652, 2657, 2667, 2682.
CopyblInst in *-pascals*, class = enumeration, declared on 60, used on 2320, 2321, 3537, 3996.
count in *-pascals-printtables*, class = var, declared on 3966, used on 4049, 4050, 4051, 4056, 4057, 4058, 4063, 4064, 4065, 4070, 4071, 4072.
count in *-pascals-block-statement-casestatement*, class = var, declared on 2417, used on 2514, 2515, 2517, 2527, 2528.
count in *-pascals-insymbol*, class = var, declared on 359, used on 482, 486, 487(2), 493.
countofnumofinputlines in *-pascals-interpret*, class = var, declared on 3031, used on 3119, 3921(2), 3924.
currarraytablesize in *-pascals*, class = var, declared on 120, used on 717, 720(2), 722, 1115, 4063, 4215.
currblocktablesize in *-pascals*, class = var, declared on 120, used on 738, 741(2), 742, 743, 1204, 1210, 2937,

2938, 4056, 4216.
currentinstr in *-pascals-printtables*, class = var, declared on 3967, used on 4072, 4073, 4075, 4076, 4077(2), 4078.
currentinstruction in *-pascals-interpret*, class = var, declared on 3023, used on 3129, 3134, 3143, 3144, 3153, 3154, 3164, 3165, 3169, 3170, 3186, 3261, 3264, 3268, 3284, 3328, 3361, 3385, 3414, 3421, 3435, 3441, 3482, 3503, 3526, 3541, 3559, 3570, 3581, 3592, 3597, 3608, 3628, 3645, 3650, 3667.
currentlevel in *-pascals-block-locinsymboltable*, class = var, declared on 949, used on 952, 965, 971(2), 972.
currentlinelength in *-pascals*, class = var, declared on 105, used on 244, 297, 320, 325, 327(2), 330, 337(2), 338, 639, 4209.
currrealconsttablesize in *-pascals*, class = var, declared on 121, used on 755, 758, 764, 765, 4218.
currsymtablesize in *-pascals*, class = var, declared on 120, used on 906, 925(2), 927, 938, 1215, 1227, 1312, 1350, 1423, 1424, 1425, 1429, 1431, 1458, 1503, 1515, 1569, 2930, 2945, 4049, 4095(2), 4097, 4099, 4214, 4266.
deadcolonsy in *-pascals*, class = enumeration, declared on 43, used on 471, 614, 1094, 1102.
debugging in *-pascals*, class = var, declared on 139, used on 4119, 4200, 4324.
defaultfieldwidths in *-pascals-interpret*, class = var, declared on 3039, used on 3122, 3123, 3124, 3125, 3645, 3651, 3652, 3653.
display in *-pascals-interpret*, class = var, declared on 3040, used on 3115, 3143, 3153, 3164, 3174, 3450, 3464.
display in *-pascals*, class = var, declared on 123, used on 916, 937, 965, 1210, 2903, 2937, 4219.
divideby0error in *-pascals-interpret*, class = enumeration, declared on 3026, used on 3885, 3894, 3909, 3939.
DivInst in *-pascals*, class = enumeration, declared on 70, used on 2136, 3880, 4033.
dosy in *-pascals*, class = enumeration, declared on 42, used on 2371, 2385, 2590, 2598, 2660, 2665, 2670, 2680, 2685, 2691, 4159.
downtosy in *-pascals*, class = enumeration, declared on 42, used on 2660, 2665, 2670, 2674, 2675, 4160.
dump in *-pascals-interpret*, class = procedure, declared on 3050, used on 3305, 3951.
elementreference in *-pascals-block-typ-arraytyp*, class = var, declared on 1088, used on 1120, 1137, 1148.
elementsize in *-pascals-block-typ-arraytyp*, class = var, declared on 1088, used on 1120, 1137, 1142, 1149.
elementtype in *-pascals-block-typ-arraytyp*, class = var, declared on 1086, used on 1119, 1137, 1147.
elref in *-pascals*, class = field in anonymous record, declared on 127, used on 1148, 4065.
elsesy in *-pascals*, class = enumeration, declared on 42, used on 2389, 2391, 4161.
elsize in *-pascals*, class = field in anonymous record, declared on 127, used on 1149, 4066.
eltyp in *-pascals*, class = field in anonymous record, declared on 126, used on 1147, 4065.
emit in *-pascals*, class = procedure, declared on 771, used on 1578, 1580, 1991, 2059, 2094, 2095, 2111, 2123, 2136, 2137, 2166, 2168, 2185, 2202, 2203, 2206, 2207, 2236, 2237, 2238, 2239, 2240, 2241, 2256, 2257, 2258, 2259, 2260, 2261, 2316, 2324, 2377, 2394, 2477, 2496, 2596, 2689, 2784, 2828, 2845, 2854, 2855, 2866, 2867, 2873, 4319.
emit1 in *-pascals*, class = procedure, declared on 786, used on 1639, 1663, 1664, 1703, 1732, 1735, 1740, 1793, 1824, 1830, 1920, 1925, 1937, 1969, 1970, 1971, 1972, 2029, 2034, 2038,

2100, 2105, 2246, 2250, 2320, 2321, 2323, 2515, 2517, 2521, 2568, 2603, 2700, 2702, 2769, 2793, 2794, 2831, 2834.

emit2 in *-pascals*, class = procedure, declared on 806, used on 1762, 1765, 1797, 1986, 2008, 2297, 2648, 2758.

endoffieldsinsymtable in *-pascals-block-typ*, class = var, declared on 1071, used on 1227, 1234.

endofstring in *-pascals-insymbol*, class = function, declared on 432, used on 441, 443, 628.

endsy in *-pascals*, class = enumeration, declared on 42, used on 1230, 1251, 1261, 1265, 2340, 2347, 2350, 2474, 2530, 2993, 3000, 3003, 4162.

enter in *-pascals-block*, class = procedure, declared on 895, used on 984, 1407, 1457, 1566, 1567.

enterarray in *-pascals*, class = procedure, declared on 702, used on 1114.

enterblock in *-pascals*, class = procedure, declared on 730, used on 1202, 2936.

enterids in *-pascals*, class = procedure, declared on 4225, used on 4317.

enterreal in *-pascals*, class = procedure, declared on 747, used on 1428, 2028.

enterstandident in *-pascals*, class = procedure, declared on 4087, used on 4228, 4229, 4230, 4231, 4232, 4233, 4234, 4235, 4236, 4237, 4238, 4239, 4240, 4241, 4242, 4243, 4244, 4245, 4246, 4247, 4248, 4249, 4250, 4251, 4252, 4253, 4254, 4255, 4256, 4257, 4262, 4263.

entervariable in *-pascals-block*, class = procedure, declared on 980, used on 1216, 1220, 1313, 1317, 1504, 1508.

eql in *-pascals*, class = enumeration, declared on 37, used on 1410, 1461, 2221, 2224, 2236, 2256, 2300, 2307, 4186.

EqualInst in *-pascals*, class = enumeration, declared on 66, used on 2236, 3766, 4020.

EqualrInst in *-pascals*, class = enumeration, declared on 65, used on 2256, 3718, 4014.

errcount in *-pascals*, class = var, declared on 138, used on 238(2), 4213, 4336, 4338.

error in *-pascals*, class = procedure, declared on 227, used on 405, 457, 529, 653, 694, 709, 712, 862, 886, 923, 975, 987, 1027, 1097, 1104, 1109, 1126, 1134, 1144, 1173, 1180, 1191, 1225, 1245, 1255, 1266, 1324, 1332, 1345, 1361, 1371, 1385, 1413, 1464, 1513, 1531, 1561, 1575, 1618, 1621, 1632, 1647, 1655, 1661, 1674, 1713, 1730, 1742, 1746, 1754, 1776, 1787, 1791, 1814, 1883, 1927, 1932, 1934, 1945, 2012, 2052, 2061, 2115, 2127, 2141, 2163, 2189, 2263, 2305, 2318, 2327, 2345, 2352, 2374, 2383, 2436, 2450, 2469, 2493, 2501, 2532, 2555, 2566, 2570, 2593, 2600, 2647, 2653, 2656, 2668, 2683, 2693, 2729, 2739, 2747, 2771, 2780, 2803, 2813, 2817, 2826, 2841, 2895, 2907, 2958, 2962, 2966, 2970, 2998, 3005, 4278, 4283, 4289, 4295, 4301, 4310, 4313, 4322.

errormsg in *-pascals*, class = procedure, declared on 143, used on 302, 4342.

errornum in *-pascals-block-test*, class = value parameter, declared on 869, used on 877.

errornum in *-pascals-block-skip*, class = value parameter, declared on 855, used on 862.

errornum in *-pascals-errormsg*, class = var, declared on 152, used on 216, 219, 220(2), 222(2), 223.

errpos in *-pascals*, class = var, declared on 110, used on 253, 258, 261, 262, 263, 310, 313, 4211.

exittab in *-pascals-block-statement-casestatement*, class = var, declared on 2421, used on 2476, 2528.

expitem in *-pascals-block-statement-forstatement*, class = var, declared on 2626, used on 2665, 2667, 2680, 2682.

exponent in *-pascals-insymbol*, class = var, declared on 359, used on 390(2), 404, 406, 409, 426, 544, 550(2), 559, 567, 569.

expoperator in *-pascals-block-statement-expression*, class = var, declared on 1842, used on 2226, 2235, 2255.
expression in *-pascals-block-statement*, class = procedure, forward on 1593. declared on 1834, used on 1652, 1720, 1886, 2048, 2312, 2371, 2490, 2563, 2590, 2665, 2680, 2799, 2809, 2822.
expressionitem in *-pascals-block-statement-call*, class = var, declared on 1696, used on 1721, 1726, 1728, 1731, 1733, 1734, 1735, 1738, 1741, 1756, 1758, 1771, 1773, 1774.
expressionitem in *-pascals-block-statement-selector*, class = var, declared on 1606, used on 1652, 1659.
facbegsys in *-pascals*, class = var, declared on 113, used on 1954, 1956, 2064, 4196.
factor in *-pascals-block-statement-expression-simpleexpression-term*, class = procedure, declared on 1862, used on 2056, 2076, 2084.
fatal in *-pascals*, class = procedure, declared on 267, used on 633, 718, 739, 756, 779, 794, 814, 907, 1207, 2438, 2933.
field1 in *-pascals*, class = field in *-pascals-instruction*, declared on 74, used on 820.
field2 in *-pascals*, class = field in *-pascals-instruction*, declared on 75, used on 800, 821.
fieldreference in *-pascals-block-typ*, class = var, declared on 1070, used on 1231, 1240.
fieldsize in *-pascals-block-typ*, class = var, declared on 1071, used on 1231, 1243.
fieldtype in *-pascals-block-typ*, class = var, declared on 1069, used on 1230, 1239.
fieldwidthitem in *-pascals-block-statement-standproc*, class = var, declared on 2719, used on 2810, 2812, 2823, 2825.
finishwithouterrors in *-pascals-interpret*, class = enumeration, declared on 3025, used on 3681, 3932.
FloatInst in *-pascals*, class = enumeration, declared on 62, used on 1740, 1824, 1830, 1920, 2100, 2105, 2246, 2250, 2323, 3595, 4001.
followingfactoritem in *-pascals-block-statement-expression-simpleexpression-term*, class = var, declared on 1859, used on 2085, 2090, 2104, 2106, 2110, 2114, 2122, 2126, 2134, 2140.
followingsimexpitem in *-pascals-block-statement-expression*, class = var, declared on 1841, used on 2230, 2234, 2248, 2249, 2253.
followingtermitem in *-pascals-block-statement-expression-simpleexpression*, class = var, declared on 1850, used on 2179, 2183, 2188, 2196.
ForfdnInst in *-pascals*, class = enumeration, declared on 59, used on 2676, 3365, 3989.
ForfupInst in *-pascals*, class = enumeration, declared on 58, used on 2672, 2699, 3307, 3987.
ForsdnInst in *-pascals*, class = enumeration, declared on 59, used on 2702, 3389, 3990.
forstatement in *-pascals-block-statement*, class = procedure, declared on 2610, used on 2915.
ForsupInst in *-pascals*, class = enumeration, declared on 58, used on 2700, 3331, 3988.
forsy in *-pascals*, class = enumeration, declared on 41, used on 2915, 4163, 4197.
fsys in *-pascals-block-statement-expression-simpleexpression-term-factor*, class = value parameter, declared on 1862, used on 1886, 1954, 1987, 2020, 2048, 2056, 2064.
fsys in *-pascals-block-statement-expression-simpleexpression-term*, class = value parameter, declared on 1853, used on 2076, 2084.
fsys in *-pascals-block-statement-expression-simpleexpression*, class = value parameter, declared on 1844, used on 2160, 2171, 2179.

fsys in *-pascals-block-statement-call*, class = value parameter, declared on 1688, used on 1720, 1770, 1782.
fsys in *-pascals-block-statement-selector*, class = value parameter, declared on 1597, used on 1652, 1682.
fsys in *-pascals-block-statement-expression*, class = value parameter, declared on 1593, used on 2221, 2230.
fsys in *-pascals-block-statement*, class = value parameter, declared on 1586, used on 2300, 2312, 2340, 2347, 2371, 2389, 2396, 2433, 2474, 2490, 2550, 2557, 2563, 2590, 2602, 2660, 2665, 2670, 2680, 2685, 2697, 2762, 2775, 2799, 2809, 2822, 2900, 2918.
fsys in *-pascals-block-typ*, class = value parameter, declared on 1059, used on 1094, 1106, 1137, 1163, 1230, 1261, 1275.
fsys in *-pascals-block-constant*, class = value parameter, declared on 990, used on 1004, 1052, 1055.
fsys in *-pascals-block-testsemicolon*, class = value parameter, declared on 880, used on 892.
fsys in *-pascals-block-skip*, class = value parameter, declared on 854, used on 864.
fsys in *-pascals-block*, class = value parameter, declared on 829, used on 1300, 1343, 1377, 1383, 1420, 1434, 1470, 1480, 1516, 1537, 1571, 2935, 2964, 2993, 3000, 3007.
funcsionsy in *-pascals*, class = enumeration, declared on 40, used on 1557, 2985, 4164, 4195.
funktion in *-pascals*, class = enumeration, declared on 46, used on 1566, 2015, 2902, 4235, 4236, 4237, 4238, 4239, 4240, 4241, 4242, 4243, 4244, 4245, 4246, 4247, 4248, 4249, 4250, 4251.
geq in *-pascals*, class = enumeration, declared on 37, used on 604, 2221, 2224, 2241, 2261.
GereallInst in *-pascals*, class = enumeration, declared on 66, used on 2261, 3758, 4019.
GreallInst in *-pascals*, class = enumeration, declared on 66, used on 2260, 3750, 4018.
GreateInst in *-pascals*, class = enumeration, declared on 68, used on 2241, 3826, 4025.
GreattInst in *-pascals*, class = enumeration, declared on 67, used on 2240, 3814, 4024.
gtr in *-pascals*, class = enumeration, declared on 37, used on 607, 2221, 2224, 2240, 2260.
h1 in *-pascals-interpret*, class = var, declared on 3033, used on 3169, 3174, 3175(2), 3177, 3277, 3278, 3279, 3293, 3311, 3312, 3313, 3323, 3340, 3341, 3342, 3353, 3357, 3358, 3359, 3369, 3370, 3371, 3381, 3394, 3395, 3396, 3406, 3410, 3411, 3412, 3421, 3424, 3433, 3441, 3444, 3450, 3456(2), 3459, 3460, 3463, 3464, 3467, 3468, 3476, 3482, 3483, 3493, 3503, 3504, 3514, 3519, 3524, 3533, 3534(2), 3539, 3541, 3543, 3544, 3545(2), 3597, 3598, 3627, 3631, 3638(2), 3640.
h2 in *-pascals-interpret*, class = var, declared on 3033, used on 3170, 3177, 3284, 3289, 3293, 3297, 3299(2), 3318, 3319, 3320, 3323, 3335, 3338, 3355, 3376, 3377, 3378, 3381, 3391, 3392, 3408, 3444, 3447, 3478, 3483, 3491, 3497, 3504, 3512, 3518, 3526, 3528, 3531, 3540, 3544, 3546(2), 3628, 3637, 3639(2).
h3 in *-pascals-interpret*, class = var, declared on 3033, used on 3171, 3174, 3176(2), 3285, 3290, 3296, 3300, 3347, 3348, 3349, 3353, 3401, 3402, 3403, 3406, 3447, 3450, 3464, 3471, 3472, 3473, 3486, 3487, 3488, 3491, 3493, 3497, 3507, 3508, 3509, 3512, 3514, 3518, 3541, 3543.
h4 in *-pascals-interpret*, class = var, declared on 3033, used on 3456, 3471, 3477.
HaltInst in *-pascals*, class = enumeration, declared on 63, used on 3680, 4006, 4075, 4319.
high in *-pascals-block-typ-arraytyp*, class = var, declared on 1087, used on 1106, 1108, 1110, 1114.

high in *-pascals*, class = field in anonymous record, declared on 127, used on 725, 1142, 4066.
highindex in *-pascals-enterarray*, class = value parameter, declared on 703, used on 708, 711, 714, 725.
i in *-pascals-interpret*, class = field in anonymous record, declared on 3043, used on 3143, 3193, 3196, 3197, 3201, 3206, 3207, 3213(2), 3219(2), 3225, 3229, 3277, 3311, 3318, 3340, 3347, 3357, 3369, 3376, 3394, 3401, 3410, 3486, 3507, 3559, 3600, 3611, 3771, 3783, 3795, 3807, 3819, 3831.
i in *-pascals-error*, class = var, declared on 235, used on 244, 245.
id in *-pascals-block-locinsymboltable*, class = value parameter, declared on 943, used on 958, 968.
id in *-pascals-block-enter*, class = value parameter, declared on 896, used on 914, 919, 928.
ident in *-pascals*, class = enumeration, declared on 41, used on 511, 892, 983, 1022, 1166, 1214, 1230, 1261, 1300, 1302, 1323, 1343, 1377, 1404, 1406, 1420, 1454, 1456, 1470, 1502, 1516, 1560, 1617, 1745, 1931, 1957, 2637, 2738, 2885, 2887, 2952, 4193, 4194, 4196, 4282, 4294.
idiv in *-pascals*, class = enumeration, declared on 37, used on 2076, 2079, 2084, 2135, 4158.
ifstatement in *-pascals-block-statement*, class = procedure, declared on 2358, used on 2911.
ifsy in *-pascals*, class = enumeration, declared on 41, used on 2911, 4165, 4197.
imod in *-pascals*, class = enumeration, declared on 37, used on 2076, 2079, 2084, 4166.
index in *-pascals*, class = type, declared on 44, used on 53, 80, 83, 127, 131, 2419.
Index1Inst in *-pascals*, class = enumeration, declared on 60, used on 1663, 3480, 3993.
indexinsymtable in *-pascals-block-variabldeclaration*, class = var, declared on 1492, used on 1503, 1520, 1521(2), 1523.
indexinsymtableoflastvar in *-pascals-block-variabldeclaration*, class = var, declared on 1492, used on 1515, 1520.
indexinsymtableoftype in *-pascals-block-typedeclaration*, class = var, declared on 1447, used on 1458, 1473.
indexmax in *-pascals*, class = constant, declared on 26, used on 44(2), 711(2), 1143, 1244, 1360, 1530.
IndexmInst in *-pascals*, class = enumeration, declared on 60, used on 1664, 3500, 3994.
indexofblockinsymboltable in *-pascals-interpret-dump*, class = var, declared on 3055, used on 3065, 3068, 3071.
indexoffirstsyminblock in *-pascals-block-enter*, class = var, declared on 903, used on 917, 929.
indexsymtablastparam in *-pascals*, class = field in anonymous record, declared on 130, used on 4058, 4267.
indexsymtaboflastobj in *-pascals*, class = field in anonymous record, declared on 130, used on 4058, 4266.
indextocasetable in *-pascals-block-statement-casestatement-caselabel*, class = var, declared on 2429, used on 2441, 2446(2), 2447, 2449.
indextoparamsinsymboltable in *-pascals-block-parameterlist*, class = var, declared on 1289, used on 1312, 1350, 1351(2), 1353.
indextovar in *-pascals-interpret-dump*, class = var, declared on 3055, used on 3071, 3074, 3075, 3093.
initinstructions in *-pascals-printtables*, class = procedure, declared on 3970, used on 4043.
inputusedasprogparam in *-pascals*, class = var, declared on 112, used on 2728, 2731, 4220, 4298.
instr in *-pascals-printtables*, class = var, declared on 3968, used on 3973, 3974, 3975, 3976, 3977, 3978, 3979, 3980, 3981, 3982, 3983, 3984, 3985, 3986, 3987, 3988, 3989, 3990, 3991, 3992, 3993, 3994, 3995, 3996, 3997, 3998, 3999, 4000, 4001, 4002, 4003, 4004,

4005, 4006, 4007, 4008, 4009, 4010, 4011, 4012, 4013, 4014, 4015, 4016, 4017, 4018, 4019, 4020, 4021, 4022, 4023, 4024, 4025, 4026, 4027, 4028, 4029, 4030, 4031, 4032, 4033, 4034, 4035, 4036, 4037, 4038, 4039, 4073.

instr in *-pascals-emit2*, class = value parameter, declared on 806, used on 819.

instr in *-pascals-emit1*, class = value parameter, declared on 786, used on 799.

instr in *-pascals-emit*, class = value parameter, declared on 771, used on 782.

instruction in *-pascals*, class = type, declared on 72, used on 135, 3023, 3967.

insymbol in *-pascals*, class = procedure, declared on 352, used on 865, 884, 889, 985, 1010, 1019, 1040, 1045, 1050, 1103, 1118, 1124, 1129, 1133, 1183, 1186, 1189, 1194, 1201, 1219, 1224, 1253, 1258, 1271, 1296, 1308, 1316, 1321, 1327, 1369, 1374, 1382, 1403, 1408, 1411, 1416, 1453, 1459, 1462, 1467, 1500, 1507, 1512, 1558, 1570, 1574, 1615, 1642, 1651, 1672, 1677, 1710, 1749, 1786, 1882, 1935, 1944, 1959, 2043, 2047, 2051, 2055, 2082, 2159, 2176, 2227, 2303, 2308, 2339, 2344, 2351, 2368, 2381, 2386, 2392, 2463, 2468, 2485, 2500, 2506, 2531, 2549, 2554, 2561, 2586, 2599, 2635, 2639, 2663, 2678, 2692, 2736, 2742, 2779, 2790, 2795, 2806, 2819, 2840, 2850, 2857, 2862, 2869, 2891, 2950, 2954, 2969, 2992, 2997, 3004, 4275, 4280, 4286, 4292, 4304, 4309.

intcon in *-pascals*, class = enumeration, declared on 36, used on 517, 1042, 2025, 4193, 4196.

integermax in *-pascals*, class = constant, declared on 27, used on 75(2), 528.

interpret in *-pascals*, class = procedure, declared on 3015, used on 4332.

ints in *-pascals*, class = enumeration, declared on 47, used on 841, 1043, 1098, 1738, 1819, 1820, 1821, 1829, 1892, 1902, 1905, 1909, 1917, 1919, 1969, 2037, 2094, 2099, 2104, 2133, 2134, 2200, 2233, 2244, 2248, 2322, 2492, 2642, 2652, 2657, 2767, 2812, 2825, 3043, 3085, 3106, 3108, 3110, 3112, 3142, 3205, 3209, 3213, 3219, 3224, 3228, 3277, 3311, 3318, 3340, 3347, 3357, 3369, 3376, 3394, 3401, 3410, 3432, 3434, 3459, 3463, 3467, 3472, 3486, 3507, 3558, 3610, 3771, 3783, 3795, 3807, 3819, 3831, 4198, 4234, 4239, 4242, 4243.

inxtyp in *-pascals*, class = field in anonymous record, declared on 126, used on 723, 4065.

isfunction in *-pascals-block-procdeclaration*, class = var, declared on 1551, used on 1557, 1565, 1571, 1577.

isfunction in *-pascals-block*, class = value parameter, declared on 830, used on 2948.

item in *-pascals*, class = type, declared on 51, used on 1594, 1598, 1606, 1696, 1841, 1845, 1850, 1854, 1859, 1863, 2277, 2361, 2416, 2541, 2579, 2626, 2719.

JmpfallInst in *-pascals*, class = enumeration, declared on 57, used on 2377, 2568, 2596, 3265, 3984.

JumpInst in *-pascals*, class = enumeration, declared on 57, used on 2394, 2477, 2521, 2603, 3263, 3983.

keyword in *-pascals*, class = var, declared on 114, used on 505, 506, 4126, 4127, 4128, 4129, 4130, 4131, 4132, 4133, 4134, 4135, 4136, 4137, 4138, 4139, 4140, 4141, 4142, 4143, 4144, 4145, 4146, 4147, 4148, 4149, 4150, 4151, 4152.

keywordsy in *-pascals*, class = var, declared on 115, used on 510, 4153, 4154, 4155, 4156, 4157, 4158, 4159, 4160, 4161, 4162, 4163, 4164, 4165, 4166, 4167, 4168, 4169, 4170, 4171, 4172, 4173, 4174, 4175, 4176, 4177, 4178, 4179.

konstant in *-pascals*, class = enumeration, declared on 46, used on 1026, 1407, 1963, 2895, 4229, 4230.

lab in *-pascals-block-statement-casestatement-caselabel*, class = var, declared on 2428, used on 2433, 2435, 2442, 2447.
lastcharinstringtable in *-pascals*, class = var, declared on 121, used on 630, 635, 650, 659, 661(2), 4217.
lastcharread in *-pascals*, class = var, declared on 93, used on 328, 329, 330, 347, 378, 380, 385, 386, 439, 441, 453, 454, 460(2), 475, 489, 490(2), 493, 497, 513, 522, 525, 535, 538, 549, 552, 556(2), 563(2), 575, 580, 589, 593, 603, 613, 636, 669, 675, 679, 687, 4203.
lastidentread in *-pascals*, class = var, declared on 95, used on 483, 493, 505, 506, 984, 1023, 1168, 1326, 1407, 1457, 1562, 1566, 1567, 1625, 1627, 1748, 1933, 1958, 2638, 2741, 2890, 2953, 4285, 4297, 4299.
lastintegerread in *-pascals*, class = var, declared on 96, used on 516, 521(2), 527, 530, 543, 566, 1044, 2038.
lastitem in *-pascals-block-statement-selector*, class = var parameter, declared on 1598, used on 1620, 1623, 1634, 1635, 1654, 1657, 1666, 1667.
lastrealread in *-pascals*, class = var, declared on 97, used on 407, 427(2), 428(2), 543, 551(2), 566, 1049, 2028.
lbrack in *-pascals*, class = enumeration, declared on 38, used on 1188, 1646, 1680, 1769, 1980, 2299, 2761, 4188.
LdboolInst in *-pascals*, class = enumeration, declared on 61, used on 1971, 3573, 3999.
LdcharInst in *-pascals*, class = enumeration, declared on 61, used on 1970, 2034, 3562, 3998.
LdintInst in *-pascals*, class = enumeration, declared on 61, used on 1969, 2038, 2793, 3551, 3997.
LdrealInst in *-pascals*, class = enumeration, declared on 61, used on 1972, 2029, 3584, 4000.
LeavefInst in *-pascals*, class = enumeration, declared on 63, used on 1578, 3689, 4008.
LeavepInst in *-pascals*, class = enumeration, declared on 63, used on 1580, 3682, 4007.
legalfollowingsymbols in *-pascals-block-test*, class = value parameter, declared on 868, used on 877.
legalsymbols in *-pascals-block-test*, class = value parameter, declared on 868, used on 876, 877.
lengthoflaststring in *-pascals*, class = var, declared on 99, used on 660, 2793.
leq in *-pascals*, class = enumeration, declared on 38, used on 590, 2221, 2224, 2239, 2259.
LesseqInst in *-pascals*, class = enumeration, declared on 67, used on 2239, 3802, 4023.
LesserInst in *-pascals*, class = enumeration, declared on 66, used on 2259, 3742, 4017.
LessrInst in *-pascals*, class = enumeration, declared on 65, used on 2258, 3734, 4016.
LessthInst in *-pascals*, class = enumeration, declared on 67, used on 2238, 3790, 4022.
lev in *-pascals*, class = field in *-pascals-symtabletype*, declared on 86, used on 933, 1358, 1526, 1986, 2008, 2019, 4052, 4104.
level in *-pascals-block*, class = value parameter, declared on 831, used on 916, 933, 937, 952, 1206, 1209(2), 1210, 1272(2), 1358, 1526, 1571, 1796, 1797, 2903, 2932, 2937, 2942.
levelofihs in *-pascals-block-statement-assignment*, class = value parameter, declared on 2273, used on 2297.
levtype in *-pascals*, class = type, declared on 77, used on 86.
lhsitem in *-pascals-block-statement-assignment*, class = var, declared on 2277, used on 2284, 2285, 2300, 2314, 2315, 2317, 2319, 2320, 2321, 2322, 2326.
line in *-pascals*, class = var, declared on 101, used on 245, 330, 338, 347, 2853, 2865.
linecounter in *-pascals*, class = var, declared on 104, used on 241, 319,

321(2), 781, 796, 816, 3102, 4207.
linenumber in *-pascals-interpret*, class = var, declared on 3038, used on 3102, 3103.
linerror in *-pascals*, class = var, declared on 136, used on 781, 796, 816, 3131(2), 3304, 3934.
linetoolongerror in *-pascals-interpret*, class = enumeration, declared on 3027, used on 3634, 3648, 3665, 3707, 3944.
linewrittentoscreen in *-pascals*, class = var, declared on 137, used on 240, 250, 322, 4222.
link in *-pascals*, class = field in *-pascals-symtabletype*, declared on 80, used on 929, 3093, 4051, 4099.
listing in *-pascals*, class = var, declared on 140, used on 1, 156, 222, 249, 255, 257, 262, 312, 319, 329, 333, 4205.
LoadblInst in *-pascals*, class = enumeration, declared on 60, used on 1732, 1735, 3522, 3995.
locationcounter in *-pascals*, class = var, declared on 103, used on 241, 319, 778, 781, 782, 783(2), 793, 796, 798, 803(2), 813, 816, 818, 824(2), 2376, 2393, 2395, 2397, 2399, 2443, 2476, 2495, 2511, 2528, 2548, 2587, 2595, 2604, 2688, 2696, 2704, 2991, 4070, 4208.
locinsymboltable in *-pascals-block*, class = function, declared on 943, used on 977, 1023, 1168, 1326, 1748, 1958, 2638, 2741, 2890, 2953.
locofactualparam in *-pascals-block-statement-call*, class = var, declared on 1697, used on 1748, 1751, 1752, 1756, 1758, 1761, 1763, 1764, 1766, 1767.
locofcalledroutine in *-pascals-block-statement-call*, class = value parameter, declared on 1689, used on 1703, 1704, 1706, 1793, 1796, 1797.
locofcodetojumpout in *-pascals-block-statement-forstatement*, class = var, declared on 2628, used on 2688, 2704.
locofcurrentparam in *-pascals-block-statement-call*, class = var, declared on 1697, used on 1706, 1712, 1715(2), 1717, 1726, 1729, 1739, 1774, 1775, 1790.
locoffirststatinfor in *-pascals-block-statement-forstatement*, class = var, declared on 2628, used on 2696, 2700, 2702.
locofjumptocasetable in *-pascals-block-statement-casestatement*, class = var, declared on 2417, used on 2495, 2511.
locofjumptoelseorend in *-pascals-block-statement-ifstatement*, class = var, declared on 2362, used on 2376, 2395, 2399.
locofjumptoend in *-pascals-block-statement-whilestatement*, class = var, declared on 2580, used on 2595, 2604.
locofjumptoend in *-pascals-block-statement-ifstatement*, class = var, declared on 2362, used on 2393, 2397.
locoflastparam in *-pascals-block-statement-call*, class = var, declared on 1697, used on 1704, 1712, 1790.
locofrepeat in *-pascals-block-statement-repeatstatement*, class = var, declared on 2542, used on 2548, 2568.
locoftest in *-pascals-block-statement-whilestatement*, class = var, declared on 2580, used on 2587, 2603.
LodaddInst in *-pascals*, class = enumeration, declared on 55, used on 1762, 1983, 2005, 2294, 2648, 2755, 3135, 3973.
LodindInst in *-pascals*, class = enumeration, declared on 55, used on 2000, 3156, 3975.
LodinsInst in *-pascals*, class = enumeration, declared on 64, used on 1991, 3696, 4009.
LodvalInst in *-pascals*, class = enumeration, declared on 55, used on 1765, 1984, 1999, 2006, 2295, 2756, 3147, 3974.
low in *-pascals-block-typ-arraytyp*, class = var, declared on 1087, used on 1094, 1096, 1098, 1099, 1108, 1110, 1114(2).
low in *-pascals*, class = field in anonymous record, declared on 127, used on 724, 1142, 4065.

lower in *-pascals-insymbol*, class = var, declared on 359, used on 501, 504, 506, 507, 509.

lowindex in *-pascals-enterarray*, class = value parameter, declared on 703, used on 708, 711, 713, 724.

lparent in *-pascals*, class = enumeration, declared on 38, used on 670, 1193, 1680, 1708, 1769, 1881, 1980, 2045, 2299, 2734, 2761, 2788, 2935, 2942, 4184, 4196, 4288.

lss in *-pascals*, class = enumeration, declared on 38, used on 597, 2221, 2224, 2238, 2258.

mainparamitem in *-pascals-block-statement-standproc*, class = var, declared on 2719, used on 2749, 2751, 2765, 2767, 2769, 2800, 2802, 2816, 2831, 2834.

MarkstInst in *-pascals*, class = enumeration, declared on 59, used on 1703, 3418, 3991.

maxamountofcode in *-pascals*, class = constant, declared on 23, used on 135, 136, 778, 793, 813.

maxerrornumber in *-pascals*, class = constant, declared on 25, used on 109, 152, 153.

maxexponent in *-pascals*, class = constant, declared on 14, used on 404.

maxinputline in *-pascals*, class = constant, declared on 13, used on 101, 325.

maxlevel in *-pascals*, class = constant, declared on 24, used on 74(2), 77, 123, 1206, 2932, 3040.

maxnumofinputlines in *-pascals*, class = constant, declared on 29, used on 3924.

maxnumofsigdigits in *-pascals*, class = constant, declared on 16, used on 527.

messagenum in *-pascals-fatal*, class = value parameter, declared on 267, used on 283.

middle in *-pascals-insymbol*, class = var, declared on 359, used on 504, 505(2), 506(2), 510.

minexponent in *-pascals*, class = constant, declared on 15, used on 406.

minus in *-pascals*, class = enumeration, declared on 36, used on 1015, 1016, 2157, 2160, 2164, 2171, 2173, 2179, 4181, 4193.

ModInst in *-pascals*, class = enumeration, declared on 70, used on 2137, 3889, 4034.

msg in *-pascals-fatal*, class = var, declared on 272, used on 276, 277, 278, 279, 280, 281, 282, 283.

msg in *-pascals-errormsg*, class = var, declared on 153, used on 157, 158, 159, 160, 161, 162, 163, 164, 165, 166, 167, 168, 169, 170, 171, 172, 173, 174, 175, 176, 177, 178, 179, 180, 181, 182, 183, 184, 185, 186, 187, 188, 189, 190, 191, 192, 193, 194, 195, 196, 197, 198, 199, 200, 201, 202, 203, 204, 205, 206, 207, 208, 209, 210, 211, 212, 213, 214, 215, 222.

MultInst in *-pascals*, class = enumeration, declared on 69, used on 2094, 3874, 4032.

multiplyingfactor in *-pascals-insymbol-adjustscale*, class = var, declared on 401, used on 410, 423(2), 427, 428.

MultrInst in *-pascals*, class = enumeration, declared on 70, used on 2095, 3898, 4035.

n in *-pascals-error*, class = value parameter, declared on 227, used on 261, 262, 264.

name in *-pascals*, class = field in *-pascals-symtabletype*, declared on 79, used on 928, 3078, 4051, 4098.

NegateInst in *-pascals*, class = enumeration, declared on 64, used on 2168, 3700, 4011.

NegatrInst in *-pascals*, class = enumeration, declared on 71, used on 2166, 3927, 4039.

neq in *-pascals*, class = enumeration, declared on 37, used on 594, 2221, 2224, 2237, 2257, 4190.

nextch in *-pascals*, class = procedure, declared on 288, used on 374, 379, 381, 387, 438, 440, 456, 461, 472, 496, 524, 536, 553, 578, 582, 588, 591, 595, 601, 605, 611, 615, 667,

672, 676, 678, 681, 688, 693.
nocaselabelerror in *-pascals-interpret*, class = enumeration, declared on 3025, used on 3291, 3938.
noreadingpasteoferror in *-pascals-interpret*, class = enumeration, declared on 3028, used on 3605, 3916, 3945.
normal in *-pascals*, class = field in *-pascals-symtabletype*, declared on 84, used on 1241, 1356, 1477, 1528, 1982, 1998, 2004, 3080, 4052, 4103.
NoteqrInst in *-pascals*, class = enumeration, declared on 65, used on 2257, 3726, 4015.
NotequInst in *-pascals*, class = enumeration, declared on 67, used on 2237, 3778, 4021.
NotInst in *-pascals*, class = enumeration, declared on 64, used on 2059, 3698, 4010.
notsy in *-pascals*, class = enumeration, declared on 36, used on 2054, 4167, 4196.
notyp in *-pascals*, class = enumeration, declared on 47, used on 845, 931, 1002, 1160, 1179, 1297, 1741, 1815, 1817(2), 1818, 1926, 1952, 2060, 2093, 2113, 2114, 2117, 2125, 2126, 2129, 2139, 2140, 2143, 2187, 2188, 2191, 2199, 2233, 2326(2), 2373, 2492, 2565, 2592, 2652, 2768, 2939, 3047, 4198, 4228, 4252, 4253, 4254, 4255, 4256, 4257, 4262, 4263.
numofcharsoutputoncurrentline in *-pascals-interpret*, class = var, declared on 3031, used on 3121, 3630(2), 3633, 3644(2), 3647, 3661(2), 3664, 3704(2), 3706, 3922.
numofinstrsexecuted in *-pascals-interpret*, class = var, declared on 3031, used on 3120, 3130(2), 3954.
numofintegerdigits in *-pascals-insymbol*, class = var, declared on 359, used on 404, 406, 515, 523(2), 527, 531.
numofkeywords in *-pascals*, class = constant, declared on 11, used on 114, 115, 502.
numoflabels in *-pascals-block-statement-casestatement*, class = var, declared on 2417, used on 2437, 2440(2), 2442, 2443, 2449, 2486, 2514.
numofpaths in *-pascals-block-statement-casestatement*, class = var, declared on 2417, used on 2475(2), 2476, 2487, 2527.
numofsigchars in *-pascals*, class = constant, declared on 12, used on 45, 486.
obj in *-pascals*, class = field in *-pascals-symtabletype*, declared on 81, used on 930, 1172, 1331, 1962, 3076, 4051, 4100.
objdescription in *-pascals-block-enter*, class = value parameter, declared on 895, used on 930.
object in *-pascals*, class = type, declared on 46, used on 81, 895, 4087.
offset in *-pascals-block-typ*, class = var, declared on 1071, used on 1211, 1242, 1243(2), 1244, 1246, 1268, 1269.
OffsetInst in *-pascals*, class = enumeration, declared on 57, used on 1639, 3260, 3982.
offsetinstackframe in *-pascals-block-statement-selector*, class = var, declared on 1607, used on 1636, 1638, 1639.
offsetoflhs in *-pascals-block-statement-assignment*, class = value parameter, declared on 2273, used on 2297.
ofsy in *-pascals*, class = enumeration, declared on 42, used on 1094, 1106, 1132, 2490, 2499, 4168.
onecase in *-pascals-block-statement-casestatement*, class = procedure, declared on 2454, used on 2503, 2507.
opcode in *-pascals-block-statement-standproc*, class = var, declared on 2718, used on 2755, 2756, 2758.
opcode in *-pascals-block-statement-forstatement*, class = var, declared on 2627, used on 2672, 2676, 2689, 2699.
opcode in *-pascals-block-statement-assignment*, class = var, declared on 2278, used on 2294, 2295, 2297.
opcode in *-pascals-block-statement-expression-simpleexpression-term-factor*, class = var, declared on 1869,

used on 1983, 1984, 1986, 1999, 2000, 2005, 2006, 2008.
opcode in *-pascals*, class = field in *-pascals-instruction*, declared on 73, used on 799, 819.
opcodes in *-pascals*, class = type, declared on 55, used on 73, 771, 786, 806, 1869, 2278, 2627, 2718, 3968.
operand1 in *-pascals-block-statement-resulttype*, class = value parameter, declared on 1804, used on 1813, 1817, 1819.
operand2 in *-pascals-block-statement-resulttype*, class = value parameter, declared on 1804, used on 1813, 1817, 1820, 1829.
ordinalvalue in *-pascals-block*, class = field in *-pascals-block-constantrecord*, declared on 842, never used.
ordvalofchar in *-pascals*, class = var, declared on 98, used on 649, 1009, 2034.
ordvaloffirstchar in *-pascals*, class = constant, declared on 32, used on 3196.
ordvaloflastchar in *-pascals*, class = constant, declared on 33, used on 3197.
ordvaloftabchar in *-pascals*, class = constant, declared on 31, used on 454, 460.
OrInst in *-pascals*, class = enumeration, declared on 68, used on 2185, 3838, 4026.
orsy in *-pascals*, class = enumeration, declared on 37, used on 2171, 2173, 2179, 2181, 4169.
outofrangeerror in *-pascals-interpret*, class = enumeration, declared on 3026, used on 3198, 3492, 3494, 3513, 3515, 3940.
outputlinelength in *-pascals*, class = constant, declared on 28, used on 3633, 3647, 3664, 3706.
outputusedasprogparam in *-pascals*, class = var, declared on 112, used on 4221, 4300, 4312.
parameterlist in *-pascals-block*, class = procedure, declared on 1282, used on 2943.
parameterreference in *-pascals-block-parameterlist*, class = var, declared on 1288, used on 1298, 1335, 1355.
parametersize in *-pascals-block-parameterlist*, class = var, declared on 1288, used on 1299, 1338, 1339, 1359.
parametertype in *-pascals-block-parameterlist*, class = var, declared on 1287, used on 1297, 1334, 1354.
pascals. class = program, declared on 1,
PbreakInst in *-pascals*, class = enumeration, declared on 58, used on 2515, 2517, 2873, 3289, 3302, 3986.
period in *-pascals*, class = enumeration, declared on 39, used on 617, 1614, 1680, 1769, 1980, 2299, 2761, 3007.
plus in *-pascals*, class = enumeration, declared on 36, used on 1015, 2157, 2160, 2171, 2173, 2179, 2201, 2205, 4180, 4193.
posinarraytable in *-pascals-block-statement-selector*, class = var, declared on 1607, used on 1657, 1659, 1662, 1663, 1664, 1666, 1667.
posinrealtable in *-pascals-block-statement-expression-simpleexpression-term-factor*, class = var, declared on 1870, used on 2028, 2029.
posinrealtable in *-pascals-block-constntdeclaration*, class = var, declared on 1397, used on 1428, 1429.
posinstringtable in *-pascals*, class = var, declared on 100, used on 655, 659, 2794.
posinsymboltable in *-pascals-block-parameterlist*, class = var, declared on 1288, used on 1326, 1329, 1330.
posinsymboltable in *-pascals-block-typ*, class = var, declared on 1068, used on 1168, 1170, 1171.
posinsymboltable in *-pascals-block-constant*, class = var, declared on 999, used on 1023, 1025, 1026, 1030, 1035, 1037.
posinsymboltable in *-pascals-block*, class = var, declared on 852, used on 2953, 2956, 2957, 2959, 2961.

posinsymtable in *-pascals-block-statement-standproc*, class = var, declared on 2717, used on 2741, 2744, 2745, 2750, 2752, 2754, 2758, 2759.

posinsymtable in *-pascals-block-statement-forstatement*, class = var, declared on 2628, used on 2638, 2641, 2643, 2644, 2646, 2648, 2649.

posinsymtable in *-pascals-block-statement-expression-simpleexpression-term-factor*, class = var, declared on 1868, used on 1958, 1961, 2020, 2021.

posinsymtable in *-pascals-block-statement-selector*, class = var, declared on 1607, used on 1623, 1627, 1629(2), 1631, 1634, 1635, 1636.

posinsymtable in *-pascals-block-statement*, class = var, declared on 1591, used on 2890, 2893, 2894, 2896, 2897(2), 2899, 2900, 2901, 2903, 2905, 2906.

posinsymtable in *-pascals-block-locinsymboltable*, class = var, declared on 949, used on 965, 968, 969(2), 972, 974, 977.

posinsymtable in *-pascals-block-enter*, class = var, declared on 903, used on 916, 917, 919, 920(2), 922.

posinsymtableoffunc in *-pascals-block-statement-expression-simpleexpression-term-factor-standfunct*, class = value parameter, declared on 1873, used on 1893, 1910, 1941.

posinsymtableoflhs in *-pascals-block-statement-assignment*, class = value parameter, declared on 2273, used on 2284, 2285, 2293.

posint in *-pascals*, class = type, declared on 50, used on 849.

posintable in *-pascals-enterreal*, class = var parameter, declared on 748, used on 767.

power in *-pascals-insymbol-adjustscale*, class = var, declared on 400, used on 409, 417, 418(2), 422(2), 424.

printtables in *-pascals*, class = procedure, declared on 3957, used on 4325.

procdeclaration in *-pascals-block*, class = procedure, declared on 1544, used on 2986.

profile in *-pascals*, class = var, declared on 136, used on 3103, 3131(2).

progcounter in *-pascals-interpret*, class = var, declared on 3024, used on 3117, 3129, 3131(2), 3132(2), 3264, 3268, 3297, 3304, 3328, 3361, 3385, 3414, 3460, 3478, 3685, 3692, 3934.

progname in *-pascals*, class = var, declared on 111, used on 4044, 4285.

programstatus in *-pascals-interpret*, class = var, declared on 3025, used on 3118, 3140, 3152, 3162, 3198, 3242, 3253, 3291, 3425, 3492, 3494, 3513, 3515, 3529, 3556, 3567, 3578, 3589, 3605, 3634, 3648, 3665, 3681, 3707, 3885, 3894, 3909, 3916, 3925, 3930, 3932, 3937.

programsy in *-pascals*, class = enumeration, declared on 40, used on 4171, 4277.

prosedurresy in *-pascals*, class = enumeration, declared on 40, used on 2985, 4170, 4195.

prozedure in *-pascals*, class = enumeration, declared on 46, used on 1567, 2012, 2898, 4252, 4253, 4254, 4255, 4256, 4257, 4262, 4263.

r in *-pascals-interpret*, class = field in anonymous record, declared on 3044, used on 3225, 3229, 3592, 3600, 3615, 3723, 3731, 3739, 3747, 3755, 3763.

rbrack in *-pascals*, class = enumeration, declared on 38, used on 1094, 1106, 1123, 1652, 1671, 4189.

rdiv in *-pascals*, class = enumeration, declared on 37, used on 2076, 2079, 2084, 2098, 4183.

RdivInst in *-pascals*, class = enumeration, declared on 70, used on 2111, 3904, 4036.

ReadInst in *-pascals*, class = enumeration, declared on 62, used on 2769, 3603, 4002.

ReadlnInst in *-pascals*, class = enumeration, declared on 71, used on 2784, 3914, 4037.

readscale in *-pascals-insymbol*, class = procedure, declared on 363, used on 557, 568.
realcon in *-pascals*, class = enumeration, declared on 36, used on 542, 565, 1047, 2025, 2026, 4193, 4196.
realconstanttablemax in *-pascals*, class = constant, declared on 21, used on 134, 755.
realconsttable in *-pascals*, class = var, declared on 134, used on 758, 761, 1034, 3592.
reals in *-pascals*, class = enumeration, declared on 47, used on 843, 1033, 1048, 1096, 1427, 1739, 1813(2), 1823, 1827, 1892, 1896, 1917, 1972, 2027, 2095, 2101, 2106, 2109, 2110, 2162, 2165, 2204, 2245, 2249, 2253, 2254, 2322, 2767, 2816, 3044, 3086, 3591, 3599, 3614, 4198, 4231, 4235, 4236, 4244, 4245, 4246, 4247, 4248, 4249.
realvalue in *-pascals-block*, class = field in *-pascals-block-constantrecord*, declared on 844, never used.
records in *-pascals*, class = enumeration, declared on 47, used on 845, 1203, 1620, 1734, 3047.
recordsy in *-pascals*, class = enumeration, declared on 40, used on 4172, 4194.
ref in *-pascals*, class = field in *-pascals-symtabletype*, declared on 83, used on 932, 1176, 1240, 1335, 1355, 1475, 1525, 1978, 4051, 4102.
ref in *-pascals*, class = field in *-pascals-item*, declared on 53, never used.
repeatstatement in *-pascals-block-statement*, class = procedure, declared on 2538, used on 2914.
repeatsy in *-pascals*, class = enumeration, declared on 41, used on 2914, 4173, 4197.
Reset1Inst in *-pascals*, class = enumeration, declared on 56, used on 2854, 3977, 4076.
Reset2Inst in *-pascals*, class = enumeration, declared on 56, used on 2855, 3978.
resultingexpitem in *-pascals-block-statement-expression*, class = var parameter, declared on 1594, used on 2222, 2233, 2234, 2244, 2245, 2253, 2266.
resultingfactoritem in *-pascals-block-statement-expression-simpleexpression-term-factor*, class = var parameter, declared on 1863, used on 1886, 1894, 1896, 1911, 1919, 1924, 1926, 1940, 1952, 1953, 1965, 1966, 1977, 1978, 1987, 1989, 1996, 2017, 2027, 2033, 2037, 2042, 2048, 2056, 2058, 2060.
resultingsimexpitem in *-pascals-block-statement-expression-simpleexpression*, class = var parameter, declared on 1845, used on 2160, 2162, 2165, 2171, 2183, 2187, 2191, 2195(2), 2198.
resultingtermitem in *-pascals-block-statement-expression-simpleexpression-term*, class = var parameter, declared on 1854, used on 2077, 2089(2), 2092, 2099, 2101, 2109, 2113, 2117, 2121, 2125, 2129, 2133, 2139, 2143.
resulttype in *-pascals-block-statement*, class = function, declared on 1804, used on 1815, 1818, 1821, 1823, 1827, 2089, 2195.
Rewrt1Inst in *-pascals*, class = enumeration, declared on 56, used on 2866, 3979.
Rewrt2Inst in *-pascals*, class = enumeration, declared on 56, used on 2867, 3980.
rhsitem in *-pascals-block-statement-assignment*, class = var, declared on 2277, used on 2312, 2314, 2317, 2322, 2326.
rparent in *-pascals*, class = enumeration, declared on 38, used on 1094, 1106, 1128, 1300, 1343, 1367, 1377, 1381, 1676, 1720, 1770, 1782, 1785, 1886, 1943, 2048, 2050, 2762, 2775, 2778, 2799, 2809, 2822, 2839, 2851, 2863, 4185, 4308.
running in *-pascals-interpret*, class = enumeration, declared on 3025, used on 3118, 3930.

scaler in *-pascals-insymbol-adjustscale*, class = var, declared on 401, used on 411, 419(2), 423.
selector in *-pascals-block-statement*, class = procedure, declared on 1597, used on 1770, 1987, 2300, 2762.
semicolon in *-pascals*, class = enumeration, declared on 39, used on 883, 1230, 1252, 1261, 1343, 1368, 1383, 1420, 1470, 1516, 1571, 1573, 2340, 2342, 2343, 2347, 2474, 2505, 2550, 2552, 2553, 2557, 2935, 2964, 2968, 2993, 2995, 2996, 3000, 4192.
setflags in *-pascals-setup*, class = procedure, declared on 4113, used on 4202.
setofallerrors in *-pascals*, class = var, declared on 109, used on 218, 219, 223(2), 264(2), 4212, 4330.
setup in *-pascals*, class = procedure, declared on 4109, used on 4274.
sign in *-pascals-block-constant*, class = var, declared on 999, used on 1013, 1017, 1034, 1036, 1044, 1049.
sign in *-pascals-insymbol-readscale*, class = var, declared on 371, used on 375, 382, 390.
simexpoperator in *-pascals-block-statement-expression-simpleexpression*, class = var, declared on 1851, used on 2158, 2164, 2175, 2181, 2201, 2205.
simpleexpression in *-pascals-block-statement-expression*, class = procedure, declared on 1844, used on 2221, 2230.
size in *-pascals*, class = field in anonymous record, declared on 127, used on 1146, 4066.
skip in *-pascals-block*, class = procedure, declared on 854, used on 877, 1052, 2660, 2670, 2685, 2964.
source in *-pascals*, class = var, declared on 140, used on 1, 299, 326, 328, 334, 335, 4204.
spaceforlocals in *-pascals-block*, class = var, declared on 849, used on 1357, 1359(2), 1360, 1362, 1527, 1529(2), 1530, 1532, 2928, 2946, 2983.
spaceforparams in *-pascals*, class = field in anonymous record, declared on 130, used on 4059, 4268.
specialsymbol in *-pascals*, class = var, declared on 116, used on 687, 4180, 4181, 4182, 4183, 4184, 4185, 4186, 4187, 4188, 4189, 4190, 4191, 4192.
stack in *-pascals-interpret*, class = var, declared on 3041, used on 3065, 3069, 3082, 3085, 3086, 3087, 3088, 3097, 3106, 3107, 3108, 3109, 3110, 3111, 3112, 3113, 3117, 3141, 3153(2), 3163, 3164(2), 3176, 3187(2), 3188(2), 3189(2), 3190(2), 3191, 3195, 3203, 3211, 3217, 3223, 3227, 3231(2), 3232(2), 3233(2), 3234(2), 3235(2), 3236(2), 3243, 3254, 3261(2), 3267, 3275, 3309, 3316, 3324(3), 3335, 3338, 3345, 3355, 3367, 3374, 3382(3), 3391, 3392, 3399, 3408, 3432, 3433, 3434, 3435, 3444, 3456, 3459, 3460, 3463, 3464, 3467, 3468, 3472, 3473, 3484, 3497(2), 3505, 3518(2), 3524, 3533(2), 3539, 3540, 3544(2), 3557, 3568, 3579, 3590, 3598, 3607(2), 3627, 3651, 3652, 3653, 3654, 3662, 3668(2), 3670(2), 3672(2), 3674(2), 3685, 3686, 3692, 3693, 3697(3), 3699(2), 3701(2), 3705, 3708(2), 3709, 3715(3), 3721, 3723, 3729, 3731, 3737, 3739, 3745, 3747, 3753, 3755, 3761, 3763, 3769, 3771, 3772, 3773, 3781, 3783, 3784, 3785, 3793, 3795, 3796, 3797, 3805, 3807, 3808, 3809, 3817, 3819, 3820, 3821, 3829, 3831, 3832, 3833, 3841(3), 3847(3), 3853(3), 3859(3), 3865(3), 3871(3), 3877(3), 3884, 3886(3), 3893, 3895(3), 3901(3), 3908, 3911(2), 3912, 3928(2).
stackfullerror in *-pascals-interpret*, class = enumeration, declared on 3026, used on 3140, 3152, 3162, 3242, 3253, 3425, 3529, 3556, 3567, 3578, 3589, 3941.
stacksize in *-pascals*, class = constant, declared on 30, used on 3041, 3139, 3151, 3161, 3241, 3252, 3424, 3528, 3555, 3566, 3577, 3588, 4321.
standfunct in *-pascals-block-statement-expression-simpleexpression-term-*

factor, class = procedure, declared on 1872, used on 2021.
standfunctnum in *-pascals-block-statement-expression-simpleexpression-term-, factor-standfunct.* class = value parameter, declared on 1872, used on 1885, 1888, 1897(2), 1925, 1937.
standproc in *-pascals-block-statement*, class = procedure, declared on 2710, used on 2901.
stanprocnum in *-pascals-block-statement-standproc*, class = value parameter, declared on 2710, used on 2725, 2783, 2844.
stantyps in *-pascals*, class = var, declared on 122, used on 1989, 1996, 2315, 2802, 2959, 3077, 4198.
startofcode in *-pascals-block-statement-casestatement*, class = field in anonymous record, declared on 2419, never used.
startoffieldsinsymtable in *-pascals-block-typ*, class = var, declared on 1071, used on 1215, 1234, 1236(2), 1238.
statbegsys in *-pascals*, class = var, declared on 113, used on 2342, 2552, 2885, 2988, 2989, 2995, 4197, 4318.
statement in *-pascals-block*, class = procedure, declared on 1586, used on 2340, 2347, 2389, 2396, 2474, 2550, 2557, 2602, 2697, 2993, 3000.
step in *-pascals-enterreal*, class = var, declared on 752, used on 759, 761, 762(2), 764, 765, 767.
StfuncInst in *-pascals*, class = enumeration, declared on 57, used on 1925, 1937, 3185, 3981.
StoreInst in *-pascals*, class = enumeration, declared on 65, used on 2316, 2324, 3713, 4013.
string in *-pascals*, class = enumeration, declared on 36, used on 658, 2792.
stringlength in *-pascals-insymbol*, class = var, declared on 360, used on 626, 630, 635, 637(2), 641(2), 647, 652, 660, 662.
stringtable in *-pascals*, class = var, declared on 133, used on 635, 649, 3637.
stringtablemax in *-pascals*, class = constant, declared on 20, used on 133, 631.
SubInst in *-pascals*, class = enumeration, declared on 68, used on 2203, 3850, 4028.
SubrealInst in *-pascals*, class = enumeration, declared on 69, used on 2207, 3862, 4030.
swalloweddeadcolon in *-pascals*, class = var, declared on 141, used on 469, 470, 539, 4199.
SwitchInst in *-pascals*, class = enumeration, declared on 58, used on 2496, 3272, 3985.
sy in *-pascals*, class = var, declared on 94, used on 471, 510, 511, 517, 542, 565, 581, 584, 590, 594, 597, 604, 607, 614, 617, 648, 654, 658, 670, 687, 864, 876, 883, 888, 983, 1006, 1007, 1015, 1016, 1022, 1042, 1047, 1102, 1117, 1123, 1128, 1132, 1165, 1166, 1185, 1188, 1193, 1214, 1218, 1223, 1251, 1252, 1257, 1265, 1302, 1305, 1315, 1320, 1323, 1367, 1368, 1373, 1381, 1406, 1410, 1415, 1456, 1461, 1466, 1502, 1506, 1511, 1557, 1560, 1573, 1614, 1617, 1646, 1669, 1671, 1676, 1680, 1708, 1745, 1769, 1783, 1785, 1881, 1931, 1943, 1956, 1957, 1980, 2025, 2026, 2032, 2045, 2050, 2054, 2079, 2081, 2157, 2158, 2173, 2175, 2224, 2226, 2299, 2302, 2307, 2342, 2343, 2350, 2380, 2385, 2391, 2459, 2462, 2467, 2499, 2505, 2530, 2552, 2553, 2560, 2598, 2637, 2662, 2674, 2675, 2691, 2734, 2738, 2761, 2776, 2778, 2788, 2792, 2805, 2815, 2837, 2839, 2851, 2863, 2885, 2886, 2942, 2949, 2952, 2968, 2974, 2977, 2980, 2985, 2989, 2995, 2996, 3003, 4277, 4282, 4288, 4294, 4306, 4308.
symbol in *-pascals*, class = type, declared on 36, used on 48, 94, 115, 116, 1842, 1851, 1860.
symbolfound in *-pascals-insymbol*, class = var, declared on 361, used on 451, 682, 695, 699.

symboltable in *-pascals*, class = var, declared on 124, used on 914, 919, 920, 927, 958, 968, 969, 1026, 1029, 1035, 1036, 1171, 1238, 1330, 1353, 1423, 1424, 1425, 1429, 1431, 1473, 1523, 1569, 1625, 1627, 1629, 1634, 1635, 1636, 1704, 1717, 1726, 1728, 1738, 1752, 1756, 1758, 1761, 1763, 1764, 1766, 1767, 1773, 1775, 1793, 1796, 1797, 1893, 1910, 1940, 1961, 2284, 2285, 2293, 2643, 2644, 2646, 2648, 2649, 2745, 2749, 2751, 2754, 2758, 2759, 2894, 2896, 2897, 2899, 2901, 2903, 2905, 2939, 2940, 2957, 2959, 2960(2), 2991, 3068, 3071, 3075, 3117, 3421, 3447, 3478, 4050, 4097.

symboltablemax in *-pascals*, class = constant, declared on 17, used on 124, 906.

symset in *-pascals*, class = type, declared on 48, used on 113, 829, 854, 868, 880, 990, 1059, 1586, 1593, 1597, 1688, 1844, 1853, 1862.

symtabindexatentry in *-pascals-block*, class = var, declared on 850, used on 2930, 2939, 2940, 2960, 2991.

symtabletype in *-pascals*, class = type, declared on 78, used on 124.

term in *-pascals-block-statement-expression-simpleexpression*, class = procedure, declared on 1853, used on 2160, 2171, 2179.

termoperator in *-pascals-block-statement-expression-simpleexpression-term*, class = var, declared on 1860, used on 2081, 2088, 2098, 2120, 2135.

test in *-pascals-block*, class = procedure, declared on 868, used on 892, 1004, 1055, 1163, 1261, 1275, 1300, 1343, 1377, 1383, 1404, 1454, 1682, 1782, 1954, 2064, 2775, 2918, 2935, 2988, 3007.

testsemicolon in *-pascals-block*, class = procedure, declared on 880, used on 1434, 1480, 1537.

theconstant in *-pascals-block-constant*, class = var parameter, declared on 991, used on 1002, 1003, 1008, 1009, 1029, 1033, 1034, 1036, 1043, 1044, 1048, 1049.

thensy in *-pascals*, class = enumeration, declared on 42, used on 2371, 2380, 4174.

times in *-pascals*, class = enumeration, declared on 37, used on 2076, 2079, 2084, 2088, 4182.

toomanylinesoutputerror in *-pascals-interpret*, class = enumeration, declared on 3027, used on 3925, 3943.

topofstack in *-pascals-interpret*, class = var, declared on 3029, used on 3116, 3137(2), 3139, 3141, 3149(2), 3151, 3153, 3159(2), 3161, 3163, 3187(2), 3188(2), 3189(2), 3190(2), 3191, 3195, 3203, 3211, 3217, 3223, 3227, 3231(2), 3232(2), 3233(2), 3234(2), 3235(2), 3236(2), 3239(2), 3241, 3243, 3250(2), 3252, 3254, 3261(2), 3267, 3270(2), 3275, 3281(2), 3309, 3316, 3324(2), 3327(2), 3335, 3345, 3363(2), 3367, 3374, 3382(2), 3386(2), 3391, 3399, 3416(2), 3424, 3427(2), 3432, 3433, 3434, 3435, 3441, 3471, 3477, 3484, 3496(2), 3497(2), 3505, 3517(2), 3518(2), 3524, 3525(2), 3526, 3531, 3532(2), 3533, 3539, 3540, 3549(2), 3553(2), 3555, 3557, 3564(2), 3566, 3568, 3575(2), 3577, 3579, 3586(2), 3588, 3590, 3597, 3607, 3623(2), 3627, 3629(2), 3651, 3652, 3653, 3654, 3657(2), 3662, 3668(2), 3670(2), 3672(2), 3674(2), 3678(2), 3684, 3691, 3697(2), 3699(2), 3701(2), 3705, 3708(2), 3709, 3711(2), 3715(2), 3716(2), 3720(2), 3721, 3723, 3728(2), 3729, 3731, 3736(2), 3737, 3739, 3744(2), 3745, 3747, 3752(2), 3753, 3755, 3760(2), 3761, 3763, 3768(2), 3769, 3771, 3772, 3773, 3780(2), 3781, 3783, 3784, 3785, 3792(2), 3793, 3795, 3796, 3797, 3804(2), 3805, 3807, 3808, 3809, 3816(2), 3817, 3819, 3820, 3821, 3828(2), 3829, 3831, 3832, 3833, 3840(2), 3841(3), 3846(2), 3847(3), 3852(2), 3853(3), 3858(2), 3859(3), 3864(2), 3865(3), 3870(2),

3871(2), 3872, 3876(2), 3877(3), 3882(2), 3884, 3886(2), 3887, 3891(2), 3893, 3895(2), 3896, 3900(2), 3901(3), 3906(2), 3908, 3911(2), 3912, 3928(2).

tosy in *-pascals*, class = enumeration, declared on 42, used on 2660, 2665, 2670, 2674, 4175.

tp in *-pascals-interpret*, class = tag field in anonymous record, declared on 3042, used on 3142, 3192, 3200, 3204, 3209, 3212, 3218, 3224, 3228, 3244, 3255, 3276, 3310, 3317, 3339, 3346, 3356, 3368, 3375, 3393, 3400, 3409, 3485, 3506, 3558, 3569, 3580, 3591, 3599, 3610, 3614, 3618, 3722, 3730, 3738, 3746, 3754, 3762, 3770, 3775, 3782, 3787, 3794, 3799, 3806, 3811, 3818, 3823, 3830, 3835.

tp in *-pascals-enterarray*, class = value parameter, declared on 702, used on 723.

tracing in *-pascals*, class = var, declared on 139, used on 447, 735, 1091, 1152, 1157, 1278, 1293, 1387, 1400, 1437, 1450, 1483, 1497, 1540, 1554, 1582, 1610, 1684, 1700, 1800, 1949, 2067, 2072, 2148, 2153, 2212, 2217, 2269, 2281, 2329, 2336, 2354, 2365, 2401, 2482, 2534, 2545, 2572, 2583, 2606, 2632, 2706, 2722, 2877, 2882, 2920, 2925, 3009, 4122, 4201, 4327.

typ in *-pascals-block*, class = procedure, declared on 1059, used on 1137, 1230, 1470, 1516.

typ in *-pascals*, class = field in *-pascals-symtabletype*, declared on 82, used on 931, 1175, 1239, 1334, 1354, 1474, 1524, 1965, 1968, 1977, 2017, 3077, 3084, 4051, 4101.

typ in *-pascals*, class = field in *-pascals-item*, declared on 52, never used.

typebegsys in *-pascals*, class = var, declared on 113, used on 1163, 1165, 4194.

typedeclaration in *-pascals-block*, class = procedure, declared on 1441, used on 2978.

typefound in *-pascals-block-typedeclaration*, class = var, declared on 1446, used on 1470, 1474.

typefound in *-pascals-block-typ*, class = var parameter, declared on 1060, used on 1160, 1175, 1179, 1197, 1203.

typeofconstant in *-pascals-block*, class = tag field in anonymous record, declared on 840, never used.

typereference in *-pascals-block-typedeclaration*, class = var, declared on 1447, used on 1470, 1475.

typereference in *-pascals-block-typ*, class = var parameter, declared on 1061, used on 1161, 1176, 1198, 1204, 1268, 1270.

types in *-pascals*, class = type, declared on 47, used on 49, 52, 82, 126, 702, 840, 1060, 1069, 1086, 1287, 1446, 1494, 1804(2), 2625, 3042, 4088.

typesize in *-pascals-block-typedeclaration*, class = var, declared on 1447, used on 1471, 1476.

typesize in *-pascals-block-typ*, class = var parameter, declared on 1061, used on 1162, 1177, 1198, 1269.

typesy in *-pascals*, class = enumeration, declared on 39, used on 2977, 4176, 4195.

typset in *-pascals*, class = type, declared on 49, used on 122, 1878.

untilexpitem in *-pascals-block-statement-repeatstatement*, class = var, declared on 2541, used on 2563, 2565.

untilsy in *-pascals*, class = enumeration, declared on 42, used on 2550, 2557, 2560, 4177.

UpddisInst in *-pascals*, class = enumeration, declared on 55, used on 1797, 3167, 3976.

upper in *-pascals-insymbol*, class = var, declared on 359, used on 502, 504, 505, 507, 509.

val in *-pascals-block-statement-casestatement*, class = field in anonymous record, declared on 2419, never used.

valofconstant in *-pascals-block-constntdeclaration*, class = var, declared on 1396, used on 1420, 1423, 1427, 1428, 1431.

valpar in *-pascals-block-parameterlist*, class = var, declared on 1290, used on 1306, 1309, 1337, 1356.
valueafterE in *-pascals-insymbol-readscale*, class = var, declared on 371, used on 376, 386(2), 390.
variabldeclaration in *-pascals-block*, class = procedure, declared on 1487, used on 2981.
variable in *-pascals*, class = enumeration, declared on 46, used on 984, 1752, 1975, 2643, 2745, 2896, 3076, 4228.
variablereference in *-pascals-block-variabldeclaration*, class = var, declared on 1492, used on 1517, 1525.
variablesize in *-pascals-block-variabldeclaration*, class = var, declared on 1493, used on 1517, 1529.
variablesize in *-pascals*, class = field in anonymous record, declared on 131, used on 4059, 4269.
variabletype in *-pascals-block-variabldeclaration*, class = var, declared on 1494, used on 1516, 1524.
varsy in *-pascals*, class = enumeration, declared on 39, used on 1300, 1302, 1305, 1377, 2980, 4178, 4195.
whileexpitem in *-pascals-block-statement-whilestatement*, class = var, declared on 2579, used on 2590, 2592.
whilestatement in *-pascals-block-statement*, class = procedure, declared on 2576, used on 2913.
whilesy in *-pascals*, class = enumeration, declared on 41, used on 2913, 4179, 4197.
Wr1fldInst in *-pascals*, class = enumeration, declared on 63, used on 2831, 3659, 4005.
Wr2fldInst in *-pascals*, class = enumeration, declared on 64, used on 2828, 3702, 4012.
WriteInst in *-pascals*, class = enumeration, declared on 62, used on 2834, 3642, 4004.
WritlnInst in *-pascals*, class = enumeration, declared on 71, used on 2845, 3918, 4038.
WrstrgInst in *-pascals*, class = enumeration, declared on 62, used on 2794, 3625, 4003.
x in *-pascals-enterreal*, class = value parameter, declared on 747, used on 758, 761.
x0 in *-pascals-enterstandident*, class = value parameter, declared on 4090, used on 4098.
x1 in *-pascals-enterstandident*, class = value parameter, declared on 4087, used on 4100.
x2 in *-pascals-enterstandident*, class = value parameter, declared on 4088, used on 4101.
x3 in *-pascals-enterstandident*, class = value parameter, declared on 4089, used on 4105.

Bibliography

Aho, A V and Ullman, J D, *Principles of Compiler Design,* Addison-Wesley, 1977.

Aho, A V, Sethi, R, and Ullman, J D, *Compilers: Principles, Techniques and Tools,* Addison-Wesley, 1986.

Amman, U, 'The method of structured programming applied to the development of a compiler', *International Computing Symposium 1973*, pp. 93–99, North-Holland, 1974.

Atkinson, L V, McGregor, J J, and North, S D, 'Context sensitive editing as an approach to incremental compilation', *Computer Journal*, vol. 24, pp. 222–229, 1981.

Bowles, K L, *Problem Solving Using Pascal,* Springer-Verlag, 1977.

Bratman, H, 'An alternative form of the UNCOL diagram', *Comm. ACM*, vol. 4, p. 142, 1961.

Brooker, R A, Morris, D, and Rohl, J S, 'Experience with the compiler-compiler', *Computer Journal*, vol. 9, pp. 345–349, 1967.

Cornelius, B J, Lowman, I R, and Robson, D J, 'Steady-state compilers', *Software: Practice and Experience*, vol. 14, pp. 705–709, 1984.

Dunn, B J and Murphy, T J, 'Llama: A compiler generator', (Honours Thesis), University of New South Wales, 1976.

Earley, J and Sturgis, H, 'A formalism for translator interactions', *Comm. ACM*, vol. 13, no. 10, pp. 607–617, 1970.

Foster, J M, 'A syntax improving device', *Computer Journal*, vol. 11, pp. 31–34, 1968.

Hunter, R, *Compilers: Their Design and Construction Using Pascal,* Wiley, 1985.

International Standards Organisation, 'ISO standard: specification for the computer programming language Pascal', 7185, 1983.

Jensen, K and Wirth, N, *Pascal User Manual and Report,* Springer-Verlag, 1975.

Jesshope, C R, Crawley, M J, and Lovegrove, G L, 'An intelligent Pascal editor for a graphical oriented workstation', *Software: Practice and Experience*, vol. 15, pp. 1103–1119, 1985.

Johnson, S C, 'Yacc—yet another compiler-compiler', Computer Science Technical Report No. 32, Bell Laboratories, 1975.

Lakos, C A and McDermott, T S, 'Interfacing with the user of a syntax-directed editor', Technical Report R82–3, Dept of Information Science, University of Tasmania, 1982.

Lecarme, O and Peyrolle-Thomas, M-C, 'Self-compiling compilers: an appraisal of their implementation and portability', *Software: Practice and Experience*, vol. 8, pp. 149–170, 1978.

Lesk, M E, 'Lex—a lexical analyzer generator', Computer Science Technical Report No. 39, Bell Laboratories, 1975.

Morris, R, 'Scatter storage techniques', *Comm. ACM*, vol. 11, pp. 38–44, 1968.

Nori, K V, Amman, U, Nageli, H H, and Jacobi, C, 'Pascal-P implementation notes', in *Pascal – The Language and Its Implementation*, ed. D W Barron, pp. 83–124, Wiley, 1981.

Riet, R P van de and Wiggers, R, 'Practice and experience with BASIS: an interactive programming system for introductory courses in informatics', *Software: Practice and Experience*, vol. 9, pp. 463–476, 1979.

Robinson, K A and Hayes, I, 'A tutorial on Llama: a Pascal translator generator', Teaching Document, University of New South Wales, 1986.

Robson, D J, 'Towards a conversational language-sensitive system for Pascal', *Software: Practice and Experience*, vol. 13, pp. 1013–1017, 1983.

Rohl, J S, *An Introduction to Compiler Writing*, MacDonald Elsevier, 1975.

Tanenbaum, A S, *Structured Computer Organisation* (Second Edition), Prentice-Hall, 1984.

Teitelbaum, T and Reps, T, 'The Cornell program synthesizer: a syntax-directed programming environment', *Comm. ACM*, vol. 24, pp. 563–573, 1981.

Wegner, P, 'The Vienna definition language', *Computing Surveys*, vol. 4, pp. 5–63, 1972.

Welsh, J and McKeag, M, *Structured System Programming*, Prentice-Hall, 1980.

White, B, 'Aardvark: a lexical analyser generator', (Honours Thesis), University of New South Wales, 1981.

Wirth, N, 'The design of a Pascal compiler', *Software: Practice and Experience*, vol. 1, pp. 309–333, 1971.

Wirth, N, 'Pascal-S: a subset and its implementation', in *Pascal - The Language and Its Implementation*, ed. D W Barron, pp. 199–260, Wiley, 1981.

Index

3GL 1–2, 4, 16, 22, 24–25, 28, 30–31

4GL 1–2, 5, 68

aardvark utility 15, 63–67, 83–84, 88
action routines 15
activation record 109ff
actual parameters 143
Ada 2, 3, 22, 30, 102, 187
Algol 22, 25–26
alphabet 22, 25, 58
anonymous type 28, 101
APL 22, 29, 33
architecture 2, 4, 12, 16–17, 108, 112, 118, 125
arithmetic 14, 30–31, 52, 59–60, 108, 120
array accesses 146, 157
arrays 29–30, 146ff, 149–150, 160, 163, 177–178
arraytable 92, 98–101, 102, 122, 128, 160, 163, 175, 178, 183
ascending analysis 71
ASCII character set 25, 51, 54, 57
assembler 3–5
assembly language 1, 3, 26
assignment statement 31, 57, 82, 88, 90, 127ff, 147–148, 155, 181, 184
assignment symbol 31
automatic generation 62, 81
axiomatic definition 24

back-end 18
backtracking 73–74
backup 77, 84
Backus-Naur Form *see* BNF
BASIC 2, 4, 7, 22, 28
binary infix operators 30
binding attributes 28
blanks 25, 52
block-oriented files 41
block-structured language 2, 22, 32, 91
blocktable 92, 96–98, 101, 103–105, 129, 161–163, 175
BNF 13, 22, 50, 62, 80, 125
bookkeeping routines 12
Boolean data 26
Boolean operations 121
bootstrap 16–17
bottom-up analysis 71–72, 74, 81, 84
break points 187
buffer overflow 44

call-by-name 32
call-by-reference 32
call-by-value 32
case label 138–140
case selector 156
case statement 76–77, 122, 138, 156
case table 122, 138, 156
chaining 95–96
character constant 28, 50–51, 55, 61–62
character data 26
character set 25, 49–50
  ordering 152
character strings 26, 29
COBOL 2, 20, 22, 25
code generation 11, 13, 18, 20, 108, 111, 124–125
code handler 38
code optimization 11, 20
code trace 127ff
compactness 1, 14
compilation 3ff
compiler 3ff
compiler-compiler 15

compiler writer 14, 20, 22, 25, 34, 94
compound statement 31, 76–77, 82
conditional expression 30
conformant array 29
constructors 29
context-free grammar 22
control transfer 31
cross-compiler 16
current character 41ff

data descriptor 27, 29
data elements 26, 29–30
data structures 1, 3, 26–27, 29, 94, 96
debugging 35, 94, 103, 153, 157, 183, 186
delimiter 50
denotational semantics 24
derivation 69–70
descending analysis 71
destructors 29
device-independence 38–39
direct derivation 69–70
directly reduced 69
display stack 92, 111ff
distinguished symbol 69ff
dope vector 27
dynamic binding 28, 32
dynamic link 109ff, 162–163
dynamic storage 32, 96

EBCDIC character set 25
edit-compile cycle 35
edit-compile-execute cycle 35
efficiency 20, 112
embold program 63ff
end-of-file condition 41
end-of-line translation 44ff
end-of-table sentinel 138
enumerated data 27
enumeration type 170ff
error checking 164
error handler 12
error message handling 45
error messages 11ff
errormsg procedure 41ff
exercises 185
explicit declaration 28
exponent 59–60
expression evaluation 124ff

extensible definition 24
extensions to Pascal-S 170ff

fixed-size data structures 29ff
follower symbol 78
for statement 136ff
FORTH 24
FORTRAN 2, 4, 10, 20, 22, 25–26, 28–29, 33, 96
fourth-generation language *see* 4GL
free-format language 22
free-standing interpreter 40
front end of compiler 11
full bootstrap 16
function entry/exit 141
function parameters 143
function result 111

grammar 69–73, 78, 81–82, 85, 88, 124–125

half-bootstrap 16
hashing function 95
hash table collision 94
high-level language 1, 3, 5, 122
housekeeping information 97, 111, 125, 141, 145, 162–163
hybrid translator 5

identifier 27ff
  attributes 27–29, 90–91
if statement 76–77, 134–135
incremental compilation 36
infix operators 30
input handler 38
insymbol procedure 49ff
integer constant 50–51, 60
intermediate code 4ff
interpretation 3ff
interpreter 3ff
interpretive semantics 24
interrupts 32
iteration 137

keywords 10, 25, 35, 50, 52–53, 57–58, 63, 66–67, 82

l-value 31
lambda calculus 24

language designer 22–23, 52
layout characters 52
left part 69
lexical analysis 10ff
lexical levels 91ff
lexical scanner 10–11, 15, 35, 49–50, 53, 57, 62–63, 66
lexical tokens 10–12, 25, 49, 62–67
linker 3
LISP 2, 22, 24
llama utility 15, 63–64, 67, 82–85, 88–90
loader 38
logical data 26
low-level language 3–4

machine language 1
Modula-2 2
module 39–40
multi-dimensional arrays 29, 146, 160
multiple-pass compilers 12, 20

name equivalence 102
nextch procedure 41ff
non-terminals 69
numeric constants 58–59
numerical data 26

object module 3
object program 4, 14–15, 35–39, 43
  attributes 14
occurrence equivalence 102
one-dimensional arrays 30, 97, 160
one-pass compiler 124
operator precedence 30
operators 30ff
output handler 39
overflow 59–60

P-code 4, 18
parameter passing 32
parser 11ff
Pascal-P 96, 184
peephole optimization 187
PL/I 2, 30
pointers 26–27
portability 4
post-mortem dump 165
postfix operators 30
problem-oriented language 4
procedures 32
program correctness 24, 28
program listing 14, 42, 109
program synthesizers 35
Prolog 2

r-value 31
real constant 50–51, 58–60
realconsttable 98–99, 163
record access 148
record data structure 29
recursive-descent analyser 78
regular expressions 23
rehashing 95
relational operators 30, 126
reliability 18
repeat statement 76–77, 79, 130
repetition statements 31
reserved words 50
return address 141, 162–163
rewriting rule 68
right part 69ff
run-time environment 108
run-time error 152, 156–157, 160, 162, 165, 167–168

Scallop language 16
scope 16, 27–28, 33, 74, 91, 94, 97, 105–106, 114
second-generation language 1
selection statements 31
selectors 29
self-compiling compilers 15
semantic checks 11, 28, 35–36
semantic definition 13, 24–25
semantics 13, 23–24, 49–50, 68
sentence 69–70
sequence of statements 31
shift-reduce parsing 74
SID 81
single-pass compilers 12, 20
skipto procedure 78
snapshot 114–117, 162, 168
SNOBOL 29, 33
software package 1, 4
source handler 39ff
source language 3ff
spelling 50–53, 58, 67

stack 108–109, 114–115
stack frame 109ff
stack-based machine 108, 118, 125–126
starter symbol 78ff
state transition 65–66
static binding 28
static link 109ff
static storage allocation 33
string constant 29, 53, 60, 62, 164
stringtable 51, 61–62, 99, 164
structural equivalence 101–102
subfields 29
subgoal 73–74
subprograms 32
subrange types 34, 179–184
subroutine call 32, 111
symbol table 12ff
symbol table management 12, 96ff
symboltable 92–94, 97–99, 101, 103–105, 128, 161–164
syntactic entities 69
syntax diagram 23, 68
syntax tree 11, 36, 68, 70–71, 74, 77
syntax-directed editor 35

T-Diagrams 5
target language 3–4
terminal symbol 69
text editor 13, 35–37
third-generation language *see* 3GL
top-down analysis 71, 74, 78, 81
tracing 84, 127ff
translation 2ff
translator 2ff
  attributes 6
translator-interpreter 4ff
two-operand instructions 118
two-pass compiler 12
type checking 28
type equivalence 101–103

unary postfix operators 30
unary prefix operators 30
update display instruction 122, 141

value parameter 143ff
variable parameter 143ff
variant record 29
Vienna Definition Language 24
virtual machine 4–5
vocabulary 69

while statement 76–77, 82, 132ff

zero-address instructions 118